Praise for

MW00564547

"Mangani charts a deep dive through the roots of our modern American food obsession with a highly personal tale of memory, character, flavor, and place."

—IAN MCNULTY, Food Writer, *The New Orleans Times-Picayune*

"A foodie from the minute she first spat out her grandmother's lima beans, Marisa Mangani was destined to become a chef—even if she didn't know such a thing existed. Swirling with tastes and scents, her memoir chronicles an unconventional life, a life beginning in near-poverty and forged in a succession of kitchens and restaurants. The kitchen became Mangani's sandbox, the place where she discovered her calling and confidence. 'Good food always gave me hope for better times,' she writes. Like a good hollandaise sauce, *Mise en Place: Memoir of a Girl Chef* satisfies the palate."

—PAM SCHMID, Nonfiction Editor, *Sleet* Magazine

"*Mise en Place: Memoir of a Girl Chef* is a bitingly honest view of a life lived in oyster bars, fish camps, and restaurant kitchens. Flavorful, rich, and evocative, Marisa Mangani's memoir offers readers not just tales of food and cooking, but a provocative examination of the choices we make and the pasts that might have been."

—DINTY W. MOORE, Author of *To Hell with It*

"Readers of Gabrielle Hamilton and David Chang will devour this memoir about Marisa Mangani's journey to become a chef. What began as a way to make a living became a passion for Marisa. *Mise en Place* takes us through kitchens from Maui to New Orleans to Oregon, and back again, with endless colorful characters and exciting adventures along the way. If you have ever wondered what is happening behind the kitchen doors at your local restaurant, this is the book for you."

—AMY FISH, Author of *I Wanted Fries with That*

MISE EN PLACE

Memoir of a Girl Chef

MARISA MANGANI

RIVER GROVE
BOOKS

The names and identifying characteristics of persons referenced in this book have been changed to protect their privacy.

Published by River Grove Books
Austin, TX
www.rivergrovebooks.com

Distributed by River Grove Books

Design and composition by Greenleaf Book Group and Sheila Parr
Cover design by Greenleaf Book Group and Sheila Parr
Cover images © iStock / exopixel, iStock / Toa55, Shutterstock / Spayder pauk_79

Publisher's Cataloging-in-Publication data is available.

Print ISBN: 978-1-63299-565-0

eBook ISBN: 978-1-63299-566-7

First Edition

For Saramaile

Mise en place (French, "meez ohn plahs"): a place for everything

CONTENTS

PROLOGUE

THE SMELLS OF THANKSGIVING filled Grandmother's house with the mouthwatering air of anticipation. Usually her house was a place of dread, of scoldings, unhappiness, and anger. But on Thanksgiving, with Mom and Grandmother in the kitchen acting like friends, and Stepdad hanging around like a slightly unwanted guest, the air was delicate with hope.

I was crouched on the floor of the screened lanai poking pegs into my Lite-Brite, my mind tight with the focus only a six-year-old can conjure, when Stepdad's voice sawed through my small and important world.

"C'mere, Funny Face." I heard his pockets jingle, and the music of it drew me away from my Lite-Brite and toward the man my mother had brought into our lives. I stepped through the open sliders and into the carpeted living room, where I could see him digging around in his work pants pockets with both hands. A crinkly candy-wrapper sound coming from his shirt accented the jingle. He then excavated coins from those deep pockets, which he dropped onto Grandmother's card table. He sat on the folding chair and the crinkling stopped.

The screen door was open, and Grandmother's dog, Mele, waggled into the house, along with the mosquitoes that buzzed around at every dusk. Through the screen, the clouds above the lavender-blossomed jacaranda tree were trimmed burnt orange, and I thought of the orange horizon at the beach, myself alone on the sand, and I wondered how that would feel. Alone, without the grown-ups and their games. But Thanksgiving Day was a special day, a day of food and usually everyone in a good mood, so I was here, at

Grandmother's. I felt a twinge of an itch and smacked a mosquito on my arm. I missed and started digging at the red bump with dirty fingernails.

Stepdad pulled from his shirt pocket the source of that crinkle sound: a pack of Marlboro Reds. He knocked out a stick and slid a coverless pack of matches from the cellophane wrapper and made a *come to me* gesture with his head.

He smoked Reds; my mom smoked Greens.

The burnt-egg smell of the match-strike drew me onto his lap. Then the stench of gray smoke flowed out from his lungs and around my head like a halo, singeing the otherwise happy aromas wafting from Grandmother's kitchen.

He centered me on his lap and bordered me with sun-leathered arms, corralling the coins into a pile with tarry hands. "What you count, you get to keep," his phlegmy voice whispered into my ear.

I sat rigid, pushing my tummy against the table, not wanting to lean against his chest, holding my breath against the stench of dirt. He reeked not of the sweet smell of damp chocolaty earth newly dug in the backyard, but of a dusty and old kind of dirt. A dead dirt. A trucker's dirt. A greasy, motorcycle dirt.

I stared at the small mountain of coins, determined to speed along the change-counting session without the usual dime argument. Mom always said I was born stubborn, and the dime argument proved this point. (Dimes, I insisted, are *smaller* than nickels and therefore *cannot possibly* be worth *more* than a nickel.) I began separating the coins into small hills, my mind drifting from the grime of money and man toward the sounds coming from the kitchen: the clink of ice hitting glasses, the oven door opening on a creaky hinge, the *whap!* of a cupboard door, and Mom and Grandmother's flat voices talking about the turkey gravy.

Thanksgiving Day, and instead of dragging my wooden red stool to the stove to see what the gravy was all about, I sat hostage on this alien lap. I had stood on my stool all morning, the one Uncle Jack had made for me, turning the crank on the metal grinder filled with vegetables for the stuffing, inhaling the bouquet of toasting garlic, sausage, and herbs. And now, the cooking was winding down. I was missing out.

He leaned in around me, his chest against my back. "You know," the wet voice began again in my ear, "when I married yer mudder, I was actually marrying you."

A shudder jiggled down my spine, triggering a reoccurring dream: walking to school naked, my body flushed red with hopelessness. As I thought of the syrupy turkey drippings' transformation into gravy, my small hands divvied up the coins with the speed of a banker: quarters into stacks of four, dimes into tiny towers of ten, nickels into twin piles of ten and pennies into ten. I pointed to each tower of coins: "One-two-three, three-fifty, four, four-fifty, five! Five dollars!" I slid off The Lap, ducked under the table, and scurried off toward the kitchen.

I skidded to a stop in the doorway, not wanting to penetrate and disturb the aroma-pulsating heart of Thanksgiving. "Mom, I got five dollars!"

Grandmother was pulling a green plastic spoon from her porcelain measuring spoon rooster. "Nonsense," she said, "that's too much money for a little girl." She measured salt into the spoon and sprinkled it over the bubbling pan of gravy, abracadabra-style.

Stepdad appeared in the doorway, holding out his empty coffee cup, grinning. "Can I have some more coffee, Nani?" His air of false innocence blatant as a tidal wave. A kid laughing at a scolding.

Grandmother ignored him. Mom was drying a dish at the sink, a sweaty glass of amber liquid beside her on the counter, always, like a best friend. She turned, hand perched on hip. "Did you give Marisa five dollars?"

Lava flowed down my stomach wall, for the tension slicing through the savory smells of the kitchen was my fault.

"Naw, she counted it; it's hers. Isn't that right, Funny Face?"

I stared at him, blank-faced.

Grandmother waved her little green spoon at him. "And what's a little girl supposed to do with five dollars?"

I could think of lots to do with five dollars. Soon I'd be riding the Honolulu city bus to school like a big girl, and I could buy food and stuff at the little Japanese grocery before the bus came. Or I could save it, add to it, and buy something big. At six years old, I already knew money was the key to all the things I lacked: freedom, possessions, independence—the things that fueled the power of being a grown-up.

Mom's hip hand resumed dish-drying and she said, "Give it to me and I'll keep it safe for her."

Grandmother scowled at my stepdad. He looked down at me and winked.

I pretended not to see him and asked the turkey-moistened air in the kitchen, "Can I get on my stool and stir the gravy?" Which was what I'd wanted to do all along.

CHAPTER 1

EARLY AND DISCERNING TASTE BUDS

BURIED IN LONG-AGO MEMORIES is a single recollection of my real dad. It's a mere snapshot deep in the recesses of my brain, but one polished by years and aged with elegance, like the frostiest piece of pale sea glass. I love the feeling of this memory, even though my mom always told me I was far too young to remember anything of those early days living in Berkeley, before Mom took me and ran home to Hawaii. But the snapshot is mine, and I had it before I was old enough to learn of my real dad's high IQ, his legal blindness, his perpetual student status at the university, and the time he tried to kill my mom. Throughout childhood I visited this memory in times of loneliness, and it has comforted me. Certainly, my mind has embellished it over the years, but a remarkable feeling is there inside it: hope.

In this remembrance, my dad's arm is my tether, holding me up on the edge of a gold-flecked Formica kitchen table. I know of nothing other than trust. He leans in next to me, presenting a can and a fork. I'm small and useless, there to accent the lives of grown-ups, and silent unless hungry or diaper-soiled. The windows in the stark white kitchen are black, so it must be nighttime. Not a new night but a strong and established night, a night that's been around a while, unlike me. The fork plunges into the can, then reappears with a blob. The blob hovers in the air and milky tears slide down it and it moves toward me. I stare at it.

"Come on, Marisa," he says, his voice low and inviting, and his head motions toward the fork. Obediently, I slurp the blob into my mouth. The explosion fills my whole mouth and it tastes metallic, salty, then sweet, the sensation catapulting me into the mysteries of the unknown world outside the black windows of our tiny apartment. Through this foreign flavor, the world looms big and teems with possibility. I want more! Mom stands across from us, against the bare white kitchen wall, arms crossed over a puffy-sleeved paisley blouse. She makes a groaning sound and twists her face. She would never eat an oyster.

In the slightly more focused and matriarchal renditions of my childhood, there are lima beans. Frozen from a box. Perhaps it was the time—the mid-1960s—or the fact that in Hawaii, they hadn't yet learned to farm in the perfect gardening weather and much of what we ate came from boxes and cans. I spent quiet evenings at Grandmother's house on Kahala Avenue, where she lived alone long after her split with my grandfather. While the memory of this place is framed by the purple flowers of a towering jacaranda tree out back, I felt as though the musty-smelling, thick white carpet would stain from my mere existence. In this house, dinner came forth from the tiny freezer compartment in her galley kitchen. One particular frosty white box and the sound of hard green disks plopping into boiling water always made my stomach drop with dread, and I would set my Etch A Sketch on the thin-carpeted lanai floor, creep toward the kitchen, and peer around the corner to confirm my suspicions. Yes, it would be a rough night ahead, engaged in a power struggle with that woman, my grandmother, looming above me with her silver bob, curious frown lines etched around her mouth, her words always angry and final. Fiddling with the nasty green pellets of mush on my plate, nibbling micro-bites from their edges, and making dramatic *ick!* faces would gain me nothing but a hard spanking and a night in my room staring into picture books and swatting away buzzing tropical mosquitoes.

Eventually Mom, who breezed in and out the doors of my childhood those early days at Grandmother's, let me in on a trick. Frozen peas had been her childhood nemesis, which she had swallowed whole to avoid her mother's wrath. But Grandmother bought *extra large* lima beans, perhaps because she now was wise to the swallowing-whole trick, thanks to my mom. Once armed with this information, though, I'd take a lima bean under my tongue, pretend to chew and swallow it, then wash it down with a gulp of milk, triumphant that I had thwarted the vegetable police.

My best food memories are of restaurants. On open-air lanais, smiling Hawaiian ladies in colorful muumuus served up frosty Shirley Temples topped with a maraschino cherry, speared with pastel umbrellas and purple orchids. These made me look as important as my grandmother ordering her mai tai, and my mom and her bourbon and water. Here, in the great macrocosm of bustling outrigger-themed dining rooms, I could detach from my tiny, frowny world, take in all the scents and chatter of the universe, and top it off with a fantastic taste-bud adventure.

Grandmother was always the hostess, her income as a Realtor affording the family dinner out when Uncle Jack flew in from California, where he was attending Stanford. These opportunities offered taste tests of grilled mahi-mahi at The Willows in Kailua, or Haiku Gardens in Kaneohe, or at Fisherman's Wharf in Honolulu (where Grandmother and I agreed on one thing: They had the best tartar sauce). The buttery fish soothed my abused taste buds and the restaurants' atmosphere made me feel as though the future held hope. If I was good—and I always was good when we went out for dinner—Grandmother, with a clandestine look, would let me have a sip of her after-dinner B&B, sending a rush of heat into my brain and stamping the night's memories of food and atmosphere into its recesses.

• • •

Mom had inherited some money from her paternal grandmother and, in keeping with her black-sheep-of-the-family status, bought a thirty-two-foot-long sailboat. She hung around the Ala Wai yacht harbor, red-lipsticked and ponytailed, waiting for someone to teach her to sail. This probably accounted for those quiet evenings I was alone with Grandmother and her damp-dog carpet, her gin scent, dive-bombing mosquitoes, and the weekly lima bean wars. Once Mom married Stepdad, when I was six, our new family unit moved on to Mom's sailboat in the harbor.

My prize for enduring the sailing and long hours of watching grown-ups doing boat stuff all day on the docks was the occasional dinner at the Hawaii

Yacht Club in the middle of the harbor. When darkness swallowed the boat masts surrounding the club, its dining room and long bar flickered with the warmth of red-orange tabletop candles. Once we were seated at our table, I'd stare into my reflection in the picture window, backdropped by the boat lights prickling the black water like upside-down stars. I couldn't help but wonder about this nub of a girl who was me: small, pale, and puffed with just a tad too much baby fat, compared to the fit little brown kids in first grade. This girl from a family of awkward *haole* transplants. This girl who didn't have *Dick and Jane* parents or a cherry tree out front or a dog named Spot, but a rebel mother and a brand-new stepdad who, well—it was unthinkable. I didn't know how to think of our secret encounters, did not have words for it, except "dark." That part of me was simply Dark, so I didn't think of the Dark on nights staring into this window, except, Who is that girl looking back at me?

This dining room, with Hawaiian nautical history-perfumed walls and waitresses in muumuus flitting around like so many color-drenched fish, was a welcome distraction from that reflection in the window. Fried won tons, tiny meatballs, and yellow-orange triangles of pineapple served on koa wood platters decorated the tables. *Pu pu* platters, these were called; this Hawaiian term for appetizers made me want an accomplice to laugh with. Being at the yacht club was better than playing outside or even watching television. This dining room was so perfect, it was like being *inside* a television show, this atmosphere created for people to be a certain way—happy! Sometimes I got attention from scruffy sailors: tossed onto someone's lap, talked to, pulled up onto the tiny stage, and sung to by a fat Hawaiian with a ukulele.

At six years old, I loved restaurants! And this was the year I began to become a food snob.

Living on a thirty-two-foot sloop with Mom, her black-and-white cat Midge, parrot Sam, and a creepy new stepdad, I was fully aware that my childhood was different from that of other kids my age. My boat-dwelling diet consisted of tepid strawberry Carnation Instant Breakfast, a school lunch that often consisted of unidentified canned food with an Asian twist, and for dinner, Chicken Delight. Chicken Delight was Oahu's Kentucky Fried Chicken and our colonel was J. Akuhead Pupule, the DJ on the KGMB's *Coconut Wireless* program, who crackled out from the AM radio in Mom's

Volvo each morning on our way to Ala Wai Elementary. Fifty years later, I still have the pidgen English radio ditty in my head: "No cook tonight, call Chicken Delight."

Picking me up from Ala Wai Elementary, Mom would say, "Let's pick up some Chicken Delight on our way home." Like she hadn't said that the day before and the day before that. But picking up the Chicken Delight was way better than calling from the pay phone at the harbor's bathrooms, then, embarrassingly, having our dinner of soggy fried chicken arrive in a Volkswagen Bug with a giant plastic chicken on top of it.

Sometimes on weekends, in our tiny boat galley, Mom made spaghetti sauce in her electric frying pan—the one she'd hurled at my stepdad during a fight; he had to put on his scuba gear the next morning and fetch it from the harbor's bottom. Cans were opened, cheap ground beef fried, and the mixture cooked all day, imparting a vomit-like smell to the galley. Although not yet an expert on Italian food, I did point nose-upward at the reddish-brown mixture. The addition of powdered Parmesan from a green can completed the mouth-bashing experience, and I'd be scolded for my not-too-enthusiastic reception of Mom's slaving over a hot electric pan all day. I don't know which I hated more: lima beans or Mom's spaghetti.

Food was not the only dread I felt while living on the boat. There were times I couldn't avoid being alone with Stepdad when Mom would dash off to the store or I'd come home from school and there he was, stretched out on the forward bunk in front of our tiny black-and-white TV, as if waiting for me.

"Funny Face!" He'd sit up as I tried to retreat back up the steps to the cockpit. "I think we need to practice the snorkel."

I'd be frozen on the steps, unsure, frightened, wondering if Mom would be home soon. "B-but I was just—"

"You wanna come diving with me, doncha? Well then, you need to learn how to snorkel in the dark, or you'll drown down there!"

"W-when's Mom coming home?"

"Oh, she'll be gone for a while." And the red bandanna he used as a blindfold would appear, and he'd follow my tiny steps to the boat's head, and I'd sit on the toilet, afraid that my mom would come home.

During the boat year I wandered the docks barefoot, my little feet toughened by splinters and heat and salt. Greedily, I inhaled the kaleidoscope of scents the harbor offered: briny seaweed from the Pacific basin the boats were moored upon; sun-dried salt crusted on the wooden piers and docks mingled with pungent fiberglass resin at the harbormaster's; stagnant dirt from boats lived on but never sailed; and my favorite, the mouthwatering scent of a smoky grilled fish dancing around in the trade winds.

There were a few other kids at the harbor who lived on larger boats—real houseboats. Sometimes these kids and I clustered at the harbormaster's, where weathered old men rigged us up with lengths of fishing line hooked with a shrimp at one end, the other end wound around a thumbtack pushed into the cork-like dock. We'd dangle bare legs and shoeless feet off the dock, the sun cooking our tender flesh, and wait for a darting needle-fish to hit our bait.

One time, a neighbor girl boat-dweller had gotten an Easy-Bake Oven for her birthday and, stricken with envy, I tried to befriend her so she'd invite me to her houseboat to cook with it. When I stepped onto her boat, however, her mother wouldn't let me play with the prized oven. Could it be that I was stigmatized, living on a little sailboat with that plastic chicken–topped Volkswagen parked alongside our dock so many nights a week? Was it because of the times I stood on the pier at their boat, hand pushed into my crotch because I had to pee so badly, yelling, "Can Shelly play?" Maybe her mother knew that the little head on our boat stank all the time and I was looking for release elsewhere. Or that I'd rather be *anywhere* than on our boat alone with my stepdad. I would've settled playing with the box the oven came in, leaning against the girl's boat bedroom wall with that glorious picture of the four-burner stove on it. But I was afraid to even ask about the box.

At a dinner at Grandmother's house that year I was six, my true culinarian emerged. Some relatives—my mom's younger sister Aunt Sandi with Uncle Doug, and Mom's younger brother Uncle Jack with Aunt Emily—had flown in on the giant prop plane from what was known to me as the mysterious mainland. As elevator music leaked out from Grandmother's stereo console, the grown-ups began arguing in an area of the house removed from the dinner smells in the kitchen. I was afraid of all the yelling and at being abandoned, but I was hungry and all I could reach in the kitchen from my red stool were the cooked frozen corn on the cobs draining in a colander in the sink. At the table I had set in the screened lanai (with strict supervision from Grandmother), I slathered my corn with butter like I'd seen Mom and

Grandmother do. Then I sprinkled salt on my plate and with both hands spun the cob into the salty melted butter. I did the same with the pepper. My mom had always prepared my corn for me, so I was simply copying her. The butter was the obvious thing and, well, salt and pepper were always together, so I was certain I had this correct. I was proud of myself, mastering the seasoning techniques of my corn with my little hands.

I was halfway chowed down on the cob, pretending there was a typewriter *ding!* when I got to each end—something I'd seen on *Bugs Bunny*—when the grown-ups appeared in the dining room, red-faced and quiet.

"Oh, look at little Marisa!" Aunt Sandi exclaimed.

"Wow, she did that all by herself," Mom said proudly.

"I guess she was hungry!" said Uncle Jack, always my favorite.

Laughter all around. I blossomed with pride. I was the center of attention!

Then: "She put *pepper* on her corn?"

Grandmother in her matriarchal voice, hand on ample hip: "Oh! We don't put *pepper* on corn."

Well, maybe *we* don't, I thought, but *I* do. I was enjoying my ear of corn, and although I tended to embarrass easily, the insecurity I felt with all those adult eyes on me melted like the butter on hot corn. Even though Grandmother maintained there was a right and wrong way to do everything, there was no longer a reason to have more rules about how and what to eat. Maybe I'd made a mistake, copying what I thought the grown-ups did to their corn, but I *liked* the pepper on my corn and I *still* like pepper on my corn, and if I could go back in time and yell something to the sneering grown-ups in that dining room on that evening in 1967, I'd say this: "Fuck you! I like *pepper* on my corn."

I liked the corn as much as I hated lima beans. And these facts could be my little secrets. I planned to share them with no one. I was afraid to be further judged by Grandmother and her gang—and the food, at least, did not judge me.

• • •

I cannot pinpoint when I began to stutter and then became silent because of it. This is not a snapshot, like the memory of my real dad and the canned oyster. The memory of my stutter is slippery, hard to grab hold of, with a multitude of strings flapping in the wind. According to Grandmother, I picked it up from a neighbor girl one summer (no memory of that at all). According to Mom, I began to stutter after one night she was accosted by a man on a street while I remained in the car, crying (no memory of that either). It seemed to me that I always stuttered, but during a therapy session when I was thirty-nine, a moment of clarity proved that this was not the case. Long-dormant memories came alive, and I was able to remember a pre-abuse girl, the kindergarten class-disturber, the chatty comedian wannabe, who'd been banished from the classroom for her disruptive one-liners, inching one toe over the threshold once the teacher had scolded: "Do not set one foot into this classroom!" The family telling of this story always labeled me a brat there, but in therapy, I finally felt the motivations of this girl. Brave, clever, shit-disturber, not shy. (Okay, maybe a little bratty.) Somehow, the chatty-bratty girl transitioned into a quiet one, secretly rejecting the adults' penchant for soggy fried chicken, canned Parmesan, and cardboard lima beans, and hanging on to her delicious secrets of pepper on corn, grilled fish, fried wontons, and turkey gravy.

No, I did not plan on being a chef when I grew up, because I did not know of such a thing. I still had comedian (which began to fade once my stutter got so bad) or architect in mind. But good food always gave me hope for better times, in spite of the judgments, scowls, and shenanigans of the grown-ups.

CHAPTER 2

WORKING FOR A LIVING

AFTER THE BOAT YEAR we moved to Kailua, where I went to school at Maunawili Elementary. Grandmother had constantly pressured my mother that a boat was no place to raise a child, so Mom and Stepdad bought a house in the Pohakupu subdivision, right down the street from Grandmother's new house. I was just happy to have a door with my bedroom, and a fat orange cat named Jo-Jo who slept with me in my *Jungle Book* sheets. From an outsider's perspective it looked like an idyllic Hawaiian childhood: walking to school, bike-riding, swimming in our new pool, watching *Hawaii Five-0* at night on our color TV. I made a friend from up the street that first year in Kailua, and Jackie has endured as my forever friend all these years later. Then little brother Christopher arrived and we looked like a complete family. But inside the walls of our house were fights, too many cats pooping in corners, week-old dirty dishes, locked doors, Grandmother scolding my mother, and my continued insecurities blooming like a smelly corpse flower.

Then in 1971, when I was eleven, Stepdad lost his foreman's job on the Dillingham docks due to a dock strike, and we moved from the island of Oahu to rural Maui, leaving Grandmother and her condescending ways behind. Mom, Stepdad, Christopher, and I settled into a subdivision of identical stucco houses in the beach town of Kihei, the desert end of the island known affectionately by locals as "that wide spot in the road." Missing Jackie but relieved to be away from Grandmother, I did miss those taste-bud-inspiring dinners at Haiku Gardens and Fisherman's Wharf. The dining opportunities in Kihei consisted of Fuku's Suck 'em Up Eats housed in a metal Quonset hut, Azeka's Ribs at the local market, and the Maui Lu Hotel's Longhouse dining room. Before long, though, our financial situation had sunk so low that eating out was considered as luxurious as a Cadillac or a world cruise.

One evening when I was twelve, the culinary wasteland years were happily interrupted when we went to Chez Paul in Olowalu, a town comprising a store, some old plantation worker shacks, and an unlikely but actual French restaurant. Stepdad had done some construction work for Mr. Callarec, the chef and owner, and the restaurateur's payment to us was dinner. The bartering system was big in our household; Stepdad did unlicensed contracting work and got paid in furniture, televisions, and once with a pot-bellied pig, much to the anger of my mom, who simply wanted the bills paid and food on the table. (What about that pig?) But I was ecstatic at this rare opportunity (the restaurant, not the pig) on this night, looking for something nice to wear in my closet of little-girl dresses left over from that era of Grandmother, and venturing off in Stepdad's fix-it car of the month—a hot pink Javelin—to the only French restaurant on Maui.

Reading the menu at the candlelit table was like holding some ancient rare parchment, the French words so alluring, taunting me from the pages. Life felt so large then, proof that there were many exciting things in the world, and in a few very long years I'd be out in that world exploring everything. English translations were listed under the French words and I read the descriptions—lyrics for all things great—with excitement and apprehension, as if I would soon be experiencing the thrill of jumping from an airplane or sailing around the world.

After Mr. Callarec had greeted us, shaken hands with Stepdad, and left us to study our menus, Mom looked at the menu and made a face. "Oh! They have those snails."

"Where?" I asked, looking at the jumble of words before me, then seeing them listed under the word *escargots* in the appetizer section.

"You don't want them, Marisa."

But I did want them!

Then Stepdad barked, "Just order a main course; that'll be enough!"

Mom ordered mahi-mahi; Stepdad, a steak. It was my turn and my heart began to pound. "C-can I have . . ." I pointed to the roast duck on the menu, saving myself from tripping over the "d" in *duck*, and avoiding judgment from my parents for my selection. I could tell by Mr. Callarec's raised eyebrows that he was impressed by my order.

The duck, with its crispy skin and smoky flesh, was by far the most elegant sensation my young taste buds had ever experienced. I yummed and hummed while eating, like a cat purring over a food bowl. After dinner, Mr. Callarec, in a heavy rambling accent, explained each dish to me: the escargots, the pâtés, the preparation of the duck. I didn't understand much of what he said, but his presence there at our table prolonged the dining experience and I wanted to remain in the small candlelit dining room and listen to his French accent forever.

That year was also the year I begged my mom to relinquish her command post—her kitchen—so I could cook dinner. She still made her spaghetti, in an iron pan instead of the electric one, which had gone by the way of the fishes, and this new iron pan made the sauce taste even worse. Mom could make some good stuff sometimes when she followed recipes from her large volume of *Joy of Cooking* ("Marisa, this cookbook is older than you"), but Stepdad didn't like anything "fancy," putting his plate on the floor next to his black Naugahyde easy chair for our multitude of cats and dogs to yowl, bark, and slurp over. These were fight nights, when I'd escape to my room to do homework, listen to Savoy Brown, and plot out how I, in the kitchen, could make a successful meal.

Mom finally gave me her kitchen one afternoon. I'd flipped through the food-stained *Joy of Cooking* and selected peanut butter pork chops, which, to everyone's amazement, including my own, were good and tender. Peanut butter, milk, diced onion, and cayenne pepper were the main ingredients—mainstays of pork satay, as I would later learn. My moment of pride, after Mom and Stepdad tasted my dish, nodding and smiling, was a rare moment in my childhood stew of insecurity and angst. Even three-year-old Christopher liked it. Here was something I could do. I would show them all.

Our move to Maui had also been a strategy to get me into a better school. My mom clearly lacked many maternal and household abilities, which riled my grandmother, but she decided that getting me out of the shoddy Hawaii state public school system was essential for my education. And on this point, the two actually agreed. In Kailua I'd overheard whispers of haoles being knifed in the bathroom at the intermediate and high schools, and that it was important to "get Marisa out of here before she leaves elementary school." I took the scary entrance exam for Seabury Hall, got a full scholarship, and a carpool was arranged. Oddly, I had no sense of the faith they apparently had in me.

So at fourteen I was attending the quaint Episcopalian, former all-girls school nestled on the verdant green slopes of Mount Haleakala. With its small classes led by brilliant instructors, cows mooing in the surrounding pastures, gorgeous girls from mostly wealthy families, and curious cute boys, I felt frumpy, awkward, and afraid to speak. I was also enduring the emerging poverty in our household and more eager than ever to get through high school and leave home.

I also wanted nice things—including better food, a surfboard, and eventually a car. Towns on Maui are spread out, with no public transportation, and having a car when I got my license at fifteen was mandatory for my freedom. I'd been babysitting and washing cars since I was twelve, but I wanted—needed—a real income.

The couple I babysat for across the street worked in Whalers Village in Kaanapali, twenty-six coastal and mountainous miles from the red-dirt flatness of Kihei. If the neighbors would let me ride to work with them one morning, I could look for a job in Whalers Village and, once I found employment, I could carpool with them for the summer. It was a great plan, until I approached my mom for her part in it—because by my wildly insecure teen years, I stuttered so badly that it was a fright-fest to engage in conversation with anyone I didn't know well, especially grown-ups.

"You should ask them yourself, Marisa." Mom was pulling weeds in the dirt in our front yard, below the upright twig she called the monkeypod tree. We had no grass.

My stomach gurgled and fell at the thought of approaching the neighbors. Why did I have to endure this curse? The roller-coaster stomach, the burning stares, my mortal fear to be called upon in class to read aloud, which further inspired more contempt from my new classmates.

I dug my big toe into the red dirt next to Mom on her haunches at the base of the tree-twig. "But, Mom, I need *you* to ask. They'll say no if I ask 'em!

Then I won't get a job!" I was ratcheting up to a tantrum, my need to earn money so strong. My need to avoid embarrassment even stronger. My need to get the hell out of there, strongest.

"Marisa, you need to—"

My face felt on fire. "Y-you want me t-to w-work, don't you? E-earn money t-to help out?" The toe-hole in the dirt I'd dug was now a small pit. Did she not understand? Did she think everything was fine with me? Or was she just plain oblivious?

Mom stood up and dusted silty dirt from her knees. She was wearing a pair of Stepdad's old jeans, faded nearly to white and cut off at the thighs, the extra denim gathered at her hip and secured with a yellow diaper pin. Her shirt, one of the dingy three she always wore, had rust-colored half-moons under the armpits. To me she looked like a homeless person, reduced to a hell I never, ever wanted for myself. I *had* to have a job. I would always have a job. I would wear new clothes. I would eat good food. She must have seen my desperation, because finally she said, "I'll talk to them this week." Then she crouched back in the dirt.

Our unkempt house of overflowing ashtrays and shitting cats showcased my mom's lack of pride. The front door and back sliding glass doors were always open for the animals, whose smell tainted the salty trade winds that breezed through our house like a visitor running from something, and blew in the talc of red dust that lay over the cat-clawed surfaces of our black Naugahyde furniture like a thin red blanket. And there it stayed. There was little dusting or vacuuming in our house, and dishwashing occurred every few days when there was nothing left to eat on. I hated my mom for this lifestyle. Later, after I left home, I felt sorry for her. Eventually, I would forgive her.

This dirty canvas of our lives was the backdrop for the fighting, Mom always yelling at Stepdad, with many *goddammits*. "You lost that job? Well we've got bills to pay, buster." Stepdad: "Oh, get off my back!" Sometimes there was her after-the-kids-are-in-bed, under-her-breath yelling, which we could hear through the cheap drywall of our bedrooms. "You're supposed to at least act like you love him; he's your son, goddammit!" The silence that followed was scarier than the yelling, and I would wonder if Christopher had heard. I wondered why Mom would say this for him to hear. I also wondered why she had married this man, let alone had a child with him.

No surprise that my five-year-old brother roamed the neighborhood in his ragged Fruit of the Looms, looking for nice neighbors to take him in and feed him. The end of each fight was usually punctuated by the storm of my mother pounding down the hall and slamming their bedroom door. The house would sit quiet except for the sound of crickets outside and the low laughter from a sitcom on the TV in the living room. Then, right when I'd finally begun to doze off, I'd hear the pop of my humidity-swelled door, and Stepdad would creep in. I'd hug my knees and roll into a ball, determined to protect myself from the world.

• • •

My drive for employment overruled my nervousness that day at Whalers Village, applying for jobs. There wasn't much to breezing into gift shops and galleries spitting out my rehearsed line: "C-can I fill out an application?" Either I filled one out, or they didn't need help. I didn't even feel rejected, I was having so much fun exploring this new potential in my life. When I happened upon the Sea Scoop, with its aroma of eggs and its black-and-white ice-cream parlor decor, the manager ("Hi, I'm Greg") read my application and then sat across from me at the wrought iron table. (How oblivious was I to this very important moment of my life. What if I'd gotten a job at one of the galleries instead?)

"I see you don't have any experience, but Bob needs some help in the kitchen."

"I learn quick. I-I help my mom in her kitchen."

He smiled at this. "How old are you?"

"Fifteen," I lied. I'd be fifteen at the end of the summer.

• • •

So that day I was introduced to Bob the grill cook, a smiling man in his thirties. I really wanted to help him. My eagerness proved worthwhile, because the following week on my first day, I found the cutting and prepping tasks simple and fun and Bob said I was the best help he'd ever had.

The cobblestone paths wending through Whalers Village led eager and pinking tourists on a sunny trek past shops and outdoor whaling displays to the beach. But at 7 a.m., before the shops opened, the sun hadn't yet climbed over the top of the West Maui Mountains and the village remained in shadow, the brightest images the lighted windows behind which shopkeepers readied cases of scrimshaw and turquoise, arranged walls of framed batik and pedestals of folk art, or simply sat with coffee and a copy of the *Lahaina Sun* in hand, each anticipating their day. As I walked the paths toward my destination on those early summer mornings, anticipation swelled in my chest. I felt special! This feeling was a precious one that had eluded me throughout my short life, and I had it now and wouldn't let it go. Sure, anyone could walk through the outdoor museum at this early hour, stop to peer into glass cases of whaling artifacts or giant, reconstructed whale bones. But I was walking to my *job*. I had purpose.

As I neared the beach, the clink of china on wrought iron tabletops penetrated the silence of the sleeping shopping village, and the scent of bacon and beach moistened the back of my tongue. I walked up the outdoor stairs, paused to view three-foot waves crashing on empty sand, and, once on the balcony, wound through tables populated by soon-to-be-beachgoers filling their stomachs with pancakes and eggs. Then I arrived at the Sea Scoop kitchen, where a haze of melting American cheese and bacon grease assaulted my already-clogged adolescent pores.

Two waitresses were leaning into the pickup window, which meant that Bob was already deep in the weeds. I dashed behind the cook's line, tying my apron, and before I could peer into the top of his prep refrigerator he said, "Need ham and cheese diced."

"'Kay," I replied, and I blazed into action. I grabbed the ham from the cutting board, tossed it on the meat slicer, whipped off a few slices, piled the slices atop each other, and, with the French knife, sliced the pile in each direction to make small cubes like Bob had shown me. I brushed the cubes into the stainless steel insert in his prep refrigerator. I did the same with the American cheese—just enough to get him through the next few orders—and then I went back to backing up the ham, filling up the insert, feeling like his savior girl, then asking, once the window was full of plated food and only one ticket remained flapping on the ticket rail, "Um, any-anything else before I do lunch prep?"

Bob turned from the stove and looked at me, his green eyes locking on mine, which sent an unfamiliar tingle up my spine. He smiled. "Fine now.

Thanks." He turned to the still-full pickup window and banged his metal spatula on the shelf. "Betty!" he yelled. "Pick up, pick *up*!"

Betty, a fifty-something bleached blonde, rushed around the corner, her black French maid–style uniform poufing at the skirt. "Coming!" she hollered in a nicotine-charged voice. "Girls! Come pick up your food!" she yelled to the others, and they all scurried in, black dresses a-poufing, plates disappearing from the window as they filed in then out.

I also wore the embarrassing black uniform dress but covered it with a long white kitchen apron, which made me feel less self-conscious about my extra inch of lingering baby fat and awkwardly blooming breasts on my five-foot frame. My brown hair, after a childhood of herky-jerky growth due to Mom's dull scissors, finally hung to the middle of my back and I twirled it into a nob behind my head and secured it with a dime-store clip.

Bob wore jeans and a T-shirt over his lanky and sun-leathered self. Each afternoon he removed the formerly white apron, which wore the war stains of every broken egg yolk and grease splatter from the 375-degree griddle. His thin brown hair was tied back into a ponytail, and those green eyes when he looked at me seemed to really see *me*, not just some stuttering and awkwardly curvaceous girl, so I talked with relative ease and comfort around him. Bob was a thirty-two-year-old Vietnam War veteran. I was in love with him.

Really, I was. I felt good about myself around him. He listened to me without any apparent judgment. When I was near Bob, the reflection of myself I perceived was of a pretty, clever girl, and therefore I stuttered less. Relieved and relaxed, I cherished these feelings like a sailor cherishes the fleeting orange glow of sunrise amid a storm.

On my birthday in August, I shared a secret with Bob. No, I didn't profess my love for him—that would come much later. I confessed that I wasn't turning sixteen, but fifteen, because I had lied about my age to get the job. While most fourteen-year-olds were still babysitting and doing paper routes, I'd been working illegally all summer around sharp whirring blades and searing hot equipment. Earlier in the summer, while positioning a chunk of roast beef on the meat slicer, I'd sliced off a piece of my thumb's knuckle, and no one pulled me up on my lie. Bob just shook his head and smiled when I admitted my age, and then he tossed two burger patties onto the griddle.

Also that summer, I bought a used surfboard and went out with a teen neighbor girl named Kalani. Caramel-skinned and slim, she looked beautiful in her crocheted bikini. She was also popular with the boys. None of this rubbed off on me, however. I just kept wiping out and getting scratched up on coral. Then the movie *Jaws* came out and I was afraid to surf anyway. But I still felt cool owning a surfboard.

Alas, summer ended and tenth grade began with the distraction of getting my driver's license, my new wealth buying a beat-up 1963 Rambler—a true Maui cruiser—and planning my escape from high school, and Maui, a year early. Once everything had settled in at school, I daydreamed of dicing ham and cheese with the big French knife, talking to Bob, and banging metal spatula on metal overshelf and yelling, "Pick up!" to the waitresses. The sound the spatula made—the release of pure frustration—was so satisfying, I wanted to duplicate it at home and school. But I had to study. I had to make something of myself and leave Maui.

One fall day after school, and without a word to anyone, I drove down Mount Haleakala, through the cane fields hugging the flat center of Maui, and instead of hanging a left at the beach toward Kihei, I turned right and headed toward the mountain (*pali*) road between the mist-covered West Maui Mountains and the sapphire-blue Pacific. I drove through Lahaina town and into Kaanapali, where Whalers Village sat nestled between the famous Black Rock at the Sheraton Maui and Chuck's Steak House. This trip was only about forty miles but narrow and winding, and the Rambler topped out at about forty miles per hour. It took me almost two hours. This seriously cut into homework time, but I was driven to ask my question.

Sitting across from Jim, Sea Scoop's weekday manager, at an outside table, I asked, "So . . . c-c-c-can I work weekends and holidays?" I didn't know Jim like I knew Greg, who'd hired me, and I feared rejection. But he went back to the kitchen and talked to Bob, then waved me back to say hi to Bob, who smiled at me.

I drove home along the coast to Kihei, the sun flirting with the Pacific horizon, my car overheating, my chest tight with anticipation to get through the school week so that on weekends I could help Bob in the kitchen.

Life at school was tense: The girl cliques shunned me and no popular boys liked me, further bruising my young and shy psyche. I focused on my studies and did well. My friend interactions didn't seem to meet the expectations of the cliques, and I was accused, more than once, of "trying too hard." But weekend mornings I'd race (as much as the Rambler could race) off to Kaanapali to work at the Scoop, where I became addicted to a foreign feeling. Confidence.

The confidence stayed with me only while in the kitchen, however. After my shift, tanning on the beach behind Whalers Village, I remained an observer of the restaurant workers not only from the Scoop but also from the neighboring Rusty Harpoon and Chuck's Steak House. Many of the Scoop waitresses worked in two or all three restaurants and they hung out together drinking, smoking pot, and playing volleyball in the sand, in crocheted bikinis that hugged their slender bodies. And the boys—men?—were tan and fit, with pure smiles and tousled, sun-bleached hair.

I'd sit on my beach towel and watch the interaction of those only a few years older than I was, and I ached to be a part of a group like that, for humanity to invite me in for full interaction. I wanted to be invited to someone's house for dinner, or to participate in a volleyball game, and to graciously accept and have people enjoy my company. Watching the restaurant workers reminded me of school, everyone appearing comfortable in their little groups of friends while I wandered the halls, trying to find a place to fit.

A few times after work I did get invited into the fold, sharing a joint of Maui Wowie—one of the island's major food groups—or being invited up to the Harpoon for beers, my age ignored. I'd sit, silent and smiling, my brain paddling around in a youthful buzz, while a hippie sunset musician strummed "Havana Daydreamin'" and "Waimanalo Blues."

So it was possible, then, that I just needed more practice. Once I graduated, this was how *I* was going to live. But I wanted to start over, somewhere else, where no one knew me.

CHAPTER 3

ON MY OWN: PORTLAND, OREGON

MY COLLEGE DREAMS HAD ALWAYS BEEN BIG, and despite the state of my home life, my mom always assumed I'd go to college. But my grandmother showed favoritism for only the male brains in our family: specifically Uncle Jack, the Stanford graduate, later a nuclear physicist with a career with NASA. The sixties and seventies were progressive times for women, but in our family, the past nipped at our rears.

In the 1940s Grandmother, daughter of a strict schoolteacher and a World War I army sergeant stationed at Schofield Barracks in Wahiawa, had herself taught school, at Punahou in Honolulu, where her children attended (and from where Barack Obama would graduate many years later). I'd gone to Punahou for kindergarten but was asked not to return to the familial school. This was a nice way to say that I was kicked out, due to behavioral issues. (Maybe the toe over the threshold had sealed my fate.) Sure, I got a D in naptime and disrupted class a lot, but I got As in all the learning stuff. So this "asked not to return," a phrase I heard constantly in my youth, could've been made up by Grandmother, who simply didn't want to pay tuition for such a brat to attend a good school in Hawaii's otherwise shoddy educational system. I'll never know. I did know that she did not hold back any of the scorn she felt about me "ruining her reputation." Anyway, the women in our family were expected to be smart, but only smart enough to land the right man. This unspoken fact had landed my grandmother, Mom, and Aunt Sandi in multiple island-to-mainland, dead-end marriages. None of them had gotten an A in the man class.

In the summer of my senior year, I finally acted on my crush and submitted to a tumultuous love affair with older man Bob at the Sea Scoop. Bob lived with his girlfriend Jane, and she arrived home from work one afternoon and caught Bob and me cuddling. A great storm had rolled in and the *pali* road was closed, so I couldn't drive back to Kihei and was going to stay in their spare room. But beer and pot had further clouded our judgment and there I was stranded, drunk, high, guilty, embarrassed, and lovesick, and made to sleep in Bob's Dodge van. The van vibrated in the wind, rain washed over it in great sheets, and I wished to hell the storm would pick the van up *Wizard of Oz*-style and deliver it somewhere. I needed to disappear.

So at seventeen, having graduated from Seabury Hall a year early, my heart filled with love and loss for Bob, I headed to Lewis and Clark College in Portland, Oregon. I was a straight-A student beginning my upward climb to be *something* when I grew up.

The excitement of arriving in a new place ready to start my life was not the balm to my woes I had hoped for. Portland was cold and gray and I was bored without my car, sunshine, and the friends it had taken me years to cultivate. Since I was only seventeen, the other students were a few years older and seemed to be of a different species. They were wrapped in coats, tight and looking inward; I was a sunshine girl, open and wanting. Once again, I didn't fit in.

My English and psychology classes were duller than dirt. Spanish had been my love in high school, with my tiny class of known peers led by a beloved teacher, and I'd placed in such an advanced level that my classmates at Lewis and Clark were in their intimidating twenties. I was struggling to get comfortable speaking to anyone in English, and Spanish class with all these strangers had me tongue-tied. There was one boy from Boston who'd invited me to a boys' dorm party, then abandoned me for some other girl. On that night, the music cranking out of the turntable was a shrill backdrop to my woes. It was 1977 and the dissonant saxophone shrieks of jazz fusion drove me to bathtub punch. Alone.

I missed Bob and the warmth he'd bestowed upon me, but not the hurt look of his girlfriend Jane when she discovered us, nestled up together in their living room. Guilt was added to my list of confidence-crushing emotions. The marijuana of the Great Northwest sent me further into doom, so unlike the nearly caffeinated Maui Wowie I was raised on. I was bored, cold, and lonely, and I wanted a confidence fix. So one drizzly afternoon toward the end of first term, I rode my bike down the hill and, bragging about my cooking timing and speed, got a job at the Marketplace, a Continental restaurant with a bearded and plaid-shirted young chef named Dewey Kelly, who agreed to teach me sauces on the sauté line.

Rack of lamb, chateaubriand, pompano en papillote—the sautéed butter-aroma-filled kitchen and my testosterone-charged cook mates grounded me to the damp Pacific Northwest soil. To the boys on the line I was the quiet new kid, the student, that food prep girl heading back to Maui soon for the holiday. Were those sneers aimed in my direction?

This stint in the kitchen was a brief one. While the sauté and grill lines were charged up in full dinner shift action, I was at the small prep table behind the hood wall, chopping, blending, and wrapping pompano in filo dough. After Dewey went up front to expedite during the rush, I was on my own, my brain locked into my tasks and how to perform them as efficiently as possible.

The fact that I rode my bike to work in the afternoon did get me some interaction with the staff, as it was usually raining, always cold, dark, and simply dangerous to be riding back up the hill at night with no lights. Dewey had promised he'd prearrange rides for me. Sometimes it was George the bartender in his giant Buick, other times Doug the sous chef (if he worked late) in his van. After work, passenger-seat chatter in the dark came fairly easy to me. Smelling of onions and garlic, I felt I had purpose.

Home for two weeks over Christmas did not grace upon me a paradise of warmth, or surfing and driving around Maui in my convertible '67 Volkswagen Bug (which had replaced the Rambler after its transmission fell out on Kalanianaole Highway). Bankruptcy had ripped what little civility there had been from our household, and everything was gone. Sold was my car, my surfboard, my *stuff*, even my collection of swizzle sticks from my little-girl days restaurant-hopping with Grandmother and Mom. The bits of good stuff that had been in my childhood—my talismans—were gone. The stucco house had been sold off and my family and all the animals with their shit smells were holed up in a partially built cinder block house down the street on Ohukai Road—all walls and no roof.

Anger was my Siamese twin on this visit. My scholarship to Lewis and Clark had netted only a three-thousand-dollar dorm cost per semester, and all first term my mom kept promising this would be paid. She was starting to sound like Stepdad: "After we get paid on this pool job." Or, "We're getting a big deposit this week for the retaining wall for so-and-so."

My brother, now eight, was off on his bike most of the time, surely avoiding the fights about money and any scoldings that would come his way, for it seemed Stepdad would invent stuff to yell at him about. I felt helpless to protect him.

But we all faked the Christmas spirit and would play Hearts at night, Mom and I slurping down eggnogs and rum, Stepdad drinking coffee like he did all day. One night I drank so much eggnog and rum that I forgot to lock my bedroom door. I awoke when my stepdad opened it and I played possum until he was close enough—and then I kicked him in the face.

The question of my overdue tuition payment came up and Mom told me, several times, "Don't worry about it." But in January when I returned to the gray-misted Northwest to register for second term, my attendance was blocked for nonpayment of the first term. With the last of my savings, I paid off what I owed so that I could access my dorm room to get my stuff (record player and clothes—it was all the stuff I had left, and I wanted it). I rode my bike to the Marketplace and whined about my situation, and Doug loaned me his couch for a few nights. With his van, we went and emptied my dorm room. I'd now bought my separation from the parents, but I didn't reregister at Lewis and Clark. I didn't like it there anyway. Instead, I signed up for nutrition and Spanish classes at Portland State and rented a house in Oregon City. Chef Dewey increased my night shifts, and I decided I would tolerate the sneers from the other cooks. I needed the money.

Early days at the Marketplace were as intimidating as the first day of school. Chef Dewey was like most egotistical men, and teaching the young maiden (me) fluffed the feathers on his rooster chest. I simply listened as he instructed me in the techniques of toasting butter and flour in roux-making. We used that roux to tighten the classic French sauces we made for the sauté station: a chicken-y velouté for the white dishes, a rich beefy bordelaise for the meat dishes. We made these from scratch, so my taste buds, after being asleep from years of tough meat and iceberg salads at home, and hamburgers and banana pancakes at the Scoop, were awakened, astute, ready for action.

These sauces were building blocks for the completed dishes we produced during service. Add the bordelaise to sautéed mushrooms deglazed with brandy for sauce Diane. Reduce red wine and add bordelaise for the chateaubriand. The velouté worked in the same manner for fish and chicken dishes. The logic and the art of these techniques trumped anything I'd learned at Lewis and Clark.

My favorite sauce was Hollandaise—which I discovered I had a knack for. Already I looked like an expert because, thanks to breakfast shifts at the Sea Scoop, I cracked the eggs one-handed before separating the egg yolks into the big metal bowl. Swiftly whipping the eggs over heat to avoid scrambling is the real technique, about which the boys would say to me, "It's all in the wrist," rich with innuendo, as I hefted the bowl onto the gas flame and whipped away in the figure-eight pattern shown to me. Chef Dewey had to explain only once about the butter's temperature (not too hot, not too cold) before whipping it ever so gradually into the cooked yolks. The hardest part was Hollandaise maintenance: finding a warm and draft-free spot in our hot kitchen to store the sauce so it wouldn't break, curdle, or separate.

One afternoon in my early days of training, Chef Dewey stood at the stove making that evening's dinner special and he said, "Get me some scallops from the walk-in." I dashed off, pulled open the big cooler door, then stood in the refrigerated air, suddenly flooded with self-doubt. Bunches of green onions mocked me from the shelf. *Scallions?* The *shallots* were in the storeroom by the onions . . . what had he said? Shallots or scallions? I looked around the walk-in shelves. He was making a special, this thing he asked for would be *it*, the special thing, not a condiment . . . scallops? Scallops? What the fuck *are* scallops? The term was vague in my mind. I was paralyzed with embarrassment, envisioning the look on Chef Dewey's face if I brought him the wrong thing, and how that would knock me to the lowest rung on the kitchen ladder. *Idiot*, I'd be called, *stupid girl*. Finally, I pivoted from the scallions to the meat shelf behind me. And there, next to the box of chicken breasts, was a clear bag filled with something lumpy and milky white. *Scallops?*

He'd said *some scallops*. I picked up the bag and inspected it. I'd never seen these in the walk-in before, so I reasoned they must be the special thing. Scallops. I took a deep breath, shut the walk-in door behind me, fixed my expression to one of great calm while rounding the corner, and hesitantly presented the bag to the chef.

Chef Dewey looked up from the stove and nodded, taking the bag. "What took so long?"

"I was just cooling off in the walk-in, straightening some shelves." The tension in my throat fell into my stomach.

As the only girl among the night cooks, I eventually enjoyed near-prodigy status. What I lacked in conversational skills I more than made up for in timing and accuracy at the stove. Once Chef Dewey had shown me all the sauces, and once I knew a scallop from a scallion from a shallot, I was rock-and-roll girl on the six-burner range. It was all in the setup, having all garnishes, spices, wine, and sauce bases ready and in reach, *mise en place*—a place for everything, as they say in cook terms. Then we'd crank up the radio and the black-vested waiters would scurry up to the window with their order slips. My focus was on sautéing and flaming multiple pans to ensure cooking accuracy and great flavor. My mission: to swamp the grill cook.

"Where's your steaks? I'm ready, slowpoke!" I chortled one night, slapping a perfectly browned halibut steak onto a plate and finishing it with the lemon-butter sauce from the sauté pan.

"Well-done steak's almost ready, hold on." This was curly-black-haired Donny, who I had a great big crush on, his responses always accompanied by a wink that melted me bit by bit each night.

On Saturday nights Chef Dewey joined Donny and me behind the line to act as a third station in the middle, searing filet mignon on Donny's grill, wrapping the meat with puff pastry for beef Wellingtons, and folding parchment paper around pompano fillets. These were delicate tasks that Donny and I were too amped up on cooking speed to handle.

On one such Saturday the three of us were pivoting around our stations, trying to keep up with all the tickets hanging in the window. Chef Dewey had three beef Wellingtons in the oven and I had a break on sauté to lay out heated plates for him. When Dewey went to spatula the pastry-wrapped steaks to the plates, one of them flipped out of the pan and onto the floor.

The three of us stopped in mid-whatever and looked at the steak in a splat of ruined puff pastry, oozing mushroom duxelles on the dirty rubber floor mat. The world stopped at that moment: This would ruin the rest of the meals and make us all failures. Right when I felt my eyes tear up in anguish for my fellow cooks, Chef Dewey, cool as ever, scooped the meat onto the cutting board and put the two intact Wellingtons into the warming oven. Donny grabbed more mushroom duxelles from the refrigerator near him. Catching on to this wordless save-the-day, I pulled more puff pastry from my refrigerator. For a minute, the waiters' calls for pickup were ignored while we redressed the meat and fast-fired it. That night reinforced something: that the key to everything is problem-solving, not finger-pointing or complaining. Just get the job done.

It was especially fun that our chef had committed the faux pas, and Donny and I joked about the Wellington episode regularly on our weeknight shifts.

"Yeah, good thing it landed on that wax paper," Donny said, carefully flipping over three steaks with long-handled tongs, his lankiness reminding me of Bob.

"What wax paper?" I said stupidly.

He rolled his eyes at me. "It's a joke—it's what we say whenever anything lands on the floor. Learn the lingo, will ya, hotshot?" Wink.

I stuck my tongue out at him. But I would use "good thing it landed on that wax paper" in almost every cooking job for the next twenty years, and I say it at home if something falls on the floor. Eventually, I came up with my own clever saying about our illustrious young chef: "Dewey unto others as you would like others to Dewey unto you," which, when the other cooks repeated it, made me feel of particular value to the operation.

Donny was off Monday nights and a man named Dennis worked the grill. Setting up the line with someone new was awkward at first, since Donny and I had settled into a system and camaraderie, but Dennis intrigued me. He was more educated than the usual kitchen ilk, and he spoke slowly and softly with carefully chosen academic words. His perfectly trimmed red beard wiggled when he smiled and he maintained a steady, inexorable pace throughout the shift. And Monday nights were typically slow, so we talked—this opportunity to get to know someone through conversation was somewhat rare for me, but much easier in a kitchen environment than in Real Life.

Dennis lived with his girlfriend, a teacher, and he had been a teacher as well and was currently working on some big academic project. The rest of our conversations have evaporated with time, but there is one thing about Dennis that always remained with me, front and center of my psyche, like a carrot twelve inches in front of my face. One night Dennis told me that he and his girlfriend were reading a book together. I asked him, "How do you read a book together?" Dennis, flipping over a steak with a shrug, said, "One night, I read a chapter to her, and the next night she reads a chapter to me." And I thought, what a damn sweet thing, two people, a man and a woman, reading to each other. I pictured Bob and me, in all our twisted lust, and I could not picture him reading to me. I thought about the fleeting sexual encounters with faceless boys the summer after I graduated; no, they would never have read to me. I thought about that kid in the dorm from Boston. Read to me? Never. I wanted someone to read to me. I wanted to be a girl like Dennis's girl and have a sweet man like Dennis care for me. Would this ever be possible?

A second job at a truck-stop joint on the nearest freeway exit filled in the rest of my idle hours. Three days a week I dished out meatloaf specials alongside scoops of instant mashed potatoes and canned green beans, choreographing moves around the crotchety old kitchen manager who looked like Li'l Abner, complete with the permanent appendage of a cigarette drooping from his lower lip. Five nights a week at the Marketplace, I whipped up Hollandaise and velouté sauces and womanned my post at the six-burner sauté station, keeping up with the grill guys, whose sneers began to melt into mild amusement.

Life had a rhythm to it. I had forged something in the wide-open world and it was mine. On days off I experimented with freeway driving, merging onto I-5 with the limited horsepower of my newly purchased 1971 VW Bug. I drove north to Vancouver, Washington, thrilled to cross into another state. I followed Pacific Highway west out of Oregon City, mapless, in pursuit of the coast. Sometimes I'd slow into a little town and stop at the local diner for a small iceberg salad, just to sit in a booth and people watch. Once I ventured into a smoky bar near Oregon City and tried to pass for twenty-one so I could watch that walk of life. No luck there. My bar life would come later.

The rush of cooking, my new repertoire of sauces, having honed my sauté-slut status to near Olympic proportions, beer-drinking, and smoking bad pot with my workmates after work—all this kept my spirits up, but I knew I needed to get on with my education. My two classes at Portland State were just a pit stop, the classes dull, with monotonous lectures in huge auditoriums. I'd been groomed on private school and small classes, with plenty of student-teacher interaction. Slinging hash at two jobs, the overburdening costs of rent and expenses in Oregon City, and a part-time school would not get me where I needed to be.

Chef Dewey came up with my next move: He said to check out the sous chef program at nearby Portland Community College's Sylvania Campus.

The stigma of community college aside, I inquired at the sprawling campus up the road for fall term of 1978. Always in a rush, I wanted to challenge the first year of the program, where they'd be teaching the sauces I'd already learned at the Marketplace. I wanted a two-year degree in one year.

Mr. Hadley, the head of the program, made another suggestion: He wanted me to enter their brand-new program in restaurant management, where I would learn what I wouldn't learn in kitchens. Stuff I might need someday if I lasted in this career.

What the hell, I decided.

CHAPTER 4

LONGHI'S ON MAUI

THE BEAUTY OF THE RESTAURANT BUSINESS is that you can make a living with very little commitment. Want to fly the red-eye, booze-infested flight back to Maui and support yourself for four months? Get a job in a restaurant. Want to fly back to Portland for school in the fall? See if that other restaurant you used to work at will hire you back. Better still, ask in advance if you can *plan* on getting your job back when you return with a Polynesian tan and Maui Wowie in your brain.

Which is exactly what I did: a summer on Maui, not living with the parents. I shared a condo in Napili with former Sea Scoop waitress Pam and gay bartender Steve, on the opposite side of the island from my parents' roofless, bankruptcy-inspired house. I landed a job in the bakery cubbyhole off the main kitchen at Longhi's on Front Street, the latest hip, rock-star-patronizing restaurant to arise on the popular street in Lahaina.

Longhi's huge prep kitchen was a Darwinian experiment of hippies, musicians, beach bums, serious surfer-cooks, and me. Most of us wore next to nothing—beachwear covered with a long apron so we didn't stain our bikinis or burn our bellies. The sound system blasted Jimi Hendrix, Led Zeppelin, and The Rolling Stones through speakers that hovered over our heads like huge, musical rain clouds. Sunsets every afternoon reinforced a ritual: removing our stained aprons, filing out of the kitchen through the bakery onto

Papalaua Street, and sauntering across Front Street to the seawall to pass a joint and watch the sun drop into the blue horizon. After nature's daily show, we'd float back to work, crank up the music, and toke hash from the communal apple pipe set out in the bathroom, conveniently located off the bakery where I constructed huge mango pies for the dessert tray and baked whole-wheat breads for the bread baskets. We were all tan, salty, high, and happy making good food.

Unlike the parchment-printed Continental menu of the Marketplace, the verbal menu at Longhi's was more of a California-hippie-Italian-comfort-food-inspired mix. Pan-sautéed fresh local seafood, bowls of steamed broccoli and cauliflower with cheddar cheese melted atop, and giant steamed whole artichokes; hand-cranked pastas by Marina Beebe, the aging-hippie artist/boat-dwelling pasta lady; and giant-size baked goods were the menu's staples. "Organic" food wasn't a thing yet, but this is the term that comes to mind now whenever I think of the food at Longhi's.

Longhi's aromas, after all these years, still linger in my olfactory memory. The open-air dining room and front production kitchen sat under a perpetual mist of toasted butter-garlic and licorice-y Pernod from the signature dish, Shrimp Longhi. In the rear prep kitchen—where salads, baked goods, general prep, and multicolored pastas were joyfully cranked out by stoned worker bees, me included—the sweet wholesome smell of whole-grain mini-breads hung in the otherwise stale kitchen air, inspiring a mouthwatering need to grab a hot roll and slather butter all over it. In retrospect, now knowing more about the mechanics of kitchens and equipment, I believe the ventilation systems may not have been up to par. Whether on purpose or to save money with a substandard hood system, the colliding aromas worked. You walked into the dining room at Longhi's and you wanted to eat, eat, eat! Or maybe the Maui Wowie had something to do with it.

Baking is a science, cooking an art. I prefer the flair and sport of cooking to hunkering down on a recipe for the exact results that baking requires. During my four months working at Longhi's, however, I was eager to learn all things culinary. Although we had a three-ring binder of handwritten, food-stained recipes, the baking there was very close to imitating art. The large oval dessert tray passed around the black-and-white-tiled dining room was laden with Thor-size slices of crumb-topped mango pie, wedges of chocolate-crusted grasshopper pie, parfaits of chocolate mousse, peach cobbler, slabs of banana cake layered with cream cheese frosting, flavored cheesecakes, and bowls of tropical fresh fruit.

Experimentation was encouraged by the ankle-length-skirt-wearing head baker, Jan. "Bring in a recipe and make it," she said. "If it sells, put it in The Book." I focused on cheesecakes, taking the basic recipe and infusing it with special liqueur or a puree topping, making all sorts of flavored cheesecakes: mango, mocha, peanut butter, hazelnut. Mornings I perused the bar for my ingredients: Kahlúa, Frangelico, and the traditional amaretto. This was play for me; I was a kid making witch's brew from found objects in the yard.

After Jan left each day, I worked evenings alone in the tiny bakery. My maple baking table sat near the walk-in cooler door, where sun-weathered surfer-cooks from the front line rushed frantically around the corner to grab more shrimp or parsley or steaks. These guys were the handsome generals of our ragtag team. Everything we did in the prep kitchen, directly or indirectly, was for them and they were held in high esteem by all. Longhi's kitchen was larger and less intimate than the Marketplace's, and although some of us in the back prep kitchen were friends with the surfer-cooks, to me they were sexy strangers and I was still an insecure, nervous stuttering person. Sometimes, when a particularly friendly cook—one who said hi to me on occasion—burst into the calm of my little nook, I'd ask if he needed me to do anything, chop some herbs, break down a tenderloin maybe?

Drugs were another advantage of the positioning of the bakery. Since the battered wood-framed screen door exiting onto Papalaua Street was in my station, cooks going out the door for a toke often invited me out with them. I was encouraged by this. My awkward communication skills left something empty in me, and being invited to share drugs with another person bridged this gap. The communal fruit–turned–hash pipe on the sink in the small bathroom adjacent to my station gave me another reason to feel particularly special. For when another prep cook came out of the bathroom winking a glassy eye and flashing me a sheepish smile, I'd wink back knowingly. I was the keeper of this thing, the apple or green mango pipe. It was in my station, after all.

Bob came by Longhi's bar after work one evening and over beers, halt-ingly, we talked of nothing. He was drunk. The awkward and improper thing we'd done when I was sixteen seemed to have happened to someone else in some other stratosphere. His girlfriend had finally left him. He was no longer at the Sea Scoop. He appeared to be a broken man, and I had been the cause. Or maybe not, I thought as I looked at this thirty-something drunken man next to me at the wooden bar. My life was full of hope, work, school, and travel, the whole world ahead of me. I even had a new boyfriend from the salad department, a wild-haired blond musician from Oakland named Jon, who did not read to me but sang to me! Bob, however, would drink and chain-smoke in some bar in Lahaina or Napili before going home to an empty apartment to smoke a joint, then awaken a few hours later, red-eyed and cardboard-tongued, and drag himself to some early-morning resort kitchen shift where he would throw broken-yolked eggs against the wall. I was no longer there to slice his ham. I had moved on.

Bob put his hand on my hair, and I ducked to avoid his touch.

"Oh, so you don't want me now that you can have me, huh?"

I shrugged. "I don't know; th-things are different now."

He leered, stood, swayed, and walked out.

I did not linger too long on the confusing aspects of feeling so strongly in love one year, then so contemptuous the next.

I ordered another beer.

A guy nicknamed Mango sometimes helped me peel mangoes in my tiny bakery. The skinny California-bred haole was known for his love of them, which he regularly harvested from the many trees in town by shimmying up their rutted trunks and filling his T-shirt with the plucked fruit. Mango's claim to fame was walking around Front Street sucking the flesh from the tip of one of the ripe beauties with both hands, announcing to wide-eyed tourists that he was sucking on "Mother Nature's tit." According to Mango, he had a deal with Bob Longhi whereby he would help the cooks, prep, and mop floors, and in return he got to eat what he wanted and could sleep on one of the cushioned dining booths at night. I don't know if this was true, or if Bob Longhi just tolerated Mango because this was 1978 Maui and it was our belated Summer of Love.

Mango was a pleasant enough character. In one sense you could envy this guy. He'd set up a system for himself: He had figured out the eating and sleeping thing without the drag of actually working, so he could suck his mangoes by day and play music on the streets at night with some of the other Longhi's-employed California refugees. Mango was a caricature of a person, always smiling like the cat who had eaten the mouse.

Bob Longhi had been an insurance salesman from New York when he came to Maui in 1976 and opened his restaurant. This is something you come across on the internet in this century. In 1978, however, the rumor among us cooks was that he'd sailed over from San Francisco on his boat and left behind quite a network in Haight Asbury, which is why rock stars frequented his restaurant: Jesse Colin Young, Jackson Browne, George Harrison, and Fleetwood Mac. Perhaps they hadn't known Bob Longhi at all until they ate at his restaurant, and the reason they ate there in the first place was because it was a hip place. However it came to be, the place was a rock-star magnet.

Fleetwood Mac that summer practically lived at the restaurant. They sat in the same corner booth, the one Mango bragged was his bed. Their album *Rumours* had been released the previous year, but it was new to us on Maui, as we were about a year late in most things and a decade behind in others, like the Summer of Love.

When Stevie Nicks's birthday rolled around in late May, an order came in on my shift for an entire sheet of carrot cake for her and the band. This was a resume milestone, and I still love the sound of it—"I baked a birthday cake for Stevie Nicks."

That night the cake went out without a hitch and I resumed my other tasks: cutting and arranging pies on the dessert platter, whipping cream, peeling mangoes, eyeing the line cooks who slung open the walk-in cooler door. Hendrix was shredding guitar from a speaker above me and all was fine in my little sugar-and-whole-wheat world. Suddenly, Hendrix dialed down to a faint pitter and the kitchen got uncharacteristically quiet. Curious, I turned to the activities behind me to see the image of flowing dresses and shawls dancing through the prep kitchen and into my bakery. Then a surreptitious blur disappeared behind the paint-chipped bathroom door. I stood still and stunned: Behind that door not twenty feet from me, Stevie Nicks was peeing. (Was there a hash apple in there?) God, I loved working in restaurants.

When not working, I went to the beach at Kaanapali, at my old spot behind Whalers Village. Sunset music at the Rusty Harpoon still featured the hippie playing "Havana Daydreamin'" and after borrowing roommate

Pam's *Changes in Latitudes, Changes in Attitudes*, I bought a few Jimmy Buffett albums of my own. I drank margaritas and dreamed of Florida in my future. The warm places far from home in these songs beckoned me. I had to remain in warm weather and palm trees, but knew I wouldn't stay in Hawaii forever. I was like a shark; I had to keep moving to survive.

The summer rolled on—working, tanning, participating in lines of coke at the bar after hours, quaaludes at the beach under a full moon, my still-shy self had a great time. I had learned to bake, a skill I looked forward to utilizing at the Marketplace. It would be time to start restaurant management school in the fall. And Jon, my new singing boyfriend, would escape the uncertain Maui life to move to Portland with me.

CHAPTER 5

WINE SO FINE, OYSTERS SO PERFECT

IT WAS A DECENT SATURDAY NIGHT at the Marketplace, mostly big parties with long lapses in between, Donny and I cooking in spurts. A rush to get out a twenty-top—mostly steaks, so I had to help out on the grill—then a dead pause during which we occupied ourselves by cutting long, thin slices of carrot on the meat slicer, nipping small triangles off an end with a paring knife, and each putting one between our lips, showing off to the waitstaff our bright orange forked tongues. Dewey Kelly entered the kitchen with a fatherly frown behind his black beard. We threw out the carrot tongues, brushed the remaining carrot scraps into the stock pot, and got ready for the next big table.

Our chef had been bumping around upstairs in the loft all night, which was odd since there was no private party going on up there. At the end of our shift, when Donny and I were scrubbing down the line, Chef Dewey pulled me aside and asked if I'd like to join the wine tasting upstairs at ten.

Not only would I get a free buzz at my underage eighteen years, but I'd also get to learn about wine! Wine, which people drank with *food*. And which I was learning about in my favorite class, Food/Beverage Management and Service. Afternoons, while setting up my station, I babbled on to Chef Dewey about my newfound knowledge: food procurement techniques, labor laws, and my favorite topic, wine and wine regions. He must have appreciated my need to have him confirm that I was learning the correct stuff, which was probably why he invited me to the wine tasting that night.

Still wearing my checked pants and having traded my oversize white coat for a T-shirt, in the loft, I sat alone at the rear dining room. The room was dim and rustic, with baskets of cubed French bread on the white-linened tables and red globular netted candle holders giving off a dreamy light. I stood out in my casual attire, and hopefully, I thought, not too obviously in my youth. The guests were all silk and linen, coiffed and perfumed. I smelled like garlic and sweat. At the head of the dining room, wine bottles were centered on a long table, flanked by sparkling stemware. Chef Dewey stood behind the table, presented a bottle of white wine, and described its region in France: *Bordeaux*. And its subregion: *Graves*. And the soil there: *gravelly*. I knew all this from my beverage class and I also knew that Burgundy was the other main winemaking region in France and not just a name for red wine, because they made white wine there as well. You could tell a Bordeaux from a Burgundy by the shape of the bottle. The Bordeaux bottle was broad-shouldered; Burgundy bottles were sloped. This was all great information to prove I was knowledgeable, but very soon, I'd get to *taste* this gravelly wine.

It was a help-yourself affair, the Portland suburbanites and me going up to the table to take a glass with an inch of wine in it and listening to Chef Dewey's description: "a blend of Sauvignon Blanc and Semillon grapes, a heady bouquet, dry finish . . . drink with rack of lamb . . ." Back at my table, the gravelly wine hit my taste buds with a metallic rush. So far, the only wine that had rolled along my tongue had been Boones Farm and Almaden Chablis, back on the beach in Lahaina on those few occasions I was not too far from the outskirts of the girl clique I hung around to be invited. But there in the Marketplace's candlelit loft, tasting the white Bordeaux elevated me. I appreciated the warmth in my brain, sipped on the Graves, and listened to the next wine presented.

Several wines in, I went up to the table to take a new glass, my mind swimming with wine buzz and not able to take in all the information. *Burgundy*, I heard Dewey say, and *Chardonnay grape*. I returned to my table and, like a wine pro, dissolved a cube of French bread between my tongue and roof of my mouth to cleanse my palate before taking a sip of the new wine.

This newest wine hit my taste buds like creamery butter, spilling along all tasting zones and shooting me through time and space to stone-walled wineries in France, which smelled of grass, lemon, and oak. I became someone else right then, not the skittish underage college girl at a wine tasting. I swooned and took another sip, which inspired more visions and sensations of other places and times.

Things were a little disorganized in the room now, people milling about the table, several wines available for taste at once. I approached the table and asked about the most recent Chardonnay. Dewey pointed to a golden-hued bottle and I lifted it, pretending to study it; when it appeared no one was watching, I took it back to my table and placed it between me and the red candle. The label was an elegant and complicated royal blue and gold. *Meursault, 1974*, I read, swirling the juice in my mouth, rolling it around with my tongue before swallowing.

When I was nine and living in Kailua, before poverty hit us on Maui, a big mango tree loomed above our pool and dropped its sun-ripened fruit into the deep end. The neighbor kids and I would dive down and fetch the mangoes, then sit on the pool steps with our booty and bite through the tough skin and eat the flesh. We discovered that if we did an underwater somersault while chewing the sweet fruit, there'd be a sensation of otherworldliness, an odd mental buzz that sent us somewhere else through our taste buds. We chewed through these somersaults over and over again, holding our breath, the cool chlorine water washing over us, our stomachs falling through the underwater twists.

This is how I felt that night at the Marketplace loft, hoarding the bottle of Meursault. It was mine. These mind-traveling sensations through my taste buds were also mine.

Here's some wine trivia: In the mid-1800s, the *phylloxera* aphid species chewed its way through French and other European wineries, causing a blight that destroyed the French winemaking industry. Two French winegrowers, Leo Laliman and Gaston Bazille, proposed that the European vines be grafted onto resistant American rootstocks that weren't susceptible to the *phylloxera*. The ethnocentric French disliked this idea, especially since it was likely the aphid had come from North America in the first place. But there were no other options to revive winemaking in France. And it worked. Eventually French wineries were "reconstituted."

This little tidbit from my Food/Beverage Management and Service class textbook* was happily summed up by my teacher Mr. Hadley as follows: "So all those so-called great French wines originated from California anyway."* I suppose he was proud of our California wines, which had recently beat out French wines in both red and white categories at the 1976 Judgment of Paris wine competition, and he wanted to make sure America got its due.

Mr. Hadley was being patriotic in this way, dissing the French in front of his classroom, and I was more than happy to spread the word among my restaurant peers about the California wines and thus showing how knowledgeable I was about such things.

As much as California had encroached upon the French in winemaking, there was also a quiet little winemaking industry going on in Oregon and Washington—"The Great Northwest." Opportunities to increase my wine knowledge came from Mark, an Oakland transplant working at a Seattle beer and wine distributor. Mark was a high-school friend of Jon's, with whom I'd set up housekeeping in a lumpy old house in Tigard, and we regularly drove up to Seattle in our sputtering Dodge van to visit Mark and his girlfriend Carol. I don't know if the boxes of beer and wine Mark and Carol kept stacked in the corner of their small apartment were legitimate perks from the job or just contraband. Carol and Jon drank the local beers, mostly Henry Weinhards, and Mark and I popped open bottles of Willamette Valley Pinot Noir, swirled, slurped, and sang out, "This is *so* much better than French wine!"

We were all underage still, so these trips to Seattle, with Mark's welcomed assortment of beverages, presented great opportunities for me to cook with wine. As in not pouring the wine in a pan to deglaze it, but actually *drinking* wine with a meal. While the other three California transplants smoked bad Northwestern pot, I planned, plotted, and shopped for whichever meal I'd be preparing in Carol's tiny apartment kitchen. Seattle's Pike's Place Market was

---

* The textbook was *Grossman's Guide to Wines, Beers and Spirits* by Harold J. Grossman (New York: Charles Scribner's Sons, 1978).

a perfect spot to hunt for the basis of a good meal. If Mark had some bottles of Chardonnay, I'd wrangle money from the trio to buy fresh seafood and vegetables. If he had Pinot Noir, the less expensive chicken parts would stew in a pot of coq au vin.

Cooking consumed me on these trips, which gave me a thing to do while the other three talked about Oakland and Grateful Dead concerts, people they knew, and how Seattleites hated Californians—especially hippies like Jon and Mark. I didn't take part in this small talk; I cooked instead. It didn't seem like anyone minded.

On one trip to Seattle in the early spring, we drove north of the city to the rocky beach on the edge of Puget Sound, with an ice chest of Washington Chardonnay and some Henry Weinhards. It was oyster-harvesting season and we'd brought butter knives from Mark and Carol's kitchen to chip oysters from their shallow beds. This excursion was simply for the fun; we planned to carve out our twenty-per-person limit of the barnacled bivalves from the shallows, then give them to other, more serious oyster connoisseurs scouring the shallow waves.

I wasn't entirely hip to the idea because the air, wind, and water were Arctic-cold and this adventure required us to wade out in the freezing water in our shoes. There were special wading boots made for this, of course, but we didn't own any. This was entirely a roll-up-your-jeans-and-dry-your-shoes-later affair, and this Hawaiian girl shivered and whined and sputtered. I cast about on the chilled water's edge for a small oyster here and there, while the boys and Carol waded in.

Back on shore we cracked beers and considered our box of briny rocks. "People actually eat these?" Carol asked.

"I-I've never seen a *real* oyster before. Only in a can," I said.

"I dare you to eat one," Mark said to Jon.

Jon shrugged, pulled out his butter knife, and selected a clump of oysters from the box. He maneuvered the knife into an opening, then another, and finally hinged open a shell, revealing a live but immobile shiny gray oyster lying in its pearly domain. The thing looked beautiful. It was the color of the overcast sky, with a suggestion of the same lavender reflecting from the tops of the Olympic Mountains to our west. Jon slurped the meat from the shell and instantly looked like the happiest man in the world.

I was not about to be upstaged by this long-haired guitar player from Oakland, and I reached for my own oyster clump and knife and began to poke and twist away at the little caves and crevices until I, too, held in my hand an open, pearl-white shell, its opaque meat reflecting the sky and mountains.

Slurp!

And like sipping Meursault and eating mangoes in the pool, this sensation also transported me out of myself. In a single mouthwatering explosion, the cold, salty, smooth flesh of the oyster jettisoned me back to the sun-dried docks of the Ala Wai yacht harbor, the aroma of grilled fish wafting on the Pacific's breeze. Then I was underwater, breathing and swimming like a mermaid. I was with my real dad, propped up on the Formica counter eating that oyster from a can. I looked up at the gray sky while chewing and tasting, swallowing the lingering memory of what had been in my mouth a mere second ago, and a religious tinge came over me and I knew that this oyster was God's gift to humankind, a tool to get closer to Her nature.

"Wow!" I said. "Do we have our limit yet?" I was suddenly ready to get cold and wet in order to harvest my share.

Mark and Jon exchanged looks. "Well, we were going to just give them away to some of these other people," said Mark.

"Naw, let's eat 'em!"

I reached for another oyster and another, each oyster opening more doors in my brain. Soon, all four of us were eating oysters, slurping and ooh-ing and yummy-ing. We needed more! I did brave the cold water, so I could cook oysters for dinner: oyster stew, fried oysters, creating a dreamy feast accompanied by a chilled bottle of Washington Chardonnay. Oysters . . . so fresh, so salty and clean, like the ocean.

CHAPTER 6

A GIRL IN THE KITCHEN

IN 1994, WHILE INTERVIEWING for my current job designing commercial kitchens, my future boss said to me across his big mahogany desk, "In order for a woman to be successful in business, she has to be twice as smart as a man." "No problem," I heard myself say, as I tamped down the fear and apprehension of leaving the kitchen after twenty years to embark on a related but new career.

His statement put words to something I've always known: The active seventies and eighties restaurant kitchen was a man-cave of testosterone-laced sweat, ego-charged banter, and puffed chests on the front line. Who could outdo whom was the order of the day, this competitive edge overshadowing each ticket handed in through the food window from a vested waiter.

And I, the demure girl by day and rocking line cook/sauté slut/prep fiend or grill bitch by night, was equally competitive, having found an outlet to prove how good I was at something. My ability to communicate didn't come easily, but it was easier in the kitchen, by way of confidence bolstered by my abilities to prepare, organize, and execute good food. Attending school, reading cookbooks, cooking at home for Jon's garage band (all of them possessing willing palates) certainly helped.

Eventually, however, I took my mission too far. I arrived at the Marketplace after class one day and went over to the hot well to taste the soup that sous chef Doug had made for both shifts. It was some creamy vegetable affair, and I felt it needed something, so I went for the spices and added some salt, white pepper, and tarragon. I had started baking the desserts for the restaurant, and Chef Dewey allowed me to come up with specials during the week. I felt like I knew stuff now. I thought nothing of this reseasoning of the soup until a few days later, when Chef Dewey pulled me out into the dining room before a shift and looked at me sternly. I felt like a trapdoor had opened in the floor and I was about to fall through.

"Marisa," he started. "Many of the cooks feel like you are overstepping them."

"Wha-what d'you mean?"

"For example, reseasoning Doug's soup the other day is just one example."

"Well, I-I thought it was bland."

"I'm sorry, but you've been disrupting the continuity of the kitchen. You just don't fit in. I'm going to have to let you go."

And that was it. In my mind, the cook's egos were more important than serving the customers a flavorful soup. But I suppose I did seem like a bull raging into a china shop.

I had risen, then fallen hard. I let anger overshadow my hurt, since that was an easier emotion to process. I didn't hold still long enough for depression to settle in. I needed to work, to move on, to keep going—that was what I knew would work. The shark metaphor, once again.

Several jobs floated me for a while. One, at the Portland Golf Club, a men-only club where female staff had to enter the building from the service entrance, had a wizened American chain-smoking chef who held on to food techniques from some other era, like putting baking soda in boiling water to keep green beans green. The soda broke down the proteins and rendered the beans mushy, like those from a can. I'll admit that it was a pretty green color, though. The young sous chef, Patty, wore a white dress and white shoes to match, like a nurse. Her Puritan outfit never got dirty because she didn't actually do much work. From time to time she did something, like hefting a twenty-pound bag of carrots onto a counter and demonstrating how it was so much faster to peel a carrot by running the peeler in both directions instead of one, but these time-motion studies didn't impress me. I couldn't even be jealous of her; she was so benign and unimaginative. And wearing a *dress* in the kitchen? She gave women in commercial kitchens a bad name.

Farrago was a gleaming new business-trendy restaurant above a twenty-four-hour dive on Burnside Street in downtown Portland, pioneering a gentrification movement in an area stretching north of downtown populated by homeless folks endearingly called "Burnside Bums." The owner of Farrago was an oily, scowling, silent man, but Charlie, the old Czechoslovakian chef, hired me to create and maintain the daily salad bar for the office lunch crowd. This daytime job required me to attend my restaurant management classes at night, but I was happy to do this, for here at Farrago I'd have an opportunity to create stuff—even if that was only the stuff of cold salads, a girl's work.

The Northern Italian cuisine of Farrago gave me food rushes after the culinary junkyard of the Portland Golf Club. Around 11:30 in the morning each day, after arranging my salad platters on the dining room's buffet table, I'd hang around the hot line and study the preparation techniques of the lunch entrées: fresh pastas with sautéed veal; pastas with salmon or chicken tossed with pancetta, capers, peas, white wine, and cream; *linguine alle vongole* (with clams) and *spaghettini alla carbonara* (with prosciutto, egg, and black pepper). Chef Charlie was a born teacher, so even though he already had his troop of macho line cooks, he happily showed me his techniques.

Charlie and I had a camaraderie that he lacked with his male counterparts. I appreciated his cleverness and mimicked him adoringly when he said *wodka* sauce for the penne and pronounced the "l" in salmon. Charlie was also somewhat of a historian, proudly relating a tale of how in the 1500s, Catherine de' Medici, the future queen of France, brought her Italian chefs from Tuscany to cook for her, and that before then the French didn't know how to cook. "The Italians taught the French how to cook!" he'd proudly announce. I was happy to tuck this little tidbit into my bank of food slogans. He also explained that Marco Polo had traveled to China and brought back the noodle, so Italy's famous pastas actually originated in China. "To love pasta is to love life!" Charlie would exclaim, after depositing a pasta dish into a wide bowl and garnishing it with freshly grated Parmesan and a sprinkle of parsley. I once asked him how a Czechoslovakian could become an Italian chef and he responded with a shrug, a smile, and a wink. Eventually I flipped and flamed food in sauté pans, repeating Charlie's mantra upon completing a pasta dish and periodically checking the salad bar in between, while the other cooks scowled at me with resentment—something I was accustomed to by then.

Mornings I'd meet Charlie in the twenty-four-hour dive downstairs to wait for front-house management to open Farrago. Charlie would chow down on SOS—shit on a shingle, creamed chipped beef on toast that lived up to its name—and slurp several cups of coffee. Charlie fit right in with the morning-after crowd, with his unkempt tangle of gray hair and wrinkled tweed. I wondered if this was where he hung out after closing, and maybe he'd been there all night drinking with the gum-smiling bums. "Morning," he'd say, followed by something clever, and we'd file out of the joint and up the stairs to start our day behind the sunny windows of Farrago.

The chef is the heartbeat of the restaurant, and when the chef is not steadily moving in his required groove, trouble starts spreading across the restaurant like water from a broken dam. After a few months, Charlie's morning coffee at the joint downstairs became a glass of something amber with ice. He wasn't smiling anymore, and this created a knot in my stomach; a sense of dread came over me, helplessness, like seeing a loved one on their death-bed. The oily owner had shown up a few times and Charlie quickly became subdued on those occasions. He wouldn't confide in me much, but he said that things were wrong with the restaurant and he wasn't sure he'd be around much longer.

Which broke my heart. I loved Charlie. I wasn't sure what loving a father was like, but what I felt for Charlie surely was close to it. My lingering sadness soon turned to anger when Charlie disappeared and the waiters' paychecks started bouncing.

The kitchen began to veer off course without its captain. We tried to pull things together, the macho line cooks and me. I volunteered to do the daily produce order. The guys would leave lists of the produce they needed, and I'd leave my lists of dry goods for them to order. We teamed up as much as we could, but with no leader, not even a pep talk from Mr. Oily, we began to lose morale.

One afternoon found me standing in the lounge across from a seated Mr. Oily, hands on my hips, stomach churning with battery acid. "Wh-what a-are you d-doing?" I managed to get out. The words left my lips with such effort; my head felt like an explosive device. With my heart pounding, face hot and red, these difficult words proved I cared, cared about the restaurant and my co-workers, even the macho cooks. Mr. Oily surely thought I was just the salad girl.

"Huh? What are you talking about?" he said smugly, black eyebrows wrinkling above a scowl.

This meant I had to force out more words. "Ch-Charlie," I said. "No chef. And n-no one knows what's happening here. W-we want to work, but—"

He interrupted my struggle with, "Nothing's happening. Get back to work."

Two days later I arrived in the morning to find a CLOSED FOR BUSINESS sign taped to the inside of the glass door.

In 1980 all manner of restaurants were scattered throughout downtown Portland, like jacks from a child's hand. Some were the dim-upholstered, wood-paneled musty hangers-on with codgy regulars who wouldn't be caught dead at the gay Hamburger Mary's or local restaurateur Horst Mager's trendy Tivoli Garden. Other establishments were shiny and new, with smiling entrepreneurs ready to charge through the recession with their hopeful cuisine. After a three-day stint cooking with some clueless housewives at the brand-new Wooden Horse in John's Landing, I decided there were too many of these Farrago and Wooden Horse–type flaky owners and that I needed to be more wary and selective of where I would earn and learn next.

On one day of combing the streets for employment, I went into L'Auberge, a tidy little French restaurant on Burnside up from the recently defunct Farrago. The dining room surprised me with its array of bent cookware hanging on the walls like unearthed artifacts—such a different look than the classy Chez Paul on Maui. A man wearing a starched white chef's coat approached me and I asked if he was the chef. "No," he said, "I'll get her for you."

Her? The chef was a *her* in a French restaurant? And why was that man wearing a chef's coat? This place intrigued and excited me more than any other.

The chef appeared to be in her late twenties and I liked her instantly, dissolving my disappointment in not seeing an old French chef and enabling my questions to flow without stammers. L'Auberge was a traditional country provincial French restaurant, hence the simple decor and the daily prix fixe menu featuring wholesome preparations of salmon, pork loin, and lamb. The chef read my application at the two-top table we sat at. She looked up. "Well, you have quite the experience. We don't have any openings right now and when we do, we start all new employees as dishwashers. It takes a few years to work up to a waiter."

"So the waiters work in the kitchen first?"

"Oh yes, the knowledge of preparing the food guarantees the best service."

I really wanted to dine there someday, when going out to dinner could be in my budget.

She had worked at L'Auberge for seven years, studying under the original chef (that must have been the old French guy) until she was promoted to executive chef the previous year. I didn't want to be at the bottom anyway; my ego, even early in my career, wouldn't allow this. But this was a restaurant above the others in Portland, and I knew I needed to find a job at a place like this, higher up than what I'd been doing. I had one more year of school, and then I would move on to somewhere else.

Two more restaurants filled in my working needs while I completed my degree in restaurant management. Robertino's was a cozy house-turned-restaurant across the Willamette River, owned by Miss Kay, who had spun-white hair. Miss Kay instantly adored me—which, I later learned, was probably due to her steady consumption of Verdicchio. Or maybe it was my response when she asked what I knew about pasta, when I proclaimed, "To love pasta is to love life!" She said she needed a chef to help her with the ordering, with organizing the kitchen, and to polish up the recipes of her otherwise homey Italian menu. And she wanted me to be her chef—an early rendition of Girl Power.

So, at twenty, I had my first official chef's job. I organized the refrigerators and freezers. I made stocks with all the leftover frozen stuff I found. I used these stocks in the sautéed dishes and streamlined the recipes for each menu item. I employed my childhood friend Jackie, who'd just moved to Portland from Hawaii, and taught her all the techniques I knew, then made her my sous chef. We filled *cannellonis* with ground veal, pesto, and spices; we sautéed petite chicken breasts with capers and lemon; we made *spaghettini alla carbonara* and *penne alla vodka*, all of which I'd learned from Charlie. And we all drank Verdicchio, because Miss Kay was very generous with her jug of white wine that was tucked into the two-door reach-in refrigerator behind the white tub of cooked fettuccine.

I needed a daytime prep cook as well, and Miss Kay placed an ad in *The Oregonian*, resulting in a parade of applicants ranging from pimply high-school kitchen virgins to the ex-con types who would probably have lifted me off the floor with one gnarled fist if I told them how to do something. But a young man named Grant I liked instantly. Grant was thin, effeminate, and respectful and had some experience working for local celeb restaurateur Horst Mager. He would fit in with us girls: me, Jackie, and day cook Gabrielle. He was my guy.

Kay validated my selection and soon Grant, with his bandanna-covered head and his own set of knives, joined the girl cooking team. He was fast, tidy, and had a sense of humor, joining in our silly musings as we chopped, sautéed, and baked, even agreeing that we were like girls who lived together and that we'd all get our periods at the same time, so he would get his also.

Of course Grant was gay, and that's why he fit in so well. He was low in the testosterone department and ego-conflicts were nil. And he always had good pot.

One afternoon after his shift, once our camaraderie had been established and Grant felt at home, he removed his bandanna and shook out a butt-length mane of reddish-blond hair, the golden highlights accented by the sun beaming in through the kitchen's clerestory window above the range hood. It was a lot of hair for such a small guy. We girls were stunned and probably somewhat jealous, for it was beautiful hair, curly, then straightened out by the weight of its length.

Gabrielle gasped, "We have to show Miss Kay!" She dashed out of the kitchen while Grant paraded around like a show horse. Then Miss Kay stepped into our sunny realm with her face polished to a shine by a day of Verdicchio sipping. Gabrielle rejoined us and we all stood before her. Grant put his hand on his hip and shook his mane.

"Well, Grant!" Her hand went to her mouth to silence a giggle. "I do believe you are the prettiest girl in this kitchen!"

During this evolutionary time in my career, I tried on different personas: boss, friend, party girl. But the shy beach girl who had returned from Maui with hippie musician boyfriend Jon was evaporating. Quiet days off, cooking a pot of something for stoned band members, dropping acid and climbing trees in our huge yard, full-moon parties, and the Grateful Dead seemed far behind me now. It had been a life to try out, I realized, and now I wanted to try more things in life.

But this life of bands and acid and full-moon parties was beautiful blond-haired Jon's life: Jon, whose father paid his rent and bills as long as he took a few classes at the community college, whose father would give him an apartment building after he graduated. To Jon, I began to understand, Portland would be his life forever.

"But don't you want to travel, see the world, meet all kinds of people?" I asked while we were discussing what to do after college, when I said I wanted to take a road trip.

"Not really." He shrugged. "I'm happy here." Surely the bells of doom must have begun to ring, although I don't believe I actually heard them at the time.

Around this time, one evening the Princess phone rang at our house and Mom's voice was bouncing off the satellite from Maui. "Your grandmother has died," she said. "Oh," I said. I felt nothing. Was I supposed to feel something?

• • •

Working in restaurants is a communal thing. You and your team work hard to make the customers happy; you exercise your brain fully to keep all the plates in the air, so to speak; and you help your workmates who may not be able to keep up. You endure eight hours of full concentration in a busy place—and Robertino's was busy—then you crash afterward, the comedown. Only you want to prolong the rush. So you go for a drink and a toke with your teammates after work to discuss the day's adventures.

Which is how it had been at the Marketplace. But Robertino's had something else going on around its invisible, raggedy edges. The sleeping around between my nearly all-girl kitchen and male waitstaff had resulted in venereal warts. And even I was at risk, for I had had a drunken and forgetful evening with Bill the smiley waiter while Jon had gone back to Oakland for a few weeks. (More bells of doom: he had an old girlfriend from high school there.) And I was trying, for reasons unknown to me, to hang on to our relationship. Jon, I was certain, would never read to me. (He no longer sang me songs, either.)

So in an odd solidarity to my rocky relationship, I quit Robertino's.

Aldo's was a downtown Portland establishment known for its Italian fare and as the last last-call bar in town. In other words, a meat market. The kitchen manager hired me, he said, to replace the dinner lead line cook, then had this line cook train me before he got the axe. This put me in an uncomfortable position because I liked Steve, the guy I would soon replace. Steve sported the typical Oregon black lumberjack beard, wore plaid flannel in his off hours, and listened to Eddie Rabbit while cooking. I didn't know why he was being canned (maybe for his taste in music?), and I felt like a traitor, knowing I'd be taking his job in a few weeks.

If the Marketplace was jazz fusion and Robertino's was emerging East Coast rock's Southside Johnny and Bruce Springsteen, Aldo's was pure rock and roll. Once Steve left (the deed thankfully done on my night off), I took over the sauté station and relaxed into a groove of Olympic cooking with the guys on the grill, ghetto-blaster above the line cranked up with the Doors and Led Zeppelin, their notes soon to fade into nights of New Wave and punk music, when Jerry the New Wave waiter turned us all on to the Ramones, Elvis Costello, and Devo. My change—or expansion—in musical tastes was another wedge in my relationship with Jon. Was I supposed to listen to Blind Faith, the Grateful Dead, and Jefferson Airplane *forever*?

I was the only girl again, preening in my rarity, commanding the line, quaffing free drinks offered by flirty bartenders, and liking everything I cooked. Gamberoni shrimp in spicy red sauce; scallops in ginger, lime, and cream; Scarpariello chicken with rosemary sprigs; all dishes sautéed with generous amounts of olive oil and garlic. I loved the aromas of Aldo's kitchen and didn't even mind how I smelled afterward—after work I would hit the bar with food under my nails and garlic in my pores, proud of my scarred hands and food aromas emanating from my skin.

Aldo's had no chef. I'm not sure how the place was managed; the restaurant was a ghost ship always somehow on course. Rumor had it Aldo's was one of a cluster of restaurants in town managed by a group of businessmen. And even though the waiters came in still drunk from the night before, and there were always lines of coke hidden under a *Hustler* magazine in the service elevator, and the diners could certainly hear our music blasting from the kitchen, Aldo's was always busy and the food was good; the paychecks never bounced, and we were all high and happy.

Saturdays at Aldo's found me and Orin, the redheaded grill cook, stumbling into the quiet kitchen around 2 p.m.—no lunch was served on weekends—and taking inventory of our reach-in boxes. We knew what inhabited our boxes, of course, since we'd closed up the night before. But that was before drinking next door at Paddy's and then coming back to Aldo's for last call at 2 a.m. I liked Saturdays for this reason: There would be no surprises in my station from the lunch cooks, like the time I found a very realistic butter carving of a penis perched atop a plate of parsley in my reach-in box.

"I know there's one in here," Orin said, leaning down to dig through the chest freezer, his right arm swallowed up by its tundra. Orin's claim to fame was the time he went to chug a screwdriver given to him from the bartender while cooking, and the straw went up his nose. That, and he could sing the entire AC/DC song "Dirty Deeds Done Dirt Cheap" while putting out a six-top.

"Thought we ran out last night."

"Yeah, but I put another one in for tonight." Then he fished it out, a frozen red blob of beef tenderloin wrapped in plastic wrap. He unwrapped the block of raw meat and placed it on the meat slicer.

Coffee was brewed, the tenderloin sliced into tissue-thin carpaccio, Dijon mustard and olive oil mixed, garlic toast points readied, and a ramekin of grated Parmesan located. Along with a couple of PainAids and water, our hangover breakfast was ready for chowing down. We stood over the cutting board in the grill station inhaling our food, making our prep lists for the evening's adventures.

Raw beef had never appealed to me, but the tenderloin shavings drizzled with Dijon–olive oil and fresh Parmesan layered on the garlic toast points were earthy-tasting and satisfying. We ate more of it than the appetizer portion served at Aldo's, but we needed the iron and vitamins contained in the red meat to fortify us for another night of epic line cooking, cocktail drinking, and coke snorting in the service elevator.

After each shift, charged up from the night's work, more fun awaited in the downtown Portland scene, something new for this island girl. Although cold and seemingly remote from other well-known cities, Portland had a style different from the other West Coast city I'd been to—San Francisco, with its beatnik and hippie heritage. Portland's proximity to Seattle and Vancouver gave it an edge: New Wave and punk came across the ocean from Europe, landed heavily in Canada, and trickled down into the Northwest. California, it seemed to me, from my soon-to-be-ex-boyfriend Jon's nose in the air about the Portland music scene, was just too impenetrable musically. San Francisco had acid concerts and flowers in the eyes, but Portland had punk bands.

That spring of 1981, I graduated from Portland Community College with an associate's degree in restaurant management. Nights after work throughout that summer, my skin shiny with olive oil and sweat, I was off with a gang of waiters and cooks to seedy lounges to see the Cowboys from Seattle or the local band the Wipers, or Seafood Mama (who later ditched our local haunts to become Quarterflash), no fake ID needed. I barely thought about my stutter, except when negotiating my split-up with Jon, which turned that part of my world black. As long as I was in the kitchen and part of the restaurant culture, I was wonderfully at ease. At that time in my life, you could replace the words in the previous sentence "in the kitchen" with "high," and that would also be true. The summer concluded with my twenty-first birthday at a Toots and the Maytals concert, and then training my replacement at Aldo's—a butch-like gal with a large sense of humor. After that, I was ready to pursue my culinary dreams.

It was time to go east.

CHAPTER 7

LAISSEZ LES BON TEMPS ROULER!

SOME MOMENTS IN TIME can stand still forever, locked and frozen, not dissipating into hazy or lost memories like smoke in a breeze. These moments are more tangible than those you get flipping through a photo album because you are in the scene again, with all its smells, sounds, and multidimensional nuances. Your mind will take you back anytime for a visit, to reexperience it as clearly as the day it first happened to you.

My moment was on a bright spring day in April 1981. I disembarked from the airport bus on Canal Street, hefted my backpack over my shoulders (the one I'd bought for camping in the North Cascades), and rounded the city corner on to stout little Bourbon Street, its tattered old buildings dwarfed by the modernity of Canal Street. It was the most beautiful thing, all that history captured alive in those old buildings and looking out at me, a modern girl with her backpack, walking to somewhere unknown. I looked up at the sky, an otherworldly, cerulean blue, and inhaled deeply the gas-lamp-tinged air, while freedom rushed into my body like the Mississippi River. Music spilled into the street from everywhere, a melody of aggressive horns and chirping fiddles, danceable and happy, and suddenly I felt special, like I was in a movie, because in movies music plays for the actors as they walk down a street, and this music played for me.

That weeklong trip was a knee-jerk reaction to my split with Jon. Travel is my balm when I'm emotionally fraught with failure, loss, and guilt, so off to New Orleans I went alone, staying in a seedy youth hostel, eating ten-cent oysters on Bourbon Street, drinking a lot, and generally treating the big wide world as my playground. The decision to actually move there came later; somewhere in my summer of punk bands the thought occurred to me that New Orleans should be the next place I would go to earn and learn. And it was close enough to Florida.

So in September, off I went with Dona (an on-and-off high-school friendship that had budded and bloomed into something full-fledged) and her parrot Manu, our worldly belongings packed into my Volkswagen Rabbit. We ventured toward the Big Easy on a road trip that included a weeklong stopover in San Francisco and two memorable food events: scrape-the-roof-of-the-mouth salsa purchased at a takeout window in New Mexico, and a bizarre pea and mayonnaise salad at the house of Grant's (from Robertino's) aunt in Fort Worth, Texas. Our plan was to live in New Orleans for a year, then head to Key West, where warm weather and palm trees would welcome two transplants from Hawaii.

We arrived in the French Quarter late on a Friday night, dodging drunks on the narrow streets; we Maui girls were thrilled and a little frightened, with Dona asking, "Where the hell have you brought me?" We crashed at the apartment of a bouncer I'd met at Pat O'Brien's bar in April, and a week later settled into an old slave quarters apartment on Dumaine Street near the French Market on Decatur.

I took the loft bedroom. Dona and Manu resided downstairs with the single bathroom and small kitchen. The former slave quarters-turned-apartment sat in the shadow of the main house across the courtyard, as did all slave quarters, hidden and forgotten. The historical aspect of the accommodation imparted a certain amount of eeriness, as we'd come home on gaslit dark nights after drinking in French Quarter bars, feeling the spirit of the dead previous inhabitants who merely slept here after a hard day of working for the white folk across the yard. I wondered how the former residents were treated, if they were abused.

I answered an ad in the *Times Picayune* for a line cook at Arnaud's, a classic old New Orleans restaurant on Bienville Street within walking distance of our apartment. Chef Claude Aubert interviewed me, and although I bragged about my seven years' experience cooking French and Italian cuisines—I had a degree in restaurant management, after all—all I got from Chef Claude was a wink and, "Yes, we have a position for you."

My fate was sealed with this guy when he saw on my application my summer baking at Longhi's—and the fact that I didn't have a penis, I was certain, once I saw the large, male-populated kitchen. Instead of the position advertised, Chef Claude offered me the position of Baking Girl. So for those first few fall months in my new home, honing my wardrobe and hairstyle to mimic Chrissie Hynde of the Pretenders, spending every night in this bar or that bar, wide-eyed and a little scared, I toiled at caramel custard, crème brûlée, bread pudding, and chocolate mousse. When my baking tasks were completed, I helped the Vietnamese girls in the salad pantry and joined them in preparing and eating boiled chickens seasoned with white pepper and lime. Eventually, Chef Claude showed me how to butcher meats and dress out ducks, hens, and quail. This kept me going for a while on the learning scale as I eyed the all-male line cook staff with envy and disdained the especially useless ones who touted culinary school educations but not much else (except the requisite penis).

At first, despite the boring baking tasks and missing the excitement of the cooking line, I liked how different Arnaud's was from those distant and amateur kitchens back in Portland. Chef Claude was a traditional French chef who cursed at cooks and flirted with waitresses. Bald and skinny, he had half-moon eyebrows that rode high on his forehead in permanent question mode, giving him the look of a jester. The huge kitchen cranked out 300 to 500 covers a night, but this excitement I missed while working days. There were stories, though, from Steve and Robert and Greg, three of the cooks who worked day and night shifts and who all had different but indigenous Louisiana accents.

"Yeah, we was in the weeds last naght," Robert would say with his word-devouring Chalmette accent. "Steve kept tellin' Chef, 'Chef I gotta pee, Chef I gotta pee,' but Chef woodn't let him leave da line. Steve kept beggin', but Chef woodn't let 'um, so fanally, he stepped off da line to the steam kettles, unzipped, whizzed into da floor trough, then got right back to cookin'."

I was appalled at this and wished I could've been part of such a cooking frenzy. I secretly wanted to know if Steve had washed his hands before returning to his station. I didn't think so.

The Arnaud's building was over a hundred years old, and some of the old Black cooks had worked there for many, many years. Old Mr. John for one, shuffling in each morning at seven, making big batches of turtle soup and gumbo in the tilting braising pans, then shuffling out by ten. Miss Bea, who always wore a colorful scarf turban-style around her wiry hair, sat on a wooden barstool because she was so old, and peeled tubs of carrots or cleaned okra pods. She spoke in some foreign tongue—or she was touched somehow—and the cooks liked to make her brandy milk punches that made her giddy, and sometimes she'd pee herself, which made Chef Claude start cursing in French.

There was another baking girl, Edie, a large Texan who did not want to be trumped in any way by this West Coast girl, me. She liked to boss me around. The boys on the line said to not mind her, so I did my best to stay out of her way.

I enjoyed mostly hanging out with Chef, as he butchered sides of pig and beef on a big butcher block table next to me in the bakery. I didn't blame him for the "woman's work" of baking and salad making, for in New Orleans it wasn't 1981, but somewhere around 1955.

Chef Claude was informative and pleasant while he taught me the butchering, which made Edie jealous (I'm sure of it) because she'd worked at Arnaud's more than a year before he taught her these things. Daily, Chef Claude ranted about how American restaurants were "Shit! with Stupid Waiters!" He resented how much money waiters made, and for having absolutely no knowledge of food. "Shoemakers," he'd say, "fucking shoemakers." In France, he explained, waiters work in the kitchen first, earning the right to work the dining room. Of course I knew this already, from that short hour I spent with the chef at L'Auberge back in Portland.

Late mornings when the lunch waitresses and hostesses streamed into the kitchen, clocking in, setting up their cash banks at the service bar, and fixing their lipstick, Chef Claude put on his debonair French act. He'd wander over to the cluster of girls preening at the service bar and say something I could not hear but that always resulted in a chorus of giggles and chirps of

"Ooooh, Chef!" Chef Claude would wink and smile and return to our end of the kitchen, content as a stuffed bird. Once, when he was butchering a pig, he put a hoof under the sleeve of his white coat, sticking it out in place of his hand. Wild-faced, eyebrows wiggling like spastic caterpillars, he said, "Madeesa! Watch this." He sauntered over to the waitress cluster and began to rub the back of one girl with the hoof. When she turned to flutter at him, he held up the hoof and she screamed a *Psycho* shower scream. The look on his mischievous face was one of pure joy. Before the hooves went into the sausage pot, all the cooks and I had a turn at them, each of us wrapping the long sleeve of our chef's coat around the base of a hoof so it looked authentically like an extension of an arm. Pig hooves were more fun than carrot tongues.

The daily staff meal was an event for Chef Claude. You didn't stand at a stove and eat. You didn't munch (though I sometimes did because I never ate "meals"). We sat down every day after the lunch rush at a banquet table set up at the end of the cooking line, in front of the forty-gallon steam kettles and braising pans (over by where Steve had peed into the floor grate). Chef Claude spent most mornings planning this lunch, after the routines of butchering and waitress-rousing were complete. He'd roast or stew some cut of meat or fowl, whip up a soup, and bark some orders to a cook: "Greg-la, sweetbreads, oui?" Sometimes he'd let me make something for him—a creamy tomato soup or baked pompano with lemon and basil, reminiscent of my Northern Italian training in Portland. In addition to the main meal, Chef would have an omelet, which he showed me how to make French-style, toasting butter in the pan and using a fork to make the eggs fluffy.

"You Ameri-cans *keel* de eggs-la," he'd say, scrambling the eggs in the hot pan with the fork as the edges browned, and folding it into thirds onto the plate with the egg still soft in the center. "You dun *know* how to eat!"

To which I'd agree and make myself an omelet too, just the way he made his. The next day, and days after that, he allowed me to make his omelet for him, a service that I was proud to perform. I don't think Edie got to make omelets for Chef.

Then, after sweetbreads, an omelet, and a salad, he'd smear a soft wedge of brie over a loaf of French bread and eat that for dessert, always making a face at how the bread's crust shattered in his hand because of our below-sea-level location. "You Ameri-cans dun *know* how to bake bread-la!"

I don't know if, all these years later, anyone remembers me at Arnaud's, but I do have some fame to claim, and I'm going to claim this historical tidbit right here in this book: I was the first female line cook at the restaurant, ever—since its beginning in 1918 when there was a fully operating bordello upstairs. Sixty-three years of an all-male crew preceded me, and there I was, one Sunday morning brunch, called upon by Chef Claude after he fired culinary school grad Chris for "finishing" an omelet in the salamander broiler. "Motherfucker-la!" Chef yelled. "Get offa da line! Out of my kitchen-la! Out-la!" Anger and hate sharpened his voice to violence. Waitresses scattered like mice. Chef may as well have been chasing Chris out of the kitchen while wielding a butcher knife.

I heard the commotion over at my station—I was deboning roasted ducks for the dinner shift—when Chris, head down, scurried past me and out the back door.

"Madeesa! Madeesa! I need you on de line! Egg station-la!"

Adrenaline rocketed me over to the line, where I cranked down flames under empty sauté pans, made a quick mental picture of the mise en place in the salad-top refrigerator, and looked for orders on the ticket rail. Only there were no orders; Chef had them all on the front of the counter, where he was expediting, yelling, "Order this" and "Pick up that" with his heavy French accent, and I couldn't recognize a thing that might have eggs in it.

Robert, the Chalmette cook, flipping steaks next to me at the grill, translated for me: "Omelet 'fines herbs,' pick up. The herbs are there, yes. Ordering: smoked salmon on toast—salmon's under da line; ordering: wild mushroom omelet; pickup: smoked salmon on toast."

With jerky moves, I said, "Okay, got it, got it," each time Robert told me how much egg, how many mushrooms, and when to put the food up. Of course, I knew how to make the omelets and that, obviously, was the most important thing.

It was drinks at the Chartroom over on Iberville and Chartres afterward with Robert and Steve and Sous Chef Gary because we were all wound up, especially me. Brunch had topped 350 guests, a very busy day. I basked in my fame. The boys were noticeably impressed, with Gary telling me there'd never been a girl line cook at Arnaud's. But then, on our second round of drinks at our communal chef's table facing the sidewalk, Robert said, "That was great how you pulled that off, but you know, Marisa, a guy will always be a better line cook than a girl."

"N-no way! Why? T-timing and skill is t-timing and skill; how can sex matter? W-what does a dick have to do with cooking? Sh-shorter pee breaks?" I was so outraged that my stutter returned in full force. I looked at Steve and he laughed at my joke. But admittedly, I was insulted. I had a long way to go in this town.

At work the next day, waiters and waitresses commended me for my new line cook stature. Chef put me on the schedule to cook Sunday brunch and a few lunches. So it was official. Now I needed to make the same weekly salary as the boys. I knew from going over to Hibernia Bank with them Friday afternoons that their checks were $165.00 and mine, $135.00. Chef agreed a raise was only fair and that he'd go to the owner, Archie Casbarian, and get back to me.

A week later, the answer was no.

Since I was not one to just suck up and take this chauvinistic insult, or to refuse to work the line unless I was paid accordingly, or to politely quit, my frustration simmered into a raging hot bad attitude. Just because I was a poor conversationalist didn't mean I couldn't hurl out the Tourette's-like one-sentence zingers in earshot of Archie's secretary as an overcompensation for my lack of truly expressing myself: "This place is run like a shit house," I'd say, or "Archie can go fuck himself." To which Chef was eventually asked by upper management to let me go.

So just after Arnaud's maven Germaine Wells led the Easter parade in her characteristic bird- and flower-emblazoned Easter hat, I moved on.

CHAPTER 8

PRETTY BABY

TO BECOME A CHEF, first you need to know how to cook, of course. But you also need to know timing, knife skills, how to set up and cook for the masses, how to produce consistently good food, and how to maintain your cool under pressure. Some are born with this timing and ability to multitask—as I'd discovered I was, from that very first job at the Sea Scoop—so you plug in all the food knowledge you can get and one day, hopefully, you'll become chef of your own kitchen. Which I wanted badly. In those days of contemplating my life's culinary goals over a Myers's rum and grapefruit juice in a smoky bar after work with "Mack the Knife" scratching out on the jukebox, I didn't yet recognize the other important aspect of one's personality that would ease the ride up the culinary ladder: maturity. Sure, I could keep my cool during the entire shift; I could be great, in fact, but if something threatened my perceived stature in the kitchen, like being refused equal pay for the same or better work, I melted into a hotheaded tirade, or a pout. Chefs were hotheads, I told myself, so this was okay. But chef *men* are hotheads; chef wannabe girls were bitches.

The tiny Creole kitchen at the Columns Hotel on St. Charles Avenue, though just uptown from the French Quarter on the streetcar line, was worlds away from the ego-driven, old-school kitchen of Arnaud's. The ivory-white hotel in the Garden District was still basking in fame from being filmed as the bordello in Louis Malle's *Pretty Baby* in 1978, Brooke Shields's first film. Walking through the narrow entry of the Columns Hotel from its marble veranda was like stepping through a virtual time portal into turn-of-the-century Louisiana.

The hotel and its thirty-five-seat restaurant had originally been built in 1883 as a dream home for tobacco merchant Simon Hernsheim. With a romantic front veranda overlooking St. Charles Avenue, Queen Ann–style furnishings, Victorian lounge, fifteen-foot ceilings, and a grandiose three-story mahogany staircase topped with an ornate stained glass window, the place oozed Southern elegance. I would've washed dishes there just to have the privilege of spending time in the classic building without having to pay an entrance fee.

Thankfully the job opening wasn't for dishwashing, but for cooking. The chef, Armand Jonte, a twenty-eight-year-old White Creole who had been Chef Paul Prudhomme's sous chef at Commander's Palace, appeared not to care that I was female, contrary to most ethnocentric New Orleanians. White Maui girls in this city simply didn't make shrimp Creole, seafood gumbo, turtle soup, or alligator sauce piquant, but Chef Armand seemed to think I'd be able to manage it.

Beholden to his culinary mission in running the small Columns Hotel kitchen, Chef Armand simply needed someone teachable. So he taught me all of those classic New Orleans dishes, and I learned well from his passionate teachings and his after-shift alcohol-infused ramblings. Armand Jonte: a Hawaiian shirt–wearing creative thinker, a lover of food, music, poetry, alcohol, and drugs, and eventually lover of me.

So taken was I by the boyish-faced, tousle-haired, married Armand and the Creole and Cajun food he taught me, and the artistic atmosphere of the tiny Columns kitchen, with WWOZ's old-timey jazz blasting on the boom box over the cooking line, I dove into the culinary love whirlpool with all my senses. The courtship was long and gradual, flirty, dangerous, stomach-flipping, angst-painted, and by the time I had mastered brown roux for gumbo and étouffée, could coax the flavor from crawfish stock for a killer crawfish bisque, win a round of rabbit-boning races, and match him shot-for-shot of Myers's rum, Armand was splitting with his wife and we were a tumultuous unit.

By now, our lease was up on the Decatur Street apartment and Dona moved in with her boyfriend David, a bartender at Pat O'Brien's. She was saving for a car so they could go to Key West, since I had found love and planned to stay in New Orleans. I found a place on St. Peter Street, just off Rampart Street.

I was awed by the rough edges of New Orleans, the dark and mysterious streets, the impending danger hidden in its recesses. Its history swarmed me, yet felt somehow contemporary. Slaves living in their quarters, cotton merchants bargaining by the river, European families reading by candlelight in gaslight-ringed Uptown mansions. I had arrived via time machine and strived to learn all about this place, its music, its food, its architecture. Armand was the catalyst to all things exciting. The city killed some people, turned others into mental mush, and made others famous, ecstatic, and happy. The city was the pied piper of my dreams, and I, the quiet girl from Maui, its follower. I felt so alive!

And now I was in love with a man who personified New Orleans. With a masterful and arrogant air of a seasoned tour guide, Armand lured me further into his birthplace, taking me to dive bars and small restaurants, all the while giving me mini history lessons of the French and the Spanish, the South, the Civil War. All this was new knowledge to me, since apparently I'd slept through American History class (had there *been* an American History class at Seabury Hall? Hawaiian History, but I couldn't recall much else in the way of history). To have a smart, creative, demanding, popular, confident man show me his world and tell me that he loved me—it was perfect! We were both so hungry for something, and we found it in each other. And maybe, I thought, he would read to me sometime.

Armand had been adopted as an infant but swore by his native Creole roots. Judging by his fair skin and light brown hair, this probably meant French, perhaps a touch of Spanish. His sister had died in a hospital as a teen, through physician malpractice, and his father was also dead—two mooring lines severed in his life. Armand was dramatic, his passion manifested in poetic ramblings on various bar napkins and stained sheets of paper taking up residence in the pocket of his checked chef's pants. He'd carefully unfold the sweat-softened paper and begin to read aloud after the dinner shift with a lighted cigarette and a glass of rum. We met up after work at various Uptown bars, drank Myers's together, played Pac-Man, Galaga, and jukeboxes. We proclaimed our love for each other in our mutual drunken state, danced in the living room of my French Quarter apartment to Neil Young's "Like a Hurricane," listened to Tom Waits, Velvet Underground, David Bowie—music from Armand's college days that I now loved also. Falling into bed, our lovemaking was passionate and desperate.

Swept under by the current of Armand's love, I thought surely I had found that once-in-a-lifetime soulmate. But suddenly he would completely let go of me, spinning off into an aloof mode, sneering at me as if I were the demon in his life, leaving me to cry and nurse the now empty place in my heart with more Myers's. I accused him of being a liar; why had he just that morning said he loved me like no other but was now shunning me, giving me no love, angrily lumping me in with the rest of his tormented world? What had I done wrong? I wanted him back!

Then time would pass and, high on black beauties and rum, we were again slow dancing to Neil Young. Like the boulder had never dropped between us, separating our currents.

• • •

"Tomorrow's Brunch Special: Eggs Back-a-Town: two poached eggs on fried ham hocks on a bed of turnip greens with watermelon sauce." Steve Manning, Armand's good friend and part-time cook, delivered this deadpan, his soft monotone rising above WWOZ's afternoon jazz show blasting above the line, French knife in hand, looming tall over his cutting board, without any irony whatsoever. Armand, stirring multiple pots of sauces at the six-burner range, cigarette nub hanging from his lips, smiled slightly to himself; that was how I knew that Steve had made a funny.

Boning rabbits at my cutting board, I laughed at the joke, an attempt to quash my feeling of inadequacy. I liked Steve when he came to help out on weekends, but I hated my jealousy, feeling more comfortable when it was just Armand and me, alone together cooking, joking, flirting. Armand and Steve shared conversations in their higher-up common space that I was not a part of, like the chatter of adults "up there" when you're a child "down here."

It was just after lunch on a Saturday; Steve had put out the thirty or so lunches by himself and now we were all prepping for dinner. Once we were set, Steve would leave. But Steve had shared with us some peyote, and we were prepping like crazy because we knew that in a half hour the three of us would be flying our brains out, and who knew how productive we'd be around sharp objects and fire.

Usually at night after the dinners had all been served and the kitchen was more or less cleaned, there was mescal or Myers's, accompanied by dramatic and candlelit poetic oratory by Armand, or we'd hit the Maple Street bars and work on our Pac-Man skills. But today—getting high before the dinner shift—was a first.

We were all focused and quiet after ingesting the dried mushrooms, until Steve's announcement of tomorrow's supposed brunch special. Running my paring knife down either side of the rabbit's spine, I tried to think of something similarly witty. I could not. There was a boulder in my brain. I didn't think it was from the peyote; I suspected the boulder lived there, a permanent dull and useless organ inside my head. My talents were cooking, partying, being cute, and sex: my lot in life. I slipped the knife between the flesh and the rib cage and began to peel away meat from bone. Armand and Steve spoke in a cellophane tunnel, parents in a *Peanuts* cartoon. Down here my mind tuned in to the flapper jazz singing out from the grease-caked boom box. I envisioned we were cooking in 1919 and the dining room was packed with dapper men and Southern belles for dinner, their worlds filled with chintz, lace, tea, and apron-tied Black mamas sweeping the front steps. I stayed in this world until all six rabbits were deboned, the meat safely wrapped and stored in the refrigerator, and the bones in the freezer for future rabbit stock. I was standing before the food processor to puree a gallon of cooked turnips for soup when the clear plastic bowl of the processor began to melt and slide off its base. My heart began to palpitate.

I inhaled deeply, thinking oxygen would calm my panic. But more oxygen in my lungs did not temper the familiar feeling of fear rising up—fear that I would fail, fear that I would be found out and confronted as a fake person. Dark tunnels of groaning beasts spiraled around me. *Inhale.* More oxygen, please. From the disobedient processor the turnip puree still sloshed about, oozing stubbornly, not in my control. My gaze panned over to the line, the humid-garlic atmosphere of the kitchen prickled with lavender and pink glitter. Where was Armand? Where was Steve?

Cook? Cook dinner for all those strangers? Hard fear slammed into me. I moved slowly toward the hot line, giant purposeful steps, dodging deformed animals skittering along the quarry tile floor. *Armand? Steve?* I said telepathically. At the stove I turned off all the flames, overcautious, stopping the flow of food preparation.

Laughter then, through a tiny, invisible speaker. I pushed open the door next to the stove and peered into the alley. Armand and Steve, standing on the stone path under broad-leafed magnolias, were smoking and laughing, the air smoke-filled and green-smelling.

"Armand?" I peeped.

He looked up, eyes wide, levity drained from his face, then walked over to me. "What's wrong?"

"I can't—" *Can't what, exactly? Can't cook, can't be a person, can't put on this facade, can't talk, can't talk, can't talk, can't stand this self-loathing, being under this giant microscope of myself.* Suddenly, I wanted to cry.

Armand snapped into his in-charge mode: "I'll take you up to a room. Steve! Tell Claire Marisa's not feeling well, she's taking a nap."

"Just an hour," I blurted, "then I can cook." My fake self stepped in to show her presence.

Steve went to the stove and clicked the flames back on, and Armand led me out of the kitchen, through the small wait station, and to the front desk to get a key. I was relieved to be out of the kitchen, away from the food that mocked me.

I followed Armand up the mahogany stairs, each step's center scooped out by a hundred years of footfalls. I could not look up to the stained glass window ceiling, for I would fall into forever darkness. Instead my eyes trained in front of me, on the grease-stained cuffs of Armand's checked chef's pants. Up, up, and up.

The third-floor rooms hadn't been refurbished yet. Here were creaky doors with giant keyholes and crystal knobs, peeling paint, sloping wood floors, milky windows, musty odors of the past. Armand led me into a room and, hands on my shoulders, kissed me on the forehead. "Just rest a while and you'll be okay. Don't worry about setting up for dinner," he said with a detached voice, like a bad actor.

Through his wire-rimmed glasses his hazel eyes were magnified, giant bugs under half-mast lids. His cheeks were puffy, hair was pasted to his forehead with sweat and grease. This man loved me; in spite of me, he loved me. "I'm sorry," I said stupidly.

"We'll be fine." He turned to leave. Then, "Maybe this wasn't a good idea," he said in his boss voice. He forced the warped door shut behind him.

I had let him down.

I paced around the bed a few times, peered out the window at St. Charles Avenue like a madwoman in a belfry, then sat on the bed, hypnotized by the porcelain sink in the corner of the room, its map of brown hairline cracks reminding me of the globe I wanted to trot around, to remain anonymous in the world forever. Finally, I fell backward on the thin bedspread, shut my eyes, wanting sleep to take me, succumbing to the rumblings and shrieks of this empty room, the whisper of white lace curtains, the pressure of thick beveled windows upon me, stale air, damp wood. The streetcar grinded by every few minutes, barely keeping me tethered to the thread of reality below, while I slept off this bad reality in rapid eye movement.

When I was a kid, if Grandmother dared tell me I couldn't do something, I'd try with all my might to prove her wrong. Once, she told me it was physically impossible for me to win a race against the neighbor kids because I was the shortest. "Your legs just won't carry you as fast; you can't do it," she said.

"Can't do it"? My face wooden with determination, I ran that race. I willed my legs to move faster than the taller kids, and my heart to pump out its last beats if necessary to propel me, for I didn't care if I died as long as I proved that bitch wrong. And I did win. Even if I couldn't slow down at the finish line and ran right into the side of the neighbor's house, bloodying my right eyebrow, where I still have a scar today.

So disadvantages be damned, I would be a chef someday, and if I had to run into the side of a house to do it, so be it.

After Armand split with his wife, things began to change at the Columns. Owners Jacques and Claire Creppel hired a restaurant manager who snooped suspiciously around the kitchen, making us paranoid about our drinking and drug use. We needed these chemical infusions for the plated Renoirs we passed over the heated shelf, you see, and this manager guy was wrecking it for us.

Steve and Armand decided they were going to jump ship and planned a road trip up to Michigan, where Steve was from. It was only after they'd

made these plans that they asked me to go with them. It felt like the two
of them were closer than I and Armand were at times; I wasn't included in
the planning, and I was hurt that this trip of theirs was all about them. If I
could save the day and run the kitchen, maybe I'd score some points. "Sure,"
Armand said, about me staying back and running the kitchen. "You can do
it!" In the week leading up to their departure, we declared our love for each
other and vowed to move in together when he returned in two weeks. They
gave their short notice, Claire let me hire some cooks, and off I went into
leadership mode.

But being chef by default wasn't my bag. I missed Armand and began to
doubt my decision. Also, it was really hard to sleep alone in the St. Peter Street
apartment. After a creepy night together there a few weeks earlier, we agreed
my apartment was haunted, and I'd begun to sleep in one of the old rooms
at the Columns. But now with Armand gone and that permission no longer
sanctioned, I tried to get over the gloomy vibe in my bedroom, but wound up
sleeping on the love seat in the living room.

Haunted by historical heavy dark shit, performing chef duties by default,
lonely and missing Armand, a week after they'd left for Michigan I cleaned up
the line, left my restaurant keys on the prep table, and returned to my apartment to pack my backpack. Something had taken over my free will, or maybe
my free will actually had freed itself from its self-imposed cage, for there I was,
walking around in someone else's life. A curtain had been drawn in my brain,
preventing a conversation with myself. Preventing reasoning, planning, or
logic. With determined but stilted movements, like in a movie where actions
do not result in real consequences, I found myself en route to Michigan. At 2
a.m. In the rain. On bald tires.

I called Armand from a pay phone in Tennessee that night. "Great!" he said.
"We'll stay here for a few days, then head off to see Tommy in North Carolina!"

CHAPTER 9

IT'S ALL IN THE FOOD

IN 1710, FRENCH ACADIANS living in Maritime Canada refused to sign an oath of allegiance to Britain. They were French, dammit, and wanted to remain as such. Some years later, during the French and Indian War, the Brits sought to neutralize the stubborn Acadian military by deporting them from their homes and burning their villages in what is now Nova Scotia, New Brunswick, Prince Edward Island, and parts of Quebec. This time from 1755 to 1763 became known as the Great Upheaval or Le Grand Derangement. The 1763 Treaty of Paris ended the war and provided eighteen months for unrestrained emigration. Many Acadians traveled by way of the French colony Saint-Domingue (modern-day Haiti) to the bayous and riverbanks of the Atakapa region in southwest Louisiana. On February 27, 1765, two hundred refugees arrived from Maritime Canada aboard the *Santo Domingo* to join family members who had previously reached what would become called the Acadian Coast through a well-known and well-charted path through the center of the continent.*

The Acadians settled into their new home, now under Spanish rule, employing trapping, fishing, and farming skills honed in Canada. These were

---

* The historical details are from William Faulkner Rushton's book *The Cajuns: From Acadia to Louisiana* (New York: Farrar, Straus and Giroux, 1979).

country people: poor, without refrigeration, and their cuisine emerged from the abundance of seafood and game and their provincial French roots. Single-pot meals reflected their simplicity, along with other influences: Spanish paella and rice farming inspired their jambalaya; the abundant rice further became a bed for étouffée and a filling with leftover pig bits for boudin, a Cajun sausage of pork and rice; local Indians introduced okra and file pow-der—ground sassafras leaves—for gumbo; and Frenchified Germans upriver from New Orleans made the finest andouille sausage in southern Louisiana.

Meanwhile, the Creoles—a description that at first referred only to the French and Spanish upper class that ruled the city of New Orleans—had their own evolving cuisine. Their preparations of the local foods tended more toward classical European styles. The French influence on Cajun cooking descended from provincial peasantry, while Creole cooking evolved in the homes of aristocrats and plantation owners. The term Creole broadened to include the wider infusion of immigrants into the city—Italians and Portu-guese—and the native-born slaves who cooked for the well-to-do, for these culinary influences were thrown into the gumbo pot of Creole cuisine as well.

Of course I knew nothing of this when I began working at Arnaud's in 1982. Shrimp with white and red remoulade, turtle soup, oysters Bienville, shrimp Creole, and Creole gumbo, all rich and spiced, were mysterious menu items for me. At the Columns, Armand explained the difference between Cajun and Creole and that there was a lot of overlap, causing people to get confused and incorrectly label certain dishes. Both Creole and Cajun influ-ences inspired us in our tiny kitchen. We made gumbo with a dark roux of oil and flour—Cajun-style—while other sauces used the traditional butter and flour roux of the classic French persuasion—Creole-style. We mixed our own Creole spice consisting of different powdered peppers, granulated garlic, salt, and oregano in a paprika base. We added cumin to a similar spice mixture for meat seasoning. These Armand had learned from Chef Paul Prudhomme at Commander's Palace, before Chef Paul began selling his own line of spice mixes in the grocery aisle.

A man named Jimmy Gaubert from upriver in Cajun country delivered rabbits to the city every Tuesday. He raised them himself, killed and skinned them, sometimes leaving a blot of fur here or there, which we'd carve out with a paring knife before deboning, usually taking place as the aforementioned

rabbit-boning races. Rabbit was my favorite food to play with. Armand's signature rabbit dish was delicious—the tender boneless chunks sprinkled with
Creole seasoning and flour, sautéed, deglazed with white wine, finished with
heavy cream flavored with Creole mustard and lime, and served on a toasted
almond rice ring. The tender rabbit tasted like . . . well, chicken, with a slight
gaminess. The rabbit was a willing meat for just about any sauce—Creole;
lemon butter with herbs; tomatoes, dill, and sesame oil—you could sauce
it with anything, and the stuff just tasted good. And the little rabbit livers
blended nicely with those of duck to make a smoky, yummy pâté.

The turtle soup was funny. The sinewy meat required a painstaking
mini-cubing by hand with a very sharp paring knife and a long time cooking
in beef stock, tomato, mirepoix, and roux before adding lots of sherry, lemon,
herbs, Worcestershire, allspice, and diced hard-boiled egg. This didn't resemble anything I'd ever encountered, and once I'd dined out and tasted the turtle
soup from a customer's perspective, I thought that the mini-carafe of sherry
served alongside made turtle soup worthwhile.

Seafood, of course, was really *it*. At 4 p.m., soft-shelled crabs arrived at
the kitchen's back door arrayed in a shallow crate. We pulled the sex and the
lungs from them and at 5:30, when the first order came in, we sprinkled two
of the fresh soft-shells with Creole seasoning, lightly dredged them with flour,
tossed them into an oiled, hot sauté pan, and—wow! Look at the legs wiggle!
No, they weren't alive, just very, very fresh. Only a light treatment of lemony
meunière sauce and a sprinkling of fresh chopped parsley were needed to send
taste buds soaring.

Redfish, flounder, sea trout, drum, jumbo lump crabmeat, oysters, live
crawfish, crawfish meat, shrimp, alligator, rabbit, quail, duck—all so fresh, so
much food to work with, and I dreamed food and food combinations. Oysters and artichoke heart brochettes with sauce meunière. Filet tips and fried
green tomatoes with béarnaise sauce. Rabbit sauté with basil, garlic, lime, and
tomato. Jumbo lump crabmeat salad with fresh water chestnuts and caramelized onions. Meanwhile, Armand wowed people with his eggplant Eloise: a
crispy fried eggplant cup filled with Creole sautéed seafood and topped with
creamy oyster sauce. And we had plenty of French street names to name our
dishes after: Duck Dufossat, Veal Danneel . . . we were a team. I had found
my home at this stove and in this man's arms.

In the 1980s, New Orleans chefs weren't household names yet around the rest of the country. Before the days of blackened redfish, Paul Prudhomme was mainly managing his long lines of tourists at K-Paul's in the French Quarter. Emeril Lagasse was still toiling as Paul Prudhomme's replacement at Commander's Palace. Susan Spicer had some regional celebrity status as a female chef who seemed to have a lot of luck helping her along; she'd been taken under the wing of Chef Daniel Bonnot at Louis XVI, a chef who put applicants through a rigorous testing and a waiting period before being hired. Greg at Arnaud's had also worked for Chef Bonnot, and it all sounded like a bunch of snobbery to me. The most famous Louisiana chef at the time was Justin Wilson, because he had a cooking show. Marketed mainly for his humor and his Cajun-ness, his cooking techniques made us laugh because he relied on a jug of white wine for everything, filling his glass and pouring it into gumbo, an aberration for us real chefs (the wine going into gumbo, that is).

This was the French Quarter in 1982: dim bars scratching out Blondie and Frank Sinatra on an old jukebox while people huddled over drinks, commiserating about their days. The smell of damp street dirt blending with truck diesel and underground gas pipes. An ancient black lamp flickering at the end of Pirates Alley, against which a man was slumped, empty plastic go-cup tilted in his hand. Gas lamps in Jackson Square casting moon glows on the ancient gray brick masonry of the St. Louis Cathedral while Andrew Jackson rode off on his stone horse. The red brick Cabildo looking out over the square through dark windows, where a few musicians were set up around a wrought iron bench. They sounded stoned. Café du Monde still selling beignets late at night, though not as many as during the powdered-sugar frenzy of the bleached-out mornings. Restaurants at closing time, cooks scrubbing greasy kitchens of burnt roux and butter. A dishwasher dumping oyster shells into a heap out the back door. It sounded like music. The cooks meeting up at the Chartroom for drinks, their stained chef's coats left behind in their kitchens, their faces shiny, with the worn look of relief. On Royal Street a cat stretching in the old bookstore window, the only movement in the beveled windows of dusty shops. An inviting light on the dark street is a doorway open to a deep diorama where shadows are bending like question marks over drinks, silent, ceiling fans alive, jukebox dead. Walking, walking these streets, there was so much to see in the oldest neighborhood in the city, the French Quarter, the Vieux Carré.

And I missed all of it, during my trip up to Michigan and our break away from cooking at the Columns. We'd road-tripped to New York and the Carolinas, too, and been away for a month, drinking, arguing, and lovemaking all the way. I loved this man when he was happy and funny, his eyes dancing when he looked at me. But there was an awful flip side between us, Armand with his moods and me with my struggle for power. Whenever I shared my angst about how I was treated as a girl in the kitchen, he shot me down by saying I imagined it. Many fights would start this way, as I pleaded for him to understand my feelings. I knew our job search back in New Orleans would net Armand a chef's job and me a line cook's job, and when I shared my jealousy, he got angry.

When we returned to New Orleans we rented a shotgun house Uptown on Valmont Street and began looking for work. Armand had a permanent Sunday position at the Bay-Waveland Yacht Club, fifty miles from the city near his family beach house, and he had some money saved up, so he took his time looking for a city job. I, on the other hand, broke and in panic mode about my car payment, grabbed the first job I could. Even New Orleans has mediocre restaurants, and my first attempt at employment landed me in one of these. Cooking lunches in Iler Pope's Dante-by-the-River's little kitchen with its resident rat and unfazed old chef, and pulling down some evening waiter shifts, paid the bills while I looked for something more inspiring.

Next up, the Upperline. When a restaurant endures for thirty years, I am proud to say that I worked there. Located on Upperline Street, the eponymous restaurant was one of those new Creole-modern places, with Jason Clevenger as chef and his mother, the matronly and red-haired JoAnn, as manager and official greeter-hostess every night. It was a pretty, converted house equipped with a range, a fryer, and a large wood-burning grill. I was hired to run the day shift and carry out Chef Jason's recipes of his lighter Creole gumbo, spinach curry soup, and numerous wood-grilled specialties served with remoulade and various dips.

The only problem was that the other cooks weren't notified of my position as person in charge, so awkwardness prevailed. It was a battle for me to get the other cooks to do things for me, my peers believing that I was one of them, not the one who had to answer—although only in private—to management. Were Jason and JoAnn ashamed they had a girl in charge? Or was this just an honest oversight of new restaurateurs? I couldn't be sure.

Meanwhile, at another new Uptown restaurant called Gautreau's over on Soniat Street, owner Anne Russell, a doctor's wife, had been looking for a chef so she could open for dinner. Gautreau's was housed in an old apothecary in the Garden District. Anne cooked lunches herself, and her fellow debutantes patronized her restaurant frequently and with praise. Word of mouth sent Armand over there to talk to her, and she gladly scooped him up. "This is my new chef!" I heard her brag to her lunch-patron friends one day when Armand took me over there to see his new kitchen.

At the Upperline I tried to handle my secret-agent day chef position responsibly, but sometimes it seemed the world was working against me. One Saturday afternoon when there was no lunch shift, I was put in charge of opening the restaurant for dinner, as the Clevengers were out of town and wouldn't return until Sunday. The place had been locked up tight Friday night, and I was the first one in on Saturday at two with the key.

My instructions, in addition to the regular ready-prep list and taking phone reservations, included scooping Friday night's ashes from the wood grill into the metal can and stocking the grill with more wood for the night. The back door of the small kitchen was at the end of the cooking line near the wood grill so it was easy to take the ash can outside, once filled with the smoldering ashes, and set it by the dumpster against the side of the building. While I was going through my routines, answering the phone, writing reservations into the big book, and setting up the mise en place for the night, I felt proud of myself. These people had entrusted their restaurant to me, after all. *I'll show those day cooks who think I'm just one of them*, I thought.

After I loaded up the grill with fresh wood, I whipped around behind the line to the walk-in cooler, loaded a small cart with all my prep items, and then struck a position at the grill station cutting board and began to dice onions and green peppers for gumbo.

That's when I smelled the smoke.

There was a slow blur of thought: the equipment wasn't to full heat yet . . . and . . . this whole city . . . and its ancient wood structures. My hand flew to the back doorknob a split second before the thought fully landed in my brainpan. There in the graying afternoon, a ten-foot-tall flame licked at the wooden siding of the restaurant, the metal can sitting innocently under its hot orange wrath.

After my shaking hand dialed 911 and the fire trucks came, I called the Clevengers at the emergency number they had left. I stuttered nonsensically when JoAnn got on the line, but she got the gist of what I was saying, that there had been a fire, a small one, and the fire trucks were putting it out. She said, "That's okay, Marisa, we'll be back tomorrow." I couldn't read any emotion in her voice.

Armand worked nights at Gautreau's and I worked days at the Upperline, which I thought was good for our relationship. Or maybe I just liked being alone in my new city to explore, unjudged. Dona and I had gotten inspired to buy Minoltas when we lived together in the French Quarter, and we'd spent days off snapping our way through city streets and graveyards with grainy black-and-white film. She was long gone to Key West now, so I picked up an evening photography class at the University of New Orleans to learn more about my new passion.

From our little shotgun house on Valmont Street, quintessential New Orleans with its worn, sloped steps and front porch with fluttering lavender hibiscus, I could walk a few blocks to Magazine Street, where on the corner sat a ramshackle building that housed a bar and nighttime blues club. The upper portion of Magazine between Soniat and Jefferson was wonderfully crumbly back then, and eerie with its dusty used furniture and antique stores tended by equally dusty old men loitering out front hoping to bring in buyers. I'd been a buyer once at one of these stores, when I'd gone in search of a used mattress for the Decatur Street apartment.

The Maple Street bars were bars Armand and I went to together. This Magazine Street corner bar was *my* bar, where I went when bored and needing some conversation with those permanently stuck to the barstools. The name of the bar is long forgotten. The best conversationalist in the place, a person whose friendly face always welcomed me and ultimately whose gender confused me, well, I've forgotten their name too. But it was my bar, and that's where I went to fuel my inner fire with alcohol and it is where I went when storming out of the Valmont house, unable to conclude an argument before it turned into a full-on raging war with the man I loved and lived with. The man who had proposed on bended knee in the middle of Hillary's bar, presenting me with a pear-shaped diamond ring.

Gautreau's was closed for lunch on Mondays for Anne's day off. Armand asked me if I could juggle my Upperline schedule to cook lunch so they could capture that business. As always, I needed the money, and I was a little honored to be a part of this special little restaurant that changed its menu every day based on what was fresh. Soon I was also working with Armand on Saturday nights after my lunch shift at the Upperline. Armand and I still didn't see each other much, and when Anne asked me to quit the Upperline to be her day chef, this arrangement remained pretty much the same.

I did not know that cooking at Gautreau's would be my last restaurant job in New Orleans.

CHAPTER 10

THE ULTIMATE MENU

CRAB AND CORN SOUP, crawfish vinaigrette, rabbit Mangani, jumbo lump crab salad with fresh basil mayonnaise, beef tenderloin tips with fried green tomatoes . . . the menu items I'd written on a bar napkin the night before scrolled down my closed lids, each item printed bigger than the one before, until the food was almost yelling at me: Wake up!

I jerked upward, then looked at Armand snoring lightly beside me, remembering the scent of garlic and Myers's rum and the culinary pillow talk when he crash-landed into bed around midnight: need eggplant cups carved, order snapper, make a third soup. Morning light peered into the fishbowl bedroom window (which was painted shut), the sun just beginning its creep over the old roofs and spires of New Orleans. The clock on the nightstand read 6:30. My feet landed on the dusty oak floor, I shuffled to the bathroom and brushed my teeth, pulled on my checked pants and a T-shirt, grabbed a chef's coat from the closet, kissed Armand on the cheek, and plunged into the bird-chirping March morning for the ten-minute drive to Gautreau's.

Armand's prep list and greasy pen awaited me on the cutting board in the darkened kitchen. I flicked on the lights, perused his list while brewing a pot of coffee, then lay his list on a spice shelf, and with another sheet of paper copied my own menu from the wadded bar napkin in my pocket. With more paper I alternately wrote out the day prep list, the seafood order, the produce and meat orders. Meanwhile, I was drinking rich coffee with chicory, turning on the exhaust hood, firing up the oven, the griddle, the steam table, pulling a tub of shrimp stock from the two-door freezer, telling each supplier on the phone that I needed my order by *nine*, hefting a large soup pot on the stove for the crab and corn soup with the phone stuck to my ear and reaching the cord across the small kitchen to my various destinations. My morning autopilot routine.

At nine the deliveries started rolling in. At ten, Timmy, the prep and salad cook, arrived and began chopping vegetables. Anne Russell arrived without so much as a "good morning" and I gave her my menu to copy into the menu templates with her calligraphy pen. She stood on the other side of the pickup counter, one hand resting on her skirted round hip, the other holding my paper, her face set in a light scowl. "Why are we having crab and corn soup again? We just had it on Monday," she said, her voice a whiny crackle, like the rumpling of foil.

I dropped a fistful of julienned basil into the food processor. "Th-that's what Armand t-told me to make," I answered, feeling smug despite my stammering, knowing that she never argued with anything Armand said.

"Oh," she said, and she hurried from the kitchen through the swinging door into the dining room.

I hit pulse and finished off the basil mayonnaise wondering if the crab and corn soup would be creamy enough for her, if she'd noticed I'd chilled the Creole tomatoes again (she insisted they be served at room temperature), or if there would be new culinary offenses I'd commit to send her running to Armand when he arrived at two, pleading, whining, could he please get me to do everything her way? Then Armand, behind the cooking line with me and starting off each sentence with, "Anne says . . . ," and me considering pouring out the Worcestershire sauce from his bottle of Lea and Perrins and replacing it with vanilla extract. And maybe even giving him back the pear-cut diamond engagement ring too.

But this, this job, this little restaurant, was about the food. And about my ability to express myself through the food. And about happy customers. And about the beautiful old building nestled between two houses on Soniat Street in the dappled shadow of ancient oak trees. And the smell of history embedded in the wood. And maybe, just maybe I'd make a name for myself here. So I sucked in my perpetually bruised ego and cooked.

At eleven Jerome arrived with his white smile splitting his black face, and he started on the pile of pots and pans awaiting him on the small stainless steel dish table.

Timmy, retying his apron, said, "I think I'm set."

I inspected the mise en place in his salad refrigerator, the diced vegetables and turkey and crumbled bleu cheese and crispy bacon for Cobb salads, drained crawfish tails for the salad vinaigrette, lump crabmeat with bits of shell sifted out, and backups underneath for all, the ripest avocados selected from the box and lying near his cutting board, waiting to be peeled and diced to order. All inserts of dressing full, backups in the main reach-in. Soups hot and in the steam table. Crawfish batter whipped up. Fryer hot.

"You're good, Timmy. Start on the eggplant cups for dinner." I resumed portioning snapper fillets for the night, seven ounces each, saving the ends and scraps for gumbo.

At 11:30 the first order came in. Timmy and I silently read the ticket and got to work ladling cups of soup and sending out appetizer-size salads; then I hit the stove for the main entrées. More orders came in. Timmy dished soups, I heated pans for tenderloin tips and rabbit Mangani, and Timmy assembled three Cobb salads. We were silent in our tasks for the first half hour.

When the rush hit, Timmy and I traded communications to coordinate our efforts: "Two Cobbs up, crawfish ready, how's the rabbit and tips?" Timmy asked. Head down at the stove, I answered, "Up now, finishing three tips and a redfish, fire two crawfish." I pivoted from the stove to the counter and dressed my plates. Adrenaline pumped us through the rush, our moves perfectly orchestrated, eighty covers between the two of us, Jerome singing across the kitchen at his dishwashing station, the clunk and clank of dishware and cutlery a musical backdrop to his blues.

At 1:45 the tickets were gone save one with salads only, and I crossed the kitchen to the beverage counter to refill my coffee. Leaning against the pickup counter, calming the blood still pumping through my veins, I considered the afternoon prep for Armand's dinner shift. Then the double-action door to the dining room opened slightly, the one that squeaked open and shut as waiters rammed themselves through it with arms full of plates. Now it opened purposefully, partially, and a head poked in. A perfumed, made-up head, the type of head that undergoes careful and artistic grooming before a beveled and ancient mirror in the hundred-year-old family home, while downstairs a housekeeper hums about her duties. A head topped with a hat, complete with shellacked poppies and baby's breath.

The head was accompanied by two perfectly manicured hands, one gripping the door, the other the frame. The head looked toward Jerome the dishwasher and drawled, "Chef! That rabbit Mangani was out of this world! Anne *told* me she had a new day chef. You keep up the good work. Lovely food, just lovely . . ." She said all this to him in a high-pitched singsong voice. And the head disappeared behind the door.

Jerome shrugged, waved where the lady had just been, and resumed singing and washing—while I stood at the stainless steel counter in full whites and chef's hat, face red-hot, tamping down my rage with gulps of hot coffee. Were there *no* rewards for me? Why did this city conspire against me so? And no offense whatsoever to happy Jerome, but why was I perceived as ranking below a dishwasher?

Armand accused me of being overdramatic. "Oh, you know you do a good job; what's the big deal?" he'd say. The big deal was that he had no idea what it was like to be me. I tried, with everything I had in me, to make him understand the humiliation I felt. But later that night the scenario played out, just like the other times I'd complained to him, with Armand, jacked up on Myers's and cooking adrenaline, and me on the rum, Galaga star wars, and all previous resentments of his emotional abuse, and a drunken argument exploded. Through disjointed speech, my pleading for understanding and recognition segued into all that was wrong with Gautreau's, Anne, Armand, and eventually me—*Listen to me! Listen to me! Why can't you listen?!* At some point red lights strobed into our living room and a uniformed cop stood in the open doorway, because the only way I could force out the alien baby of thoughts and feelings within was to scream at the top of my lungs and hurl objects (Armand's vintage Civil War soldiers, glassware, the phone) against the plaster walls of our shotgun house.

If spontaneous human combustion could happen, it would have happened to me during these times of blind rage. Lucky for me we humans are made up of mostly water. My determination to succeed at being a chef and needing to be loved by Armand, and Armand's penchant to flip a switch emotionally, as if the fights never happened, kept up this cycle of love-hate throughout the fall and winter of that year.

I attempted to tamp down my rage by ignoring the triggers. I wanted to keep the peace, but there were times when Armand's apathy toward me threw me into self-doubt and there I'd be again, crying for love and attention. On more than one occasion when he was driving, I opened the passenger car door at a red light and dashed out to find the nearest bar to drown my sorrows. Or if I was driving, I stopped the car and attempted to push him out. I even called the cops on him once when he had my car—because it was my car, after all. His ex-wife had gotten his Celica in the divorce, and that's how vengeful I was toward him when he got the way he got.

I've always been a little superstitious, interpreting external events as a sign of something either ominous or promising. Perhaps this was a built-in safety valve, because clearly I ignored the obvious clues that this was not a healthy relationship. Two fiery chefs living in a one-hundred-year-old shotgun house with no air-conditioning or regular cleaning schedule resulted in something so awful to me one late fall evening that it remained as a backdrop to the next few months as I did my best to navigate work and love.

Steve and his wife, Denise, were over for dinner, and we had the front and back doors open for the breeze. While we were out in the rear court-yard for before-dinner drinks, the air had cooled a bit, so I went into the bedroom to get a sweater. When I opened the closet, a million little scurrying sounds exploded into a multitude of three-inch-long shiny, city-dwelling cockroaches. I screamed as they ran up the hanging clothes, out onto the floor, and under the bed. Armand came running in from the kitchen, meat fork still in his hand, and speared one running up the bedpost. He held it up in front of me like a tormentor, the roach pierced all the way through, legs still scrambling. I ran outside, crying. Fork held high, roach still wiggling, Armand chased me, as if forcing me to look at it. I didn't run off to the corner blues bar that night—but I probably should have.

CHAPTER 11

IN GOD WE FISHING

—COiNeD BY CAPTAiN KeNNY NeiZMAN,

MAUi, SOMETiMe iN THE 1970S

MY RELATIONSHIP WITH ARMAND may have been competitive and fiery, with much rum-swilling, passion, and fighting, but I still thank the man for teaching me how to fish.

Our ancestors had it right. They didn't need candlelight, contrived decor, or fancy silver to enjoy a meal to its fullest. Because they caught or captured their food, cleaned it, cooked it, and ate it, they enjoyed the satisfaction of a fresh, unadulterated, and wholesome meal. This was all from necessity, of course, but with our modern-day grocery aisles lined with food from obscure origins smashed under plastic wrap, there is an element of sustenance that many don't get to enjoy.

But some do. Captain Kenny Neizman, a street character and artist in Lahaina, the Maui of my youth, knew the satisfaction of catching his food, specifically fish. His main art subjects were also fish, although caricatured in Day-Glo paint and sporting huge fangs—these fish possibly depicting some guilt-shredding fish revenge.

My experiences fishing in Hawaii were few. There were those early days dangling my feet off the dock, watching my shrimp-baited nylon line entice

the menacing needlefish. I always ate fish when we dined out with Grandmother, and I envied the boaters grilling up some freshly caught mahi-mahi,
the scent permeating the sultry harbor air. We never ate fish at home, for it
was too expensive—the irony of this fact while living in a place surrounded
by water not hitting me until much later.

Waveland, Mississippi, is fifty-seven miles from New Orleans, a sleepy
pocket of a beach town on the Mississippi Sound—a body of water that eventually morphs into the turquoise Gulf of Mexico. The Sound's muddy bottom
and murky water are home to blue crabs, shrimp, flounder, trout, drum fish,
redfish, and probably more, but these were what we caught regularly when
we stayed at Armand's family's beach house. Except for shrimp, that is, which
were brought in daily by giant shrimp boats with winglike nets at the west end
of the bayou where now stands—to my absolute horror—a casino.

The accessibility of fishing in Waveland, unlike in Hawaii, is what makes
it great. You can walk down to the beach with baited rod in hand, cast it into
the small lapping waves, and pull in a trout or a redfish for lunch. You can
drive to any number of rock jetties and sit for a morning, pulling in enough
flopping fish for dinner with some left to freeze for a rainy day. You can row
out past the waves in a small dinghy and drop a crab trap baited with chicken
necks and return the following weekend for dozens of blue crabs; after cooking them up in a spicy boil and eating your fill, you sit around drinking beer
and picking the meat from them with little forks, to wrap and freeze for those
future pots of gumbo.

My favorite fish to catch and to cook is flounder. Sunday mornings in
Waveland, I'd fish alone on the docks, while Armand dished up eggs Sardou
in the pearl-white building above me that was the Bay-Waveland Yacht Club.
Flounder fishing is a little more active than sitting and waiting for a trout or
redfish to hit: Flounders are flat, bottom-swimming fish and have the ability
to spit out traditional hooks. So a special flounder jig is used, which is a length
of line with two staggered red-and-white fish sinkers with hooks under them.
People fish for flounder without baiting these hooks, but I bait both fish lures
with shrimp, just to be sure.

Line ready, I'd drop it around a dock piling, then stand and jerk it along
the muddy bottom. "Dragging for flounder" this is called, walking slowly up
and down the dock in shorts and bikini top, stopping only to take a pull of

beer or to yank up a flopping gray-brown flounder, de-hook it, and flip it into the bucket. Such purpose, such an excuse to hold nearly still in nature with the kiss of the salt breeze, the rushing of the grasses edging the bayou, the hum of cicadas, the sun warm on my arms and face, the prospect of fresh dinner, my pride to prove to Armand I am a fisherman—all these things welling up and forcing out a happiness I'd never felt before.

Armand monitored my fishing progress while he worked, peering down periodically from the dining room window saying, "Catch anything?" I'd give him the Hawaiian "shaka" sign, extending my thumb and little finger while curling down the three middle fingers. Once, he happened to look out when I pulled up a very long green eel, whose maniacal S-flopping had me squealing and stomping around on the dock, pulling on my fishing rod, unsure of what to do. "Cut it loose!" Armand yelled into the wind with a laugh in his command—which I did, sorry to lose my last flounder jig, but wrestling a strong eel jaw from my hook was not something I was prepared for. After the eel episode, there were eel food jokes aplenty: eel gumbo, eel Creole, eel pie.

Catching my flounder was only half the fun. Cooking and eating the trophy was the reward of such enjoyable work. After scaling and cleaning the fish, Armand showed me how to slit it from head to tail down one flat side to the backbone, peel away the flesh, and carve out the bones in one full piece, leaving a fish wallet. With a perfect flap of flesh to season and fill with crab stuffing from those little packets in the freezer from last month's crab-haul-beer-drinking-meat-picking-session. Sprinkle with Creole seasoning, lemon juice, and dot with butter, bake until sizzling and—God's gift to you from Her waters.

Since we're on fish, fishing, eating fish, and passion for fish, we'll talk about sushi, another close-to-God-experience. The Japanese sure know how to do it. You'd think being from Hawaii, I'd have been raised on raw fish. But no, remember, fish was expensive, and the parents, unadventurous with food.

My first sushi bar experience was in the Castro District of San Francisco during the road trip to New Orleans with Dona in 1981. Dona was off somewhere with another high-school friend that day and I met up with beautiful long-haired Grant, who had moved from Portland to San Francisco soon after I had left Robertino's. Grant showed up with a girl—her odd name long forgotten—with the bottom half of her black hair bleached blonde. The girl ordered for us in Japanese and an array of little chilled fish-on-rice snacks arrived. I copied the girl, mixing soy sauce into wasabi mustard in the tiny black bowl provided, feeling quite inadequate, for her personality shoved mine off the table. She wore a tight black skirt and a sheer little white blouse unbuttoned at the top and exposing a swell of cleavage; her face was heavily plastered white, with corpselike purple-black lips. I was wearing an awkward sweater and bell-bottoms I'd bought at the local Salvation Army store. This girl was obviously a sushi whore, and I was just a virgin. Since I was usually poor on a cook's wage and currently unemployed while traveling, I didn't dine out much and Grant was paying. But I could certainly handle chopsticks, thanks to my Hawaiian upbringing, so I pretended *not* to be a sushi virgin.

Expertly, I shoved pieces of hamachi, saba, maguro, and ika into my mouth, savoring each rush of salty and sweet chill, the hot bite of wasabi mustard, the sense of the sea, unaware and uncaring what I was really eating. This would come later, you see, for I was no longer a virgin.

The actual art of dining at a sushi bar I learned from Armand, naturally. Once settled in New Orleans, wandering into a sushi bar after a night of drinking seemed the healthiest of vices. It's important to sit *at* the sushi bar and gain eye contact with your sushi chef. Armand knew certain sushi chefs and would start off by handing the chef a five-dollar bill, thus cementing our status at the bar and therefore the sushi chef's attention.

Dear reader, if you are under forty, your sushi bar experiences probably involve a rectangular paper menu and a stubby yellow pencil to check boxes across from English fish names, which you then hand over your shoulder to a waitress. Then you sit and watch lustily as the sushi chef prepares your entire meal on a platter and places it in front of you to eat all at once, American-style. Absolutely sacrilegious! Spit your gum out in that paper menu and order, as needed, in Japanese. This is crucial. The sushi chef will treat you with much adoration, possibly making up a little something special for you, something not on the menu. And of course you've respected him with that advance tip. After you order your first round of warm sake and a miso soup from the kimonoed waitress, smile at the sushi cutter and say, "Hamachi, two orders, please." And he will know that you know how it's done.

Sushi bars of the eighties had picture menus, either in the form of a plastic tent on the bar or a mural on the wall above the sushi chefs. The pictures of the fish-on-rice were large and colorful, the Japanese names a little smaller, the English names tiny or nonexistent. This is how I learned to order in Japanese.

Eating sushi is about the fish, of course. But it's also about the style of eating, the leisure of it, how it's conducive for conversation, eating slowly, with pauses in between for digestion, of eating only until you're full.

Once at a Mid-City New Orleans sushi bar, a very attentive sushi chef bowed and nodded when we were done and said, "Ice cream cone!" I shook my head, not even believing they had ice cream at a sushi bar. But he wasn't asking. He repeated the phrase, nodded again, and set about toasting something in the little home toaster oven. It smelled like bacon. He rolled rice around the toasted stuff along with radish sprouts, avocado, and other mysterious ingredients, and folded it all into a seaweed wrapper shaped like an ice cream cone, handing it over the refrigerated fish case to me. "Hand roll, dried salmon skin, ice cream cone . . . dessert." He nodded and bowed again, smiling as I took the gift. Which was wonderful, of course. We regaled this chef with much tipping that night and on future trips to this particular sushi bar. To this day, I always order a smoked salmon skin hand roll for dessert when I eat sushi.

I am not a religious person, though I am a spiritual one and I believe fishing and eating fish is one of the most spiritual things a person can do. There are fishermen all over the Bible, after all, if you want to go there. Fish are a symbol of plenty, Mother Nature's best gift to Woman and Man. To me the staff of life is fish, not bread. Maybe they should feed you little fresh anchovies in church instead of crackers . . . okay, maybe I go a bit too far.

Back in Mississippi, I lived for fishing and cooking my fish into a buttery gastronomy. Now, many years past the New Orleans and Waveland days, I still long to fish. I don't fish enough (between my day job, writing this book, and living in Sarasota, which is not right on the Gulf), and I dream of a time when I'm the old lady on a dock with a bucket and a beer. Sure, I have fished since Mississippi—I've caught flounder under a bridge in the Florida Panhandle, whiting in Australia, tuna and mackerel off the shores of Sarasota. I even taught my daughter to fish when she was three, and she loved it.

So there I was at twenty-three, fishing on the banks of the Mississippi Sound, drinking too much, fighting for my own space in life, and unknowingly carving out what would later become my retirement dream.

To fish.

CHAPTER 12

IT HAD TO END

UNDER THE APATHETIC SCOWL of the late April sun, the hood of my four-year-old Volkswagen Rabbit boomed under each assault of my fists. *In need of a new engine,* the service man was saying. The vortex sucked me in, yanking my legs into the pit I always narrowly avoided. Everything I had worked for—my job at Gautreau's, my meager savings account, and my roller-coaster engagement to and breakup with Armand, the Asshole—had been yanked out from under me. And my car, my symbol of freedom, the thing I hopped into when angry or frustrated or lonely to explore the narrow and potholed streets of New Orleans, or to drive out to the green rolling hills of River Country, now added to the things I'd lost. I had spent four years paying for this four-wheeled tube of tin, whose fallible instrument panel hadn't flashed the oil light while a leak silently dried the engine of my freedom. The bent oil pan lay atop my engine like roadkill, proof of all my failures. "Were you driving on a bad road?" the service man asked.

"Bad road? Bad road?! This is *New Orleans*!" I shrieked back at him.

It was one of those perfect sunny days before the stagnant humidity of summer would begin to curtain the city like a hot fog. As I listened to the mechanic tell me the fate of my car, all I could think about was the April of my beginnings in New Orleans three years earlier when I'd exited the bus onto Canal Street, starry-eyed and hopeful. Prominent in my frontal lobe now was Anne Russell scowling at me at the restaurant, Armand's parrot-like "Anne says," "Anne says," "Anne says" ("Why don't you marry Anne, then!" I'd screamed during one fight), my cookery becoming rote hell. Nightly fights and daily silent treatments pushed me down, down, down into the city's below-sea-level dregs, with longer nights in air-conditioned bars, escaping the heat, physical and otherwise, fortified with Myers's and rocking and rattling the Galaga machine to kill enemy insects fast coming at me.

Finally, something (self-preservation?) in me pleaded for escape. I had hit survival mode. A change was mandatory. Anne agreed to let me take off for three days; she'd work my lunch shifts and I'd go visit Jackie, who had moved from Portland to Seattle to further her culinary career. After the seventy-five bucks I'd just spent on service and detailing, my car was acting funny, so I dropped it at the dealership and took a bus to the airport.

Under the watchful sway of giant fir trees at Jackie's house, I made gumbo and shrimp Creole with Northwestern ingredients, which seemed wrong somehow, making me want to get back to New Orleans to pick up the pieces and trudge up the sheer cliff that was my life. Not even the cool mountain air relieved me. I wanted the heat of New Orleans, the impossible spicy damp-ness and fury of swamp weather, the long hot nights, the sun burning through waves of humid clouds, afternoon thunderstorms erupting with earsplitting thunder, then emptying hot water onto the city's streets. While sitting in Jack-ie's carpeted living room, front door open to pine-scented breezes, I felt I had left something big behind. I had stepped out of the line of my life to watch from a precarious position. Then the phone call came: "Take a longer vaca-tion," Armand was saying. Apparently Anne had found my replacement.

Vacation . . . ? My replacement . . . ? I'd spend my last four hundred dollars on airfare and I'd return to New Orleans *jobless?* Standing in Jackie's kitchen with the phone held fast to my left ear, with my right hand I twisted the pear-cut diamond repeatedly around my ring finger as I listened to Armand's actor voice. The realization arrived in huge, crashing waves: I had not found a man who would read to me like Dennis and his girl at the Marketplace so long ago. This man couldn't even stick up for me. This man holds a pierced roach in my face! Frustration, anger, and my usual dose of melancholy erupted into tears as I slammed down the phone, yanked off the engagement ring, and hurled it into the dining room, where it landed silently on Jackie's white carpet.

I returned to New Orleans from the airport via bus to the Volkswagen dealership. The white-yellow blob of sun above me as my witness, I took hold of the bent oil pan, smashed it repeatedly onto my defunct engine, and hurled it across the parking lot, ignoring the service man's threat of calling the cops (one hysterical chick, and all those cars!), and stormed off to the bus stop, violently swinging my suitcase.

When you hit rock bottom, homeless, jobless, and broke, you go on a few drinking binges, sleep on some couches, tell your sad story to the local barflies, whine and carry on—because you deserve to, and you stab and rip holes in the canvas of the cruel world that has done you so wrong. Then you drag yourself up from the wallowed-upon dregs and stand, dust yourself off, dry out, and vow to reach a higher peak than the one from which you previously fell. At least this is what I did.

CHAPTER 13

WORKING AT THE EUROPEAN VILLAGE

ICE CREAM CONES, the electric plug, Cracker Jack, the elevator, hot dogs, the automatic dishwasher, Dr Pepper, the sewing machine, Belgian waffles, and iced tea all were first introduced to the public or made popular at World Expositions, also known as World Expos or World's Fairs. The French Industrial Exposition of 1844 kicked off the era of national exhibitions, followed by the first World Expo at the Crystal Palace in London in 1851, called the "Great Exhibition of the Works of Industry of All Nations." I don't think they sold size small T-shirts at that one.

In 1939 to 1940, New York City held an International Exhibition and began the trend of expos based on a theme of cultural significance. The New York Expo's "Building the World of Tomorrow" embarked on futuristic and utopian themes. Another New York Expo in 1964 to 1965 was called "Peace Through Understanding." And in Montreal in 1967, the theme was "Man and His World."

When I moved to New Orleans in 1981, eighty-four acres of neglected riverfront warehouses and railyards were being demolished to make way for the 1984 Louisiana World Exposition, one hundred years after the 1884 World's Fair, which had also taken place in New Orleans. Designers, architects, and international muckety-mucks were infiltrating the city to transform those eighty-four acres into a magical stage of music, architecture, art, food, and whimsy while I, centered in my small world of cooking, partying, and managing a dysfunctional relationship, was oblivious to all of this high-level planning. I didn't read newspapers, I certainly didn't drive around *that* part of town, and I suppose my peers—cooks and barflies—were of the same self-centered mindset.

So I was unaware of this great thing being planned in the city I already found so multidimensional that the overstimulation of it nearly hurt. But when I decided to make my big change, the 1984 fair was where it began.

At first I couldn't stand Chef John Giurini, a fifty-something, silver-haired Italian chef who spoke mainly in sexual innuendo and who constantly made goo-goo eyes at the Black girls. He ran the midnight shift at the massive European Village Food Festival kitchen on the riverfront at Louisiana World Expo '84.

My job as lead shift cook had seemed a perfect one—this temporary job during the six-month-long World's Fair would fund my new apartment on Chestnut Street and my post-meltdown escape to Maui, for I had decided I was Going Home to Mother. Cooking career be damned: I needed palm trees, endless beach, and good marijuana. Perusing the want ads in the *Times Pica-yune* had landed me in a test kitchen in the Warehouse District a month and a half before the fair's opening, where I worked with a nicotine-saturated chef and a fat sous chef, whipping up dishes from processed food donated by local suppliers. It seemed that potential menu items were being attempted, but there was no real format to anything. Each afternoon, the company's owner and president, Chuck Sanders, arrived at the test kitchen in an oversize suit and puffing on a stogie, to lord over the array of dishes we'd prepared, mostly flicking his cigar ashes into the plates to show his disdain. One week before the fair was to open, the nicotine chef and fat sous chef were gone and John Giurini appeared from somewhere in Chuck Sanders's past.

The European Village on the Mississippi Riverfront, with its semicircular central kitchen, would open in seven days and there were few recipes formulated for the eight European cuisines we would feature. There was no training system in place for the sixty or so four-dollar-an-hour, mostly Black cooks hired by a main office somewhere, and they all milled about the incomplete kitchen without guidance or aim. Equipment was brought in and hooked up. Cases of food were thawing out on the dock because the walk-in coolers and freezers weren't working yet. A dishwashing system with a conveyor upstairs had a huddle of technicians consorting over it, while assistant managers whispered and laughed about how the so-called state-of-the-art conveyor had a two-foot drop at the end of it. It didn't connect to the dish station downstairs. Who was running the show, anyway?

And John Giurini lurched around the kitchen with purposeful strides, barking orders to no one—everyone—and pinching the Black girls' asses.

Thankfully, all this chaos took my mind off my empty bank account, loss of freedom (now having joined the ranks of those who relied on public transportation), burning heartache for my asshole former lover, and the fact that I'd actually be leaving my beloved/despised city in six months. It was as if the requirements for this crazy job had been "You must be in the midst of an emotional breakdown," for the frenetic pace was exactly the prescription for my ailments. For twelve hours a day I hunkered down and worked, using all my organizational skills and logic—it seemed I was the only one who possessed these skills—to get the culinary asylum going in time for May 12, opening day. It was a welcome distraction from my otherwise exploded life.

I assigned cooks to stations. "Do you want to cook German, Italian, French, English, Greek, Belgian, or Irish?" I asked them. (The pizza, Belgian waffle, and Swiss ice cream stations were handled directly by Chuck's brother, Dick.) These cuisines were all Greek to the cooks, dark-skinned folks who had floated up from a New Orleans I had seldom traversed, with camaraderie, culture, and a sharp patois I'd never before experienced. When I asked them where they lived, their response was, "Night Wawd." Eventually I got it: Ninth Ward, an area downriver, several neighborhoods past the French Quarter, known for its solid Black population, rough streets, and crime. I'd gotten gas there once on my way to Waveland, and when I'd gone up to the bulletproof window to pay the glowering Black attendant, I'd realized my mistake: wrong country for this White girl.

My cooks read Bibles on their breaks, talked casually about who fathered whose kids, and when they engaged in passionate and loud verbal exchanges, I couldn't understand a word they said. But they were going to be the first mates in this rudderless kitchen and I, the unofficial captain, worked hard to bond with them and form a coalition against the chaos bred from upper management. I calmed my staff's opening-day fears by drawing charts of the menu items to put into their steam tables and refrigerators, made them prep lists, and encouraged them to just keep producing food for the counter girls who yelled orders to them from service windows at each station.

I'd been hired to run one cooking line in one cuisine and on opening day I had all eight of them going, with happy cooks cranking out sausages, croissant sandwiches, gyro pitas, and Irish stew, amid the yelling of management behind us in the main kitchen while thousands of dishes clacked and clanked under multiple handwashing efforts in the three-compartment sink, dishwasher techs still trying to get the dish machine and its associated conveyor up and running. Chuck Sanders strolled through the kitchen in his suit, with a shock of white hair falling over one eye, proudly puffing on his stogie—a king regally walking through his fallen empire, oblivious to the rubble, the emperor proudly showing off his new clothes. This was his normal.

But Chuck Sanders, bold and off-putting with incredulity plastered on his face, hands invisible except for the stogie fingers poking from his sleeve, could yank an innocent into his world and make a sublime person cry, or a stronger one want to punch his lights out. So on this opening day, when hordes of hungry people flooded the restaurant and it was all hands on crazy deck, Chuck Sanders looked for someone with whom to make a point.

"You!" he yelled at a tray-wiping busser, a plump Black woman wiping the detritus of straw wrappers and crumbs from stacks of orange service trays. She didn't hear him through the cacophony of dish-crashing and Ninth Ward yelping. "You!" he said again, approaching her until she looked up.

"Yeah?" she said aggressively, the *Who the hell are you?* oozing from this single word.

Chuck Sanders pointed to the floor around the trash can, littered with sugar packets, straw casings, and crumbs, as he began a slow, challenging, condescending tirade: "Now . . . You're *paid* to work here. Am. I. Right?"

The woman squinted at him, no doubt wondering who this old White man was, telling her how to do her job.

"If *I* did this"—he waved his stogie hand around *this* on the floor, as if the stogie were a paintbrush and the floor his canvas—"in *your* kitchen, would you . . . pay . . . *me*?"

The woman didn't respond, but thankfully for her, there was a broom handy. She grabbed it and, head down, began sweeping. Chuck slowly continued his stroll through his realm. And I, bearing witness to this, and in no way *ever* wanting the man to speak to *me* like that, and needing to protect all that I had organized, trained the tray-wipers to keep their areas swept up.

In a few weeks things settled into a more consistent frenzy and I was promoted to day sous chef. John Giurini continued to manage the midnight receiving and prep crews, oblivious to the string of figurehead chefs who continued to pass through the restaurant. He appeared each night around six and was still there mornings when I arrived at seven, ready to give me pointers while I, so thankful for this distraction that was my job, inventoried refrigerators and made stock lists for each station.

"*Madeesa*," he said one morning when I opened the upright refrigerator in the Irish station and gazed into it blankly, "you must be like a mouse!" And with fingers and thumb pinched together on each hand, he tiptoed toward me dramatically, his legs in his checked chef's pants bowing out like a jester's.

I slammed the refrigerator door shut, embarrassed at being seen doing my job. "W-what do you mean, a mouse?"

He launched into stories of great chefs he worked for in Europe as a youth, who taught him that to truly know the inside of the kitchen, how the staff worked, how the food was being handled, you had to snoop around their stations before they arrived, like the aforementioned mouse.

So I did this each morning, before the coffee-mug-gripping, slang-talking staff streamed in to gossip and find their prep lists and me standing there, possibly to scold them about unwrapped tomato slices or overweighed meat portions. "What are you doing?" I'd say. "I thought you liked me—I help you and you're throwing away my salary?" And it worked: Each station became shipshape. Chef John was right.

Some mornings, after Chef John knocked back a few brandies upstairs at the VIP Club, he'd return to the kitchen to cook a feast before he went home to bed, to wake up at 5 p.m. and do it all over again. He'd wrangle freebies from the suppliers: duck, hens, pork feet, and, once, a rabbit for me to cook. I missed actual cooking, for at the fair it was all consistent food production and staff management and making oodles of dough for our master—which enabled me to shake loose my degree in restaurant management somewhat, but food-wise, we were serving European fast food. So cooking something delectable and showing off a little was a bright spot in the day. Chef John turned his nose up at New Orleans food and American food in general; the opinionated European actually called it "trash," so when I cooked with him—and we had especially good duck-cooking sessions, rendering all that fat for future roux and trying to grab the fatty "pope's nose" before the other did—I leaned more toward my Northern Italian culinary beginnings. We talked while we cooked; I told him about Armand in general terms, how I needed to go home for a while, and how, although Chef John didn't much like New Orleans, I loved this city and would miss it. As long as he wasn't distracted by booze or women or going into a tirade about some idiot, well . . . he could be kind of nice. Our cooking and bonding sessions were a welcome break from feeding the hordes, until he'd accuse me of having that "fresh fucked look" after a date, or conjecture on how the accounting girl did the nasty with her boyfriend ("You think she's ever on top?"), or he'd slap the butt of a Ninth Ward woman on her way to the walk-in to grab sliced tomatoes for the French station.

"God, John, is th-that how all men act in Europe?"

"Ah, *Madeesa*," he'd say, shaking his head, "you Americans take life too seriously."

As the fair rolled onward through the syrupy hot summer, I began writing schedules for all three shifts. As day sous chef I'd been put on a weekly salary. I worked six days a week, my job a relief from the rest of my shattered life. But attendance at the Louisiana World Exposition didn't meet expectations; the fair was losing money, and vendors scrambled to stay afloat. So it was wasteful to have each shift write their own schedules, as had been protocol from opening day. I created a twelve-to-eight swing shift, straddling day and night shifts, so many cooks worked for both me and the scowling night sous chef, Spencer. This money-saving scheduling maneuver for Chuck Sanders staved off condescension from him—he was not much for compliments—but inspired more scowls from Spencer, who John Giurini referred to as "a useless clipboard-carrying twit."

Chef John appeared to have a straight line of communication with Chuck Sanders, who had apparently told his longtime chef friend that this daytime sous chef girl had something in the brains department. Many of my insecurities seemed further away now. I wasn't being recognized for cooking great food, but my personhood, my being, my *self* was accepted and praised, and this acceptance cultivated that nugget of pride buried deep within, and it healthily grew and grew, blossoming into a nice, ego-petaled flower. I accepted my stature as rockin' awesome kitchen-people manager. I asked for more money, and John Giurini, not wanting a single day without me there to keep the kitchen on course, went to Chuck Sanders on my behalf.

The proposed arrangement disappointed: I would work *every day* for the rest of the fair, no days off, and in return I'd get a bonus after the fair, equaling a raise for all the hours worked. Chuck Sanders's wheeling and dealing with my livelihood gave me the familiar sensation of feeling insignificant, and I wanted to walk right out of the asylum called a kitchen and into the arms of a chilled Myers's rum and grapefruit juice at the nearest bar. Why couldn't I just get a normal raise? Why was I hired at such a meager wage, while the clipboard-carrying twit made more than I did? After nearly four years in the city, I just couldn't break through its historically ingrained stereotypes. But John Giurini begged me to stay, promising it would be worth it, that Chuck Sanders never forgot loyalty.

Since my one day off a week usually had entailed not much more than barhopping, I wouldn't miss out on much by *not* having a day off. And I loved the excitement of the fair, the international pavilions, taking pictures of the pastel Wonderwall and visiting the various neighborhoods on my breaks, catching glimpses of parades and street musicians. I made Chuck Sanders put the deal in writing, and I slogged onward for another three months.

So began the circuitous marathon of work, party, a little sleep, and work again. An endless cycle of adrenaline-charged days and nights, of scheduling, of orchestrating food production in the now-understaffed kitchen (for as cooks left or were fired, they were not replaced—a cost-cutting measure), of learning to throw pizza dough under duress, of splitting myself six ways in the European Village kitchen, of stopping only briefly to scan the Mississippi River out front, of cruising the remote Warehouse District bars after work in search of relief from all the pressure.

When my twenty-fourth birthday arrived in August, the day began as any other: early mouse-creeping among the stations, calling in the pastry order, chatting and flirting with the cooks, doing my usual check and rechecks to ensure all would go smoothly when the masses would grin hungrily into the kitchen from the service windows, wanting European delights to fortify their stomachs for their trek around the fair.

Around 10:30 a.m., when all stations were rolling along smoothly, Chef John appeared (I thought he'd gone home) and said, "*Madeesa,* take off your apron; we're going upstairs."

So at 11 a.m., after rechecking each station, decked out in checked pants and too-large chef's coat, sweaty hat line imprinted on my forehead, I found myself sitting upstairs in the VIP Club with Chef John, sipping from a snifter of Grand Marnier and looking out at the Mississippi River from the quietest place on the entire fairgrounds.

The vantage of the Mississippi from the bar's giant windows rivaled that from the Huey P. Long Bridge, with its two reinforced webs stretching across the river to the West Bank. Or from the gondola, built especially for the fair, whose shiny bubble floated out over the river. Below us, passengers spilled out from the docked 382-foot-long *Mississippi Queen* like so many red ants ready to infiltrate our Belgian waffle station. Behind the massive paddle wheeler, a rusty barge and an array of small tugboats putt-putted up the river to destinations unknown. Across the river's wide gray-muddy expanse, the West Bank's green scrub sat sleepily under the late morning's golden cast.

"So," I said to John, "this is the mysterious VIP Club. No one but us and a lonely bartender."

John set his cigarette in the ashtray, lifted his snifter to mine, tapped glasses, took a sip, and stood. "Hold on," he said. He disappeared behind the grand piano to our rear, and I swiveled my stool around to face him. He sat pensive for a moment and then began romping out an intro that resembled Bach or Beethoven, something classical and complicated and impressive. A man of many talents! His music was a great soundtrack to the river's antics below. Then a familiar tune climbed up through the notes, its simplicity enhanced by the jazzy, extended play of John's fingers dancing along the keys and soon, through a gumbo of fatigue, loneliness, depression, and appreciation, tears leaked from my eyes and down my cheeks, I was so moved by his gift.

He was playing "Happy Birthday."

One September morning, the air no different from the stifling hot mornings of August, I was standing in the Belgian waffle station; I had begun to help out at Dick Sanders's outpost stations as well. Chuck Sanders strolled over to check the strawberries. The thickness of the slices and the amount of sugar were two of his many peeves and he monitored the strawberry situation regularly. I vowed that once this became my kitchen responsibility, the strawberries would always be perfect.

I hardly ever talked to Chuck Sanders; I wasn't about to go stuttering along to make small talk with this guy. I talked to him through Chef John. But on this day, I had something very important to ask. For obviously he was using me, and I planned to get mine from him as well; a successful relationship must go both ways. Chuck had been doing food concessions at World's Fairs since 1964 and the next one was 1985 in Tsukuba, Japan, and I wanted to go. Badly. I deserved to travel around the world because of the skills I possessed, to run a frickin' big kitchen on an international stage.

So as Chuck Sanders hunched over a white Styrofoam bowl of strawberries, flipping them around with a white plastic fork, I sputtered out my question, after which he looked at me for a long moment before speaking. "Hmm. Japan?" he asked, looking over my head thoughtfully (oh, the perils of being short!). Me thinking, mantra-like, *I need to go, I need this opportunity, I need this excitement, I need to feel special.* Chuck Sanders looked up at the striped awning protecting the Belgian waffle station from the sun and rain, as if trying to remember something. "Yes, well. Tsukuba . . ." *I need*—"Well . . . we're doing only ice cream and waffles there. Not enough time to do all this." He waved his hand around all this, his fake European Village. "Dick is already over there. No, I don't think we need you there."

My heart sank. What would I do?

He took a bite of his sugar-soaked strawberries and looked at me thoughtfully, still chewing. "Hmm," he sounded behind closed lips, and I wasn't sure if it was a thinking kind of a *hmm* or a yum strawberry kind of a *hmm.* "You're like a machine, a horse," he said, "the way you work." He took another dripping forkful of strawberries and his focus went from me to the red fruit.

Had that been a compliment?

"Well . . ." He looked at me again. "There's Vancouver in '86. I could use you there," he said matter-of-factly, and then he turned and walked off with his dish of strawberries.

My heart began to jump. I would go traveling with the World's Fair.

CHAPTER 14

A DAY AT THE FAIR: GETTING READY

A TYPICAL DAY AT THE FAIR begins before dawn. I exit the bus onto brick streets surrounded by crumbling warehouses near the fair's rear employee entrance. The air is thick with humidity and history, smelling of rotting wood and sidewalk grit, all the action and bustle of ancient wharf activity still hanging in some nearby dimension. Ahead, the Wonderwall, a fantastical sculpture swimming with mermaids, King Neptune, gators, pelicans, pineapples, and sea nymphs, rises up against the brown brick of old downtown, with lavender, teal, and coral hues muted in the dawn. I flash my pass to the sleepy fair attendant and enter the dormant world of international party.

Crossing the overpass above the Italian Village, I see the whimsical Wonderwall and the mighty Mississippi, the river's current the only movement save for a few sweepers outside the pavilions below. Every day I am lucky to see this: the wonderment of the fair, from its yawning beginning until the nightly parade and fireworks finale. Others pay dearly to get in, only coming in once and fighting the crowds, while I get to live here for six months.

Entering the International Marketplace above the European Village, I think of my day ahead. I consider moving Granville Sommers from a floater for England and Ireland to burger-patty making. He's very consistent, disciplined because he's a Marine, and it's a job to keep up on our house-formed burger patties. Willie hopefully made it through last night's cleanup and will be back in pot-washing after a few hours' nap upstairs. Mentally I scan each station, considering the day's schedule tattooed in my brain. I descend the stairs to the riverfront and breathe in the rush of muddy scent. I am the conductor of this massive and messy kitchen, ready to orchestrate it all.

The front of the restaurant faces the river, and mornings are the only times I glimpse the European Village's facade—individual facades, actually. Each station's indoor order and pickup window is set into an artist's rendering of a European shop front, hence the name. It is ingenious, really, Disney-esque, so perfectly World's Fair. I enter at the left of the semicircle of facades, between pizza and pot-washing, and begin my mouse-snooping in each station on my way to the central rear of the kitchen, to main prep and the back dock.

Chef John is leaning against the loading dock wall, facing the awakening day, smoking a cigarette, his usual position of old-man-against-lamppost after a night of food receiving and prep. His shift now entails mostly receiving, for the midnight crew has been whittled down to only John and a helper, most of the bulk prep now the responsibility of my day crew.

I stand next to him, sharing the view of the service road and a hot beam of September sunlight. "Um, what do I need to know?"

"Produce's not here yet. Motherfucker!" He flicks his cigarette butt onto the service road. "I'm going to bed his wife!" He looks at his watch, his lower jaw jutting out in semi-repressed anger.

"So . . . w-what about the tomatoes?" We go through three to four cases a day. A gurgle of panic rumbles in my stomach. Every station uses tomatoes and we slice them not on the automatic slicer but by hand, because this is the Chuck Sanders way. "Shit! You called them?"

"Yes, *Madeesa*. No answer."

"Is the guy in jail?" The standard midnight crew excuse if there's a no-show. "W-what about another company?"

"I'll take care of it. Go set up."

Back in the kitchen I slip a chef's coat over my T-shirt, double wrap an apron around my waist and tie it in the front, and twirl my long hair up under a paper chef's hat.

I stop in the main prep area to say good morning to Ben. The tomato-slicing task on hold, he's forming burger patties. Ben Jacobs had been a steady day shifter with no string of Ninth Ward children to babysit for—none that he brags about anyway—and no serious personality flaws that would prevent him from showing up every day and doing a good job. So I went to him when I needed someone reliable to work with Chef John at night and offered him the seven-day-a-week-with-rewards-after plan, which was becoming a common scheduling maneuver.

"Morning," he says and smiles sleepily. *Whap!* He slams a ball of ground beef onto wax paper.

"Hey, Ben, there's a full Lexan of patties in the cooler from last night; finish that layer and go get some sleep."

"What about dem tomatoes?"

"We'll take care of it; get some rest."

After excusing Ben to a day of rapid eye movement, I emerge back into the semicircle of stations and head to the upright refrigerator in Germany, which, when I pull open the stainless steel door, assaults my nose with over-steamed sauerkraut and three pans half-full of grilled and chilled sausages. So many left over! Claire had gotten crazy on the grill at the end of the dinner rush last night while I was helping the pot-washers-turned-pizza-dough-flippers. Where had Spencer been during the dinner rush? Smoking on the back dock, no doubt. Chuck Sanders would blame *me* for such sloppy par-cooking. I put the wasted sausages back for now, to make an example of when Claire arrives at noon. Then I'll whisk them away to the back for a staff meal without Chuck Sanders seeing them. Cha-ching! Money down the drain.

Next stop Greece, to check out the salad fixings, pita bread, and what's left of yesterday's gyro meat. Snoop-snoop-snoop. Yep, they need diced tomatoes, feta, shredded lettuce, more shish kebabs, olives; pretty low on everything. Crystal will have this station shipshape in no time. Then over to France to inventory the croissants for the morning pastry order. Yvonne opens France, and she's steady, keeps up with things.

After my once-over of each station, I inventory the five-gallon buckets of homemade dressings in the prep kitchen's walk-in cooler. Bleu cheese: full; creamy Italian is one-third full with no backup; the Thousand Islands are three-quarters full. I'll make the Italian and leave the Thousand Islands for

Spencer later. From the walk-in shelves I grab a flat of eggs and a gallon of Dijon mustard. I separate the egg yolks into the forty-gallon mixer; *blop*—in goes a serving spoon of Dijon, six cloves of garlic mashed with the back of a French knife, a handful of fresh chopped parsley, salt, sugar, white pepper, and dried oregano; turn the mixer on medium and drizzle in cider vinegar and juice from six lemons. Next up, several quarts of olive oil and salad oil, dribbled in slowly to create and maintain the emulsion. We have a tool for this, Chef John's invention, to minimize the human standing over the mixer for an hour: a clean number ten can, the top removed with the crank can opener, three holes punctured in the bottom and two holes in the top sides threaded with string and hung from the mixer's hub, positioning the base of the oil dribbler over the open mixer bowl. Turn mixer on medium, fill can with oil, walk away. Return in fifteen minutes to refill with oil. Genius.

Just after 8 a.m., cooks begin shuffling in. They get coffee, huddle in mini social circles. Chef John lurches in from rear prep carrying two cases of tomatoes. He deposits them on the prep counter, where Ben had been working an hour ago.

Mitch had wandered in earlier, my strongest cook who works busy England with its Americanized menu featuring the iconic hamburger plate. He stands out for his height, and for being the only other White cook besides me. I prop one case of the tomatoes between my hip and right arm and search for the self-proclaimed "coon-ass"—a racial slur for Cajun, though Mitch wears it as a badge of honor. He emerges from the coffee station, big-footed, eyes bloodshot, apron dirty and untied. Always cocky, laughing at my seniority, my age, my petite stature, undressing me with his eyes. Mitch needs ego stoking, then regular scoldings. He frightens me a little, and I work hard to cover my nervousness and stay on his good side. He's the only real professional cook here and I need him, in spite of those countrified coon-ass eyes.

"Mitch, go clock in. Need your ah m-manly knife skills on these here tomatoes."

"Sure," he says, tying his dirty apron, full of cordiality, then with a wink, "Do ah get paid extra, dahlin'?" The last term drips with sarcasm.

"Yeah, clock in now, y'get an extra twenty minutes." I nod at the ladies in the coffee klatch and say, "We're a little behind this morning, everyone! Go clock in and get started." Authorizing extra, non-overtime hours for all.

The ladies scatter, tying aprons, finishing sentences, coffee mugs in hand, zipping to the time clock, and then anchoring themselves in their respective stations. After depositing the tomatoes in Mitch's station, I return to fill the oil dribbler and with the second case of tomatoes on my hip, I'm off to pot-washing/pizza/Italy where I leave twelve tomatoes on the counter for Rita (who's not in yet) to slice. Then I circle back through England, where Mitch is slicing and nodding like there's still music in his head from last night. I fill the oil dribbler.

"Morning, Miss Bea." In Ireland, Beatrice is filling her steam table with a bain-marie of water. She's my steady Ireland worker—some do better when you leave them in one station instead of the rigorous cross-training to which I have subjected the others. Miss Bea is a fifty-something woman who applied for a job as a tray porter or floor cleaner, but with her lovely disposition I snagged her up and tossed her in Ireland that first day, and here she has remained.

"Moorn-ing, dear," she says while stirring a pot of Irish stew on her stove, her head jerking with each little whip-stir.

"Miss Bea, Granville's your floater today, but I'm going to have him in the back doing burgers. He'll be checking on you, though."

"Okay, Miss Marisa."

Miss Marisa. I am frequently addressed this way by my Ninth Ward minions and I like it. It's funny, in a way, being addressed as "Miss" when I'm younger than everyone. But I'll take respect when I can get it. And it's charming, in a Southern sort of way.

"Get your sliced tomatoes from Mitch," I say and pass right through Ireland, not normally a busy station. On to the combined stations of Belgium and the Netherlands.

"Marcela! Fryers on, please! Kerry, get back over to Germany; you have work to do *there*!" I tell Marcela and Kerry to get their tomatoes from Mitch.

Big Kerry scurries back to Germany like a chased dog.

"He wuz just getting my fries from the back, thatzall," says Marcela with a defensive little snip in her voice. Marcela always has a snip in her voice and a chip on her shoulder, which used to intimidate me, but through joking with her I think I've got her on my side.

In Germany I instruct Kerry to save the cooked sausages for Claire, get roast chickens from the back, put sauerkraut on the stove, grill sausages to order until eleven. He hangs his head and says, "Okay."

Crystal in Greece is young and mocha-skinned. Piled onto her counter
is a case of spinach pies, a Lexan container of green salad, and a pan of shish-
kebabs, a hunk of fresh gyro meat already turning on the vertical grill. Kerry
has obviously been here delivering goods from the back, which explains why
his station is untouched. Crystal smiles demurely when I point to her bounty.
She'll be set up in no time, then will have to go help Kerry. Ah, the Ninth
Ward social structure.

"Hey, Crystal, got your Jy-ro Peter mojo goin'?" I dole out a dozen tomatoes onto her cutting board. "Gotta slice your own today."

"They's ain't none in the back?"

"Nope. Steal 'em from Mitch when you run out." I eye her station, knowing that she needs mainly to restock and get some salad bases made up before
we open at ten. No need to linger here.

In France, Yvonne is assembling tender and pretty croissant sandwiches.
Her steam table on, onion soup heating on the stove, quiches have been
fetched from the back. (Kerry strikes again.) Her coffee cup sits on the cutting
board, filled to the brim with light brown milky liquid.

"Still like those light-skinned mulattos, yeah, Yvonne?"

"Oh, yes, Miss Marisa, I always lack my coffee the color I lack my men."
She winks. I learned this particular piece of information from her early in
the fair and keep it with me as a way to relate to my dwindling troops from
the Ninth Ward.

There's a walkway behind the stations and I hurry back toward England
via this route, eyeing the Crystal/Marcela/Kerry situations. Mitch has sliced
the entire case of tomatoes and I deposit the half-full case from my hip onto
his cutting board. He rolls his eyes and yells, "You owe me!" as I hurry off to
fill the oil dribbler, then to Italian pasta/pizza/pot-washing.

Rita is here now. There's a problem with Rita's hormones because sometimes, under her heavy cake makeup, the black dots of beard look like measles
across her cheeks. But Rita is steady and practical, and after Mitch, she is my
most knowledgeable cook, if a bit moody.

"Hi, Rita, we have a sliced tomato shortage today."

"Yeah," she says, her voice a cartoony faux voice-box tenor. "I see that."
She's at the stove, primly poised and marshalling several stock pots of water
around from burner to burner. Sauce pots of Alfredo, red sauce, and meat

sauce are lined up on her cutting board, waiting for open burners. She turns from the stove, places a hand on her hip, and tells me, "You know, there was no fettuccini cooked last night."

"We haven't had a full night crew for a few weeks now and we're not going to. Just gotta pull together, ya know? Have Miss Bea heat these up for you on her stove."

"No, I'm fine," she whines, not sounding fine.

The pizza and pasta station has the biggest pickup window in the restaurant, through which there's an expansive view of the empty dining room, a wedge of the Belgian waffle station banner outside, and beyond that a slice of the Mississippi, shimmering jewel-like in the morning light. On each morning round, I stop and look to the outside beyond the stewards straightening the sea of metal dining chairs. It's the finish line and I catch my breath here, take note that there is another world out there beyond my own, the view rejuvenating me for another warm-up lap through the kitchen. Once the gates open at ten, however, hungry heads stuff the window and block the view, jailing me in the kitchen where I marathon-supervise through the stations for the next nine hours.

Behind Rita in pizza, Jimmy James is chopping, slicing, dicing, package-opening, pizza sauce can-opening. The pizza oven is on, the overworked conveyor chains click-clicking on each rotation of both platforms. The first tray of doughballs is on the counter, proofing in the kitchen's natural humidity. Against the wall in pot-washing, pots, pans, and sheet pans tower on the three-compartment sink, waiting for Willie to return from his upstairs nap.

The combined station of pizza/Italy, otherwise known as "the pit," is the busiest part of the kitchen. The six-well steam table joining pizza and pasta is filled and refilled hourly to the brim with pasta sauces, meatballs, Italian sausages with peppers and onions, lasagna. Rita keeps it stocked and dishes up the multitude of sandwiches and pasta plates from it. Meanwhile, two pizza cooks flip dough, dress, cook, and slice pizza, and keep the garlic bread rolling through the lower conveyor for the pasta plates.

Together with the pot-washing station at Italy's far reaches, Italy/pizza/pot is a kitchen within a kitchen. For the first three months of the fair, it operated as such, with a pizza manager named Steve and his entourage of seasoned dough-flippers creating the theatrical effect required by Chuck Sanders. But the little microcosm became too big for itself and pizza cooks and pot washers began clocking each other in and out, logging sixteen-hour shifts for all. My instructions when I'd discovered this while tallying time cards upstairs in the office was to go down there and fire them all. *Fire the kitchen during the lunch rush? With all those hungry staring eyes?* Fire them I did, afterward grabbing anyone I thought could flip a pizza crust without making too many holes in it, to keep the station afloat while I trained and retrained to keep the ship on course while millions of judging eyes looked upon us novice pizza schlubs through the pickup window.

Shawn, a mild-mannered gay man, had been a quiet prep cook of the midnight shift when this all happened. I'd put him on days as a floater when the night shift was abolished and he appeared to be friends with Rita. Shawn, with his careful and artistic handling of the dough, after a little practice became my new dough flipper. Since I was as bad as the macho men trying to flip the stuff, producing holes the size of ostrich eggs, Shawn's emergence next to Rita's station was a relief. A deal was struck: Shawn would work 10 a.m. to 8 p.m., every day for the rest of the fair, so we would always have a proper dough twirler. And Rita would have someone to relate to, maybe.

At 9:20, forty minutes until showtime, I zip to the back to see what Chef John is up to. Nothing—he's slipped upstairs, winding down over a Grand Marnier for his daytime sleep. I fill the oil dribbler and take a quick mental panorama of the giant walk-in cooler and freezer. Two more cases of tomatoes to slice—I'll leave one for Spencer; Granville will definitely need to make more hamburger patties when he arrives at ten. I wipe my olive-oil-slimed hands on my apron, grab a raspberry-filled croissant from the newly arrived pastry order, and head to the coffee station between England and Ireland.

Fortified with French pastry and sugar and with coffee in hand (with cream, which I suppose means that I like lightly tanned guys), I climb the rear stairs to the mezzanine to awaken Willie the pot washer—hoping, as I do every morning, that he is there sleeping and hasn't wandered off, tired of the round-the-clock game.

CHAPTER 15

A DAY AT THE FAIR: SHOWTIME

THE MEZZANINE IS DARK, its floor littered with bus tubs brimming with dishes. Like a bridge to nowhere, the infamous conveyor only delivers dish tubs three feet from a rear wall before a bus boy or girl needs to empty the thing by hauling the tubs downstairs, labor costs Chuck Sanders was trying to avoid by the ill-conceived conveyor. Alongside the conveyor's cliff are several broken dining room chairs that have been made into an uncomfortable-looking daybed. The daybed is empty; Willie is nowhere to be seen.

Heart lodged in my throat, I storm through the mezzanine and scan the deserted upstairs dining room. "Willie?" I knock on the men's room door, even look *inside* the restroom. Empty. "Shit!" My mind races around the mental kitchen I have stored in my brainpan, calculating how to pull a pot washer from the air. Not how, but *who?*

I think of my future job at the Vancouver Fair, hoping there will be a better staffing situation. My Ninth Ward staff is endearing, sure, but the steely stress I undergo to keep the shifts running whittles me to a nub. There is scant help from management, and I do not expect this to change. Chuck Sanders operates in this way: throw a bunch of chefs and management types together, some of whom have stellar resumes to bolster their laziness, and see who rises to the top. I have risen to the top—but the top of what, exactly? If only I had more reliable staff, and more of them.

"Willie?!"

Dull silence. It's ten minutes to ten, but getting the stations open takes precedence over dirty pots.

Downstairs I set my empty coffee cup in dishwashing, fill the oil dribbler one last time, and begin my preopening station checks in France.

"Ready, Yvonne?" With my pocket thermometer I check the temperature of the onion soup in her hot well, pull open her refrigerator and peruse her backups, and scan her sandwich refrigerator's mise en place for a day of croissant stuffing.

"Mah counter girl's not here, Miss Marisa, but ahm ready."

In Greece, I yell through Marcela's window to the girl tying an apron around her Euro-uniform dress, "Hey, Na-risse, where's France!"

"In the batroom!"

"Cover France 'til she gets back, please?" Now I have to deal with counter staff too?

"Ah weel."

Crystal's gyro meat's outer layer is crisping up nicely in the vertical broiler and last night's leftover gyro meat is hot in her steam table. The rest of the pans are empty, to be filled at eleven, just before the lunch rush. Her upright refrigerator is stocked with salad mix, sliced and diced tomatoes, spinach pies, and ready-to-grill shish kebabs. Her salad refrigerator's mise en place is perfect, with olives, pepperoncinis, crumbled feta, sliced red onions, and more sliced tomatoes arrayed in fresh inserts along the top. She has plenty of plates.

"Great, Crystal, looks like you're ready to rock, as usual."

She smiles at the compliment.

In Germany, well—big Kerry is the weak spot.

"Kerry! You need to put these sausages away. Have you sliced the buns yet?"

Kerry hangs his head like a scolded child.

The steam table is wafting steam into the air, its open spaces not covered by pans or lids. "Kerry! Where's your pans? You're heating the kitchen!" I want to yell and yell and yell, but he is shunning me, and I see that he simply isn't capable of what a station needs to get ready. It's not in his makeup. He'll simply lose respect for me, and I need respect and set stations in order to keep the ship afloat.

"Crystal! I need you to help Kerry." Crystal comes over, looking at her station behind her.

"Yvonne! Sweetie! Watch Greece while Crystal helps Kerry, please?"

"Okay, Miss Marisa," she sings out.

Kerry smiles greedily when Crystal arrives and I smack him on the arm. "No hanky-panky."

"Hankee-pankee," he echoes as I dash off. "Wuz dat?"

Marcela has Belgium's refrigerator stocked with cubed cheeses, herring, shredded lettuce, fruit cups, apple pie wedges, and shrimp salads. Her freezer is packed with bags of fries and breaded shrimp, her fryers are on, and she's slicing kaiser rolls for the ham sandwiches.

"Lookin' good, Marcela!"

In Ireland, Miss Bea is leaning against the steam table's cutting board, coffee mug in hand, a contented smile on her face. "Ahm ready!"

I poke my thermometer into the Irish stew. "Great, Miss Bea. 'Member what I told you about Granville."

"Yep, Miss Marisa."

On to England then, where Mitch is pregrilling rare burgers for the lunch rush. The second box of tomatoes is still sitting on his counter. I don't double-snoop his station; this will insult him.

"You good, Mitch? Y-you need anything?"

"More coffee."

"Y'got it. Cream?"

"Black."

I slip behind the station and pour him a cup, wondering if this means anything about his sexual preferences.

I deposit the coffee on Mitch's counter and head for the pizza-pot pit where, against the far wall, pots and sheet pans are still towering on both drain boards of the three-compartment sink.

Where is Willie?

Rita is pouring the last of the sauces into steam table pans. With a paring knife I trim the edges of unsauced lasagna noodles from the two full-size pans in the steam table. The Alfredo and clam sauces I give a stir with the

ladle and check the temperature: 160 degrees. I turn the heat down a notch;
150 degrees is what I need—any higher and the cream sauce will separate.
I temp-check the rest of the steam table's contents. Rita's slicing hoagie
rolls for meatball and sausage sandwiches. Melons, pudding, and pastry are
stocked in her refrigerator. Garlic bread coming out of the lower conveyor
of the pizza oven? Check. Hungry faces are peeking through the window
and ordering a gargantuan first meal of the day. Counter girls ring up and
call in orders with Ninth Ward patois: *one Alfray-do, one sashase sand, one
cheese pitza slace!*

Shawn is here now, twirling the first dough balls of the day, one cheese
pizza already emerging from the top conveyor. Jimmy James is still running
around getting pizza toppings and garlic bread backed up, then stopping in
mid-garlic-butter-on-bread swipe to dash over to the oven, slide out the pizza
with the big paddle, deposit it on the cutting board, and go at it with the
pizza wheel. Jimmy James is like a child buzzing underfoot compared to the
slender classy moves of Shawn. *Buzz-buzz-buzz*, goes Jimmy. Cheese pizza
slices in the window. *Buzz*—back to garlic bread detail, stop to open a bag of
pizza cheese, something he forgot; *buzz*—back to garlic bread. *Buzz*.

"Hey, Shawn, morning."

"Morning," is the monotone reply, his eyes following his flying saucer
dough into the air and back onto his fists. *Buzz-buzz-buzz*, and I'm afraid
Shawn will smack Jimmy away from him, that buzzing bug.

"Jimmy James—man with two first names—stop for a minute. Talk to
me. You ready?"

Buzz-buzz-buzz, and then he stops moving, nearly crashing into himself.
"Um," he says, his eyes, so white in his onyx face, search something in his
head. "Oh, yeah, I need more garlic bread!" Almost a whine.

"Jimmy, you're good, okay? Just do the bread in between rushes; you'll
keep up fine. Keep steady, man. Rushing around like that you'll drop something and fall behind. Sometimes you gotta slow down to speed up. Got it?"

Jimmy nods and skulks off to his garlic bread buttering station.

And now, at the end of the line, the dead end of the kitchen, the garbage
dump on the outskirts of suburbia, stands Willie, his skinny frame barely
holding up his baggy nonuniform pants. Slowly he arranges the pots and pans
by size and shape, making neat stacks while the sink bowls fill with hot water.

His arms are also skinny and he's purposeful in his languid movements, like moving through Jell-O.

"Willie!" I'm on him now, part of me wanting to fire him for being late, for being out of uniform, for just stressing me the hell out, the relieved part of me wanting to hug him for showing up.

"Ye-ah?" He turns slowly, heavy lids half-mast over bloodshot eyes in his mocha-colored face.

"You're late; where were you?"

He shrugs. "Ah-oh-no."

"Well, stay put, okay?" Willie's penchant for disappearing commonly results in choruses from the cooks: *Wheeere's Willie?*

Back to Germany for a recheck, I see Crystal has it all going, and I flash a thumbs-up. In the prep kitchen I check seasoning and turn off the mixer, pour the creamy Italian dressing into three five-gallon buckets, and start dragging them into the walk-in.

Granville is here now, tying his apron behind him, polite, smiling, and ready; my pleasant day-floater, prep guy, a Marine trainee with skin the color of dark chocolate. He can do anything at any station, so I keep him handy, just in case. The thing about Granville is this: In seventies terms, he's a stone fox.

"Morning, Granville, it's burger time!" I drag the last bucket of Italian dressing across the floor to the walk-in. "I need you to keep an eye on Mitch and Miss Bea while you're preppin', okay?"

Granville bends, taking the metal handle of the bucket from my hand, grins, and in a low voice like honey rolling over caramel, he says, "You got it, Marisa."

Chef John returns, sleepy as a nightcap, and smirking at the nonverbal male-female interchange between White girl and Black boy.

"*Madeesa,* your gal in Germany looks flustered!" He smiles impishly.

"If K-Kerry looks like a gal to you, then you really n-need some sleep."

He shrugs. "See you later."

"Sweet dreams."

And off to Germany I go, to see what minor event inspired such sarcasm from my mentor.

Noon. All staff on deck, burger patties in the making: *Whap! Pat-pat-pat-pat-pat,* tomatoes artfully hand-sliced, pots and pans crashing, office and floor management running around in some other dimension. The masses tidal-wave into the dining room from the Mississippi and line up at all the windows—hungry, flashing money, their demands needing to be met.

Counter girls' orders ricochet off the kitchen walls:

"Tree Jy-ro Peters, one Greek salad!"

"Two ham and cheez craw-sant, one keesh lor-aine!"

"One salad, one brawt-knock, two brawt sanwich, one sauerbraten, tree torte!"

"One Arish stew!"

"One fried swimps and two fries, one herring!"

"Four burgers, tree fish and chips, six side chips, and two bread puddin'!"

"One whole pepperoni, two whole deluxe, two lasagna, one fetta-chini clam, two saushase sand, one meatball sand, one side garlic bread!"

And so on. I cruise the arc of cooks who support their counter girls tending to the needs of Mr. and Mrs. Mass. Back and forth I go, from France on one end to Italy on the other, stopping to wipe a plate, assist in dishing, or running to the back to fetch, to restock, to bolster the morale by being one of them.

The food goes out like clockwork; the kitchen is a series of whirs and clicks, each station a cog supporting the next by keeping the pace, handing over the food to the chorusing counter girls, who in turn sing out more orders. But at 1:15 p.m., the synchronization crashes, like so many china plates.

I'm in England, setting up burger platters for Mitch, when Craig the manager suddenly materializes like a ghost near the grill and says in a managerial voice, "Jimmy James cut himself and—" I'm off to pizza, visions of spurting blood forcing my heart into my throat.

There Jimmy stands, a blood-soaked towel wrapped around his left hand. He's even smiling; no blood surrounds him. Wendy, another day manager, holds up his wrapped hand, her other arm around his shoulder. On the pizza-making table, the slicer is still a-whir, a pile of paper-thin onion turned pink under the blade. I click off the slicer.

Wendy says, "We're taking him to the infirmary, but we need the rest of his thumb."

"Oh, Jimmy, what did you *do*?" I pick around the pizza detritus on the cutting board.

"Sorry, Miss Marisa, I be okay. I be back soon to help Shawn. Jus' need my knuckle sewed back on."

"Willie!" I yell over to pot-washing. "Come do pizza!" Heart pounding, I recall my own slicer-thumb accident at the Sea Scoop, all those summers ago: my thumb carefully holding in place an end of roast beef below the guard, the heat of the blade as it whirred through my skin, my knees weakening at the sight of my own blood soaking into the beef slices lying under the blade. I pick through the pepperoni, cheese worms, mushrooms, and sausage crumbles at the slicer's base. Finding no chunk of black thumb, I locate a black olive end and hold it up to his arm to match color. "Is this it?" Humor calms my nerves.

"No, Miss Marisa, that's an *olive*."

"Could work, though. Let me see that." I reach for his wrapped hand.

Inside the wrap of red, I dab away the blood to reveal a pink slice in the cap of his thumb knuckle. A thin black flap of skin has been shaved off, but nothing that would be reattachable. And the errant skin flap could be anywhere. I rewrap the wound, hold up my scarred thumb. "Here's what you'll have, Jimmy, a black version of this. You'll only do it once. All this time wasted cuz you were rushing too much."

He hangs his head. "Ah know."

"T-take him and get him b-back," I say to Wendy. Willie hovers behind me like a shadow and I direct him to clean down the station before making any more pizzas. I race off to see what disasters may have occurred in the other stations during my absence. Six hours into my day, six hours to go.

At seven thirty I'm off the clock, chef's coat removed to reveal my food-smell-infused T-shirt, hair flattened from the chef's hat, which I still feel rimming my forehead, even though it hit the trash in a crumpled wad twenty minutes ago. Twelve hours of adrenaline-pounding pressure and now I'm off, to get my first beer in a go-cup and slowly peruse the fair, take in the magic of the fairy-lighted Wonderwall curving its way through the Water Garden, Bayou Plaza, and the fountains of Centennial Plaza. The plate-crashing and counter-girl-yelling day at the European Village is now a full howl of people cheering street musicians, calling downward from the Ferris wheel, or plain drunken yelling, a common sound in New Orleans anyway. The hubbub, the colors, the wet-earth scent of the Mississippi mixed with garlicky and sweet food smells comfort me and I inhale it in like prescribed medicine. Walking through the melee with my cold beer, I'm relieved and happy to occupy that wedge of the outside visible each morning from the pizza/pasta station. This is the right dose of the real world, any more and I would plunge back into those failures and loathing that haunt me, the love lost, angst over leaving New Orleans and facing whatever my future holds, the constant pressure of wanting to be more than I am. In the kitchen the pause button is depressed, and the distractions of the kitchen do everything to justify my existence.

I wind through the Entertainment District on Fulton Street, with its overpriced drinks and contrived Mardi Gras theme, and I'm out the city gate to catch the bus to the corner of Napoleon and Magazine Streets, where there are several dark and quiet bars to choose from, where I can drink cheap, then walk to my apartment on Chestnut Street and hit the bed, to get up at 6 a.m. to do it all over again.

CHAPTER 16

HAVE MIXING BOWL, WILL TRAVEL

WHEN I WAS A LITTLE GIRL, when asked what I wanted to be when I grew up, one of two answers would burble from my lips: "A comedian!" I'd say, or "Famous!" Settling for a little humor every day to soften the hard edges of life, the comedian dream faded, but fame, well—doesn't everyone want to be famous? On Maui, an island of just under 730 square miles with a population of 76,000 at the time, with a twice-weekly newspaper thinner than a fish wrap, it's easy to be famous. How many of the island's 76,000 residents had traveled to New Orleans and managed a large international-multicuisine kitchen serving 7,335,279 people in six months? *The Maui News* thought I was famous and proudly featured an article about my endeavors, hence the headline "Have Mixing Bowl, Will Travel."

Mom and Stepdad had divorced while I was in New Orleans, and Mom and Christopher were living in a small apartment off a residential street in Kihei. With Grandmother gone now, Mom was alone with her rebellious teen, supplementing her sporadic welfare checks with cash earned from cleaning condos. (The irony of this was not lost on us.) She'd been diagnosed with lung cancer the last days of the fair, and I couldn't leave to be with her for her surgery to remove the tumor. I rolled into my island home full of guilt, flush with cash from my end-of-fair bonus, wielding an almost-new Hasselblad camera I'd bought and a bursting fresh ego. Thankfully, Mom's surgery was a success. She quit smoking and had a frightening scar on her neck where they'd cut her open from ear to ear to remove the tumor. She liked to show off the scar.

I kissed the sand when I got to the beach.

After my little step into the limelight and days lying faceup on the sand at Kamaole II Beach, and nights playing cribbage and drinking cocktails with my mom, proudly sunburned, and camping out on her couch, I hunkered down to look for a chef's position to carry me a year. For in one year, I would leave for Vancouver's Expo '86.

Finally I could apply for an actual chef's position! No need to brag about *what* I could cook (although New Orleans food did raise some eyebrows in my island home); I could train others less talented to cook consistently and under pressure and for a profit. Since managing high-volume stuff back at the fair, I could do anything now. I was ready for any kitchen.

The Mana Kai Maui, a beachfront hotel at the south end of Kihei Road, sat in the shadows of newly constructed Japanese-owned hotels farther south in Wailea. These fancy high-rise hotels smacked of Waikiki-style tourism and were situated on previously remote beaches reminiscent of hot dog grill-outs for my preteen birthdays (Grandmother pointing to my bathing suit top and saying, "Oh, look! Marisa's got that fat between her armpit and breast; your aunt Sandi has that too!") and where later I camped, skinny-dipped, and smoked fat Hawaiian joints with hippie-musician friends from Lahaina. So there was *no way* I would venture past the spot where Kihei Road once turned into sand, and where now people were enjoying *my* childhood beaches for 450 bucks per night. One must have morals.

Besides, I already had a future working for Chuck Sanders. I didn't need or want to get involved with a corporate hotel chain.

So the humble Mana Kai Maui, with its fleet of powder-blue rental Ford Mavericks in the parking lot, cozy outdoor bar that smelled of salty boat planks, and a kitchen that reeked of aged grease, is where I got a job as restaurant chef. Their current hotel chef, Roy, was demoted in a sense to luau chef in order to make room for me. Two chefs in one kitchen could be a precarious situation, especially when the first chef has responsibilities removed, but in this case, it worked. Roy, a demure older man, seemed relieved to have the help. He didn't want all the responsibility of running the three-meal-a-day restaurant or the hotel's weird Pritikin diet program, a gung-ho aged hippie diet, seemingly the love child of Euell Gibbons and Richard Simmons. Roy was happy to simply prepare and execute food for the twice-weekly luaus, and fill in line shifts for me while I rampaged silently through the dirty kitchen, making schedules and checklists, dissecting menus into standardized recipes, food-costing the ingredients, working the line, making specials, getting odd looks from the surfer-cooks, and simply being my twenty-four-year-old self-righteous self.

Extreme discipline was exactly what the Mana Kai needed, however. Its food reputation had gone down in recent years, the otherwise beautiful dining room an amenity where mediocre food was tolerated because of the serene view of rolling waves and the smooth lavender island curves of Lanai and Kahoolawe beyond. The view was so beautiful that diners could be hypnotized into eating anything, even bad food.

I would have none of this.

Soon after I returned to Maui, Dona showed up from Key West with a husband and baby girl in tow. We had some good times at the beach catching up on our respective lives, and how crazy it was that we'd both shown up on Maui at the same time, neither of us knowing that we were both heading home.

The days at Mana Kai were long, starting from breakfast, working with staff who spent their off time on the beach smoking pot, reviving themselves from hangovers, then coming into the Mana Kai with half a brain. I tried to lead by example, for I was also at the bar every night after scrubbing down the line, and drinking the wonderful and authentic mai tais. But I'd be at work every morning at eight, ready to go. Although I had twelve months to whip the place into shape and there was no guarantee it would stay that way after I left, I did not treat my mission as futile. All this hard work and mai tai drinking were another great distraction from that Creole man who broke my heart into irreparable little pieces, and that bitch Anne Russell, who single-handedly nixed my opportunity for brief unemployment benefits that I needed while recuperating and job-searching, post-fair, by writing on the pink form that at Gautreau's I had "walked off the job." At the Mana Kai I would continue my denial of life, the tasks and pressures of another kitchen job justifying my existence and enabling me, along with alcohol and pot, to skirt the other, more emotional responsibilities of love, heartache, healing, and personal growth.

The key to a popular and successful restaurant, aside from its location, is consistency. I had learned this in school, but it's also common sense that when Mr. and Mrs. Customer have a wonderful meal of crisp green salad on a chilled plate, followed by a tender fillet of mahi-mahi in an almond butter sauce with freshly sautéed zucchini and a side of oriental fried rice, served to them on a hot plate by a smiling waitress (they were still called that in the eighties), that on their next trip to the restaurant they receive exactly the same experience. If, on the other hand, the portion of fish changes, if the sauce tastes oily, if the oriental fried rice has been replaced by something unidentifiable, or if the salad appears wilted on a warm plate, the restaurant is doomed.

Mana Kai had the location, certainly, but it had no backbone, no structure. So I went to work on dissecting the menus—a contemporary (for 1985, anyway) mix of Continental cuisine with Hawaiian and Asian influences—into standardized recipes, complete with photographs, all which formulated a reference manual for the kitchen: the Book, the Kitchen Bible, It. Then, my job was to enforce It. Which wasn't so hard, really, because people in general—especially my ragtag crew of beach bums—appreciate direction and like to know what's expected of them. And the Book did exactly this.

Roy appeared to be slightly amused but respectful of my endeavors. He was an old-school guy—you jump on the ship that is the kitchen and steer it wherever the weather takes you. It's a common way to command, I suppose, but we were all there for one reason: to make the owner money. And through our differences, or in spite of them, Roy and I became friends. First, we both made efforts to help each other out whenever we could: me helping out on the luaus, him getting behind the line to work the middle when we got slammed. Each of us was amenable to cover for the other's preferred days off. I didn't rag on Roy for not cleaning up the line to the new standards, and he didn't tell me to shush when I got particularly anxious. Being nice goes a long way.

I got very attached to Roy and his partner Don, an artist who sold his paintings and painted coconuts on the beachfront patio most afternoons. Roy had a silly sense of humor that lightened up my days. We shared an amusement with puns and playing with words as if they were toys. Born from this wordplay to alleviate stress were a series of birthday and Christmas cards about cows, even after I left the Mana Kai for Vancouver: A-Mooha (a picture of a cow wearing a flower lei), Lettuce Quiche (two cows kissing), Happy Moo-day.

When I think of that Mana Kai year of 1985 to 1986, a few stories come to mind, some of which I will share here, but first I must mention two Hawaiian memories of great fondness: real mai tais and Hawaiian food.

The real mai tai: First of all, if you think you're drinking a mai tai and it is pink or red, please run the other way screaming. I do. Living in Florida now, I see horrific bastardizations of the truly elegant cocktail of my homeland. Rum with red dye number-something-grenadine a mai tai does not make! A real mai tai is very simple: a half-ounce each of orgeat syrup and orange curaçao, a quarter-ounce of simple syrup, the juice of a lime and an ounce of very good dark rum, add ice and top with another half ounce of dark rum. That's it! Don't forget the pineapple-cherry-purple orchid on a sword pick and the paper umbrella. I'm certain that the Mana Kai had some pineapple juice in their mai tais and that was perfectly okay. The color was a rich brown yellow, and two or three of these babies, enhanced by the smell of the ocean and the sound of rolling waves, made for a solid night's sleep.

In 2010 I returned to the Mana Kai and found it had been converted into a condo hotel with an enclosed fancy restaurant and bar (what?!), and no more seventies Mavericks out front. I ordered a mai tai—which seemed to cost about a hundred dollars—and took it out to the beach chairs to drink it. It was just as good as before, that flavor igniting so many memories of warped bartop, smelly kitchen, laid-back Roy, and his partner Don's painted coconuts.

Hawaiian food: The Hawaiian food of my youth was minimal; sometimes we were invited to neighborhood luaus that appeared to be big family reunions of many Hawaiians celebrating a birthday or a birth or an anniversary. Folding chairs abounded across several backyards, fat Hawaiians sang with tiny ukuleles, and there was always pork and fish and poi and some macaroni salad in the works. My mom and grandmother were the awkward haoles, not comfortable in all the chaos unless they had in hand a bourbon and water or a gin and tonic, standing out like awkward parents in the microcosm of Primo beer and loud carrying-on. But I had other kids to run around with while smoky food smells invited and plumeria flower leis adorned grandmas—*tutus*—and the time would finally come to *eat*! And eat we did: the pig lifted from the pit in the ground—the *imu*—with great fanfare, freshly caught mahi-mahi unwrapped from steamed parcels of green ti leaves, and all the accoutrements filled the sections of paper-white Chinet plates. I was lucky enough to maybe experience this a half dozen times.

The biweekly luau on the beach during the year I worked at the Mana Kai conjured up these few but great memories of my childhood. On Wednesday and Saturday mornings, out on the hotel's lawn near the beach, a whole pig was lowered into a permanent *imu*, the pit lined with banana leaves, hardwood, and fiery lava rock. This task was performed by bronze-skinned Hawaiians who worked at the Mana Kai as waiters, performers, or stewards. The pig was covered with more lava, ignited hardwood, and banana leaves, and all day that area of the lawn smoked and steamed like a subterranean porcine volcano. Meanwhile I tended to the duties of running the restaurant kitchen while Roy and a helper cut and chopped vegetables and sweet potatoes, made macaroni and Namasu salads and coconut pudding—*haupia*. Mahi amandine was on my dinner menu and I thawed slabs of the fish imported from Taiwan (a subject for another book), so I cut and wrapped the portions of fish in green ti leaves for steamed *lau laus* for Roy's luau buffet later.

At sunset, as I checked the dinner mise en place, torches were lit around the hotel and on the beach. The horn sound of a conch shell against the pinking sky announced the start of the luau festivities. Hawaiian music began and the foxy Hawaiians who had lowered the pig into the *imu* earlier, now dressed in traditional *lava-lavas*—printed fabric worn like a skirt—ceremoniously lifted the smoked beast from the pit on a huge stretcher and hurried it around the hotel to the rear dock of the kitchen. Here, two more *lava-lava*-wearing stewards sat cross-legged on the concrete dock. Between them sat two parchment paper–lined sheet pans, each steward armed with two meat cleavers and a box of kosher salt. The meat and fat of the pig, now easily separable from bones and carcass, was dumped onto cutting boards and sprinkled with salt, and the stewards went at it in a double-chopping motion, removing bones and tossing them into the dumpster below. As hunks of meat, fat, and skin were transformed into a shredded, salty, smoky manna, another steward with two long spatulas scooped the meat into hotel pans and started stacking them crosswise. Then Roy or I whisked them into the kitchen, covered the pans with foil, and put them in the warming box. On these nights I made sure the dinner line was set so I could assist in the pork transport. Payment for my services to the luau department? The pick of the best chunks of the shiny, juicy, smoky meat from the pans en route to the warmer. (Eat your pork-loving heart out, Anthony Bourdain; RIP.)

Other Maui stories from 1985 include the following:

A funny smell. When you work on the beach in an open-air restaurant, you share your digs with creatures who are enticed by ocean-rotted wood, rancid kitchen grease, and food-infested sneaker juices not completely hosed from the rubber floor mats hanging outside to dry overnight. German roaches scurry around in floor drains, and the big bastard roaches boldly march in from nearby banana patches anytime they feel fit to do so. Pest control is a major undertaking, and the Mana Kai's maintenance man regularly put out poison for mice and rats, and roach motels for those creepy unwanted critters. And I, an anal-retentive clean freak, scrubbed and sanitized constantly, and made my staff scrub and sanitize constantly to ensure that the atmosphere was as pest-unfriendly as possible.

In the middle of the summer season of 1985, a United Airlines pilot strike effectively killed tourism in the islands. Cooks were laid off and my duty as a salaried chef required that I pull double shifts and, on Roy's day off, triple line shifts. This meant that my usual 8 a.m. arrival was now 6:30 a.m., to set up and cook breakfast for the few guests still staying at the hotel. In March, my friend Dona and I, mutually homesick for New Orleans, had celebrated Mardi Gras in Lahaina's Front Street bars. I'd fallen asleep at the wheel of my seventies Dodge Dart on the unlit sugarcane-lined road back to Kihei after dropping her off in Kahului. Waking up in jail was the ultimate embarrassment, and I surrendered my driver's license as my penance. So mornings at 5:45, I embarked from my apartment across from the beach on a bicycle, riding along sleepy South Kihei Road to the dark and dormant kitchen of the Mana Kai.

One morning when I got to the kitchen, a funny smell greeted me: a different funny smell among the usual funny smells of grease, salt, day-old pork, and gas from an expired pilot light on the range. But I paid the scent no mind and flicked on the exhaust hood, grabbed eggs and bacon from the walk-in cooler, and began cracking eggs and mixing pancake batter. The smell intermittently prodded my nostrils, but my morning-after mai tai brain was on autopilot prep.

After the breakfast rush of all thirty hotel guests eating at once, I refilled my coffee cup and began to prep for lunch. It was Monday; Roy was off and there was no luau, so the skeleton crew consisted of me, a dishwasher, and a helper cook who would be in at five to assist with dinner and closing up the line. I called the front desk and left a message for maintenance about the funny smell.

I spent most of lunch standing in the wait station off the kitchen, gazing past the empty dining room to the blue-green Pacific, contemplating the crashing waves and the smoky islands beyond. Pausing, much like I had paused at the sight of the Mississippi from the pizza-pasta station at the New Orleans Fair, wanting something but not knowing what that was. The deep ocean view pulled sighs from me, each sigh asking what the hell I was doing here, then disappearing into the sound of the waves, to be replaced with another sigh.

At four o'clock I was behind the line finishing up a batch of gumbo ya-ya when the condenser on top of the walk-in cooler began to *whirrrr* like a car with a loose radiator belt. Suddenly there was a *clunk!* and the funny smell became a not-so-funny stench with clods of black fur flying up from the top of the walk-in. I was out the double doors of the kitchen into the patio bar in a flash, retching.

The bar patrons were also retching.

The restaurant and bar were shut down, and I sat out on the beach fully engulfed by my previously contemplative ocean view, while poor Mr. Maintenance Man climbed a ladder to the top of the walk-in to find that a rat had curled into the condenser near the fan and died, the fan eventually catching on the dead rat and grinding it into rat burger. This was the result of the rat poison put out, which made the rats thirsty and on the prowl for moisture—plenty of which was up there atop the walk-in cooler.

As for me? What a way to get a night off.

Guess who I almost *cooked for.* As you know by now, I'm a fame whore. My biggest cooking accomplishment up to this point had been baking the carrot cake for Stevie Nicks that summer at Longhi's, and after that was the time

Armand and I cooked dinner at the Columns Hotel for Ray Walston of *My Favorite Martian*. Among cooking circles, many alcohol-infused after-work conversations start with, "Well, there was that time I cooked my [insert dish] for so-and-so." To which I can respond with, "Well, there was that time I baked a birthday cake for Stevie Nicks," or "Well, there was that time I cooked I-don't-remember-what for Ray Walston. He was tall, shook my hand, and I looked for antennas coming out of his head but didn't see any."

During that long slog of a tourist-free summer at the Mana Kai, post–rat homicide, a big event happened: Bruce Springsteen came to Maui. And I, having seen him in concert in Portland with Jon for an eight-dollar third-row seat, fell in absolute love with his charismatic music and persona. He was staying at one of those snotty, upper-crust Wailea hotels, of course—shame on him—but the front desk gal at his hotel lived with the front desk steward at our hotel, and the girlfriend phoned the boyfriend from Wailea to say she had recommended the Mana Kai to the Springsteen entourage for dinner. "There's a new chef there, trained in New Orleans"—surely this is what must have been said to convince them to leave the resort bubble up there in Wailea to join us commoners. This delicious rumor wended its way into my kitchen, where I was cooking alone. After learning how many were in the party and that they were actually, yes, Coming Over Here, I thawed out more shrimp and prepared more tomato concassé, sliced limes and julienned fresh basil and tarragon for shrimp Marisa. Yes! Some excitement on an otherwise very boring night—week—month—summer—life.

Now, stars take their time, of course, but we—the staff—and our empty beachfront restaurant were ready for their arrival. Glasses were polished, the tables nearest the railing overlooking the darkened beach were reset, and everyone was suddenly abuzz with professionalism.

Except for one person. Our assistant manager, Dean, was a bit of a suit-wearing doof. None of us actually took a two-by-four and beat him over the head saying, "Guess what? Bruce Springsteen is coming for dinner!" and apparently someone should have, for when the Springsteen entourage arrived at 8:40 and the front desk called over to the restaurant to ask if we were ready for a ten-top (why? why would they do that?), Dean the Doof said, "No, we've been slow and we're closing up and sending everyone home," and he recommended another Kihei restaurant to them.

When word of this management aberration got to the kitchen, I turned off all the equipment, shoved my mise en place into the walk-in uncovered, hurled an empty wine jug into the metal dumpster for a satisfying sound effect for my woes, slurped a mai tai at the bar, got on my bike, and rode home—really missing New Orleans where things happened, things that could bolster my fame, in spite of that damn city's shortcomings.

That year on Maui, I bought a one-bedroom condo in the Waipuilani complex in central Kihei. Long-term rentals in Kihei were rare, and Mom was having a hard time finding a place to put down roots. I also wanted to invest in my future. I now had an investment with a permanent rent-paying tenant.

In March of 1986 I left the Mana Kai, passing the cooking and management baton to a gal I trained as my replacement. I said goodbye to Roy and Don, to my mom, to my brother, and to Dona. From the plane, I looked down upon the sensuous mountains of my beloved Maui with tears of sadness and longing, but also excitement—I was going to another country to work.

CHAPTER 17

SOMETHING'S HAPPENING HERE: WORLD EXPO '86

IF MY FIRST MEAL IN VANCOUVER was any indication of the city, then I was impressed. I dropped my bags at a boarding house in the West End and headed for the first sushi bar I could find, which was easy among the international dining options along urban Robson Street. It was a sunny day in late March, a little more than a month until the fair would open, and I was hungry, jet-lagged, and anxious about my new position as executive chef for Sanders International Ventures at Expo '86.

Entering the Japanese restaurant was like taking yet another trip somewhere, with serene lute music piped in and syncopated smiles and nods from the Japanese staff. I sat at the sushi bar, and losing myself in a mural of a cherry-blossom-bedecked countryside above the back bar, I ordered tuna, hamachi, saba, ikura, and sake, thinking of what tomorrow would bring when I met up with the standoffish Chuck Sanders at his office near the fair site.

After my meal I strolled down Robson Street in exploration. Oddly, I didn't see any bars, so I wandered in and out of shops, stimulated by the colorful and silky wares and perfumy smells, realizing that I would at some point need to introduce winter clothes into my hippie beach wardrobe. I would have to actually go shopping. I would rather put porcupine quills in my hair.

The sun began to set, shooting a dazzle of pink and lavender bolts across nearby skyscrapers and distant mountains. I was close to water. I could smell it, but my feet were getting tired. I ducked into a restaurant to sit at the bar and get to know the locals a bit.

A hostess greeted me at the door, smiling. "One for dinner?"

"No, thanks, just a drink at the bar," I said, looking around for one.

"Oh! Sorry," she said, glancing downward. "You must not be from here. You have to eat to consume alcohol."

"What? But I just ate!" I whined, and I returned to the sidewalk. The sushi bar's great influence on my perception of the city was now highly overshadowed by weird drinking restrictions.

Chuck Sanders's newly formed company, VanFair, included a massive cafeteria-style grab-your-own-food joint that would introduce into popularity the buffalo burger with a Fuddruckers-style burger garnish bar. There was a combination Swiss deli and fried seafood joint, a German sausage takeout restaurant, and an English pub. These were the restaurants scattered throughout the fair whose kitchens I would manage. Eventually they all had cutesy names, but we started out by calling them by their building names, F-49, F-11, F-8, and F-6; we ended up calling them these throughout the fair, so the cutesy names are long forgotten. The menu planning and vendor selections were nearly complete by the time I arrived, but I participated in the hiring of my crews for each location, thrilled that I would actually be chef, in charge of other chefs and cooks under me. I also acted as a sort of culinary consultant to Chuck Sanders as he grabbed food ideas from the ether to put into action. A *German sausage* restaurant? What, me? German food?

Chuck Sanders thought as much, so there we were one night sitting near the window in a German restaurant looking out on a rubbery-wet Robson Street. I pushed around on my plate red cabbage, sauerbraten, and German potato salad, happy for the beer at least, although alcohol, any alcohol, increased my nervousness around my overbearing boss.

"Do you think," Chuck queried, pointing a fork-stabbed chunk of bratwurst at me, "we could get those cans of boiled new potatoes and turn them into something similar here?" His sausage pointer now hovered over the German potato salad on my plate.

Push those little cooked potatoes through a slicer? Mush. No, that wouldn't work. "Th-they need to be presliced," I said. My mind calculated a bulk recipe for the German joint so the potato salad would be easy to make, with sugar, bacon, and caramelized onion, somehow cost effective and consistent.

Chuck ate his sausage pointer, made a head motion toward the bread roll on my plate, and said, "See that bread?"

Of course I saw the bread. "Yes," I said, looking at the oval-shaped roll on my plate. It had a little flap on it, like an edge of it was pulled over onto itself before baking.

"You need to find bread shaped like this, only a little bigger, for sandwiches, and with a little more, more substance." He brought his bread to his mouth and tore a chunk with his teeth. "This is too soft for sandwiches," he mumbled around the bread.

So I'd need to find bread like this bread, but not like this bread; I'm supposed to go, what . . . chomping bread at every German restaurant in Vancouver and when I find it, *if* I find it, I ask the owner if he can put his business on hold for six months so he can bake massive amounts of bread for us at the fair? Definitely an undertaking.

Chuck waved over a stocky man in a blue suit and introduced him as the restaurant's owner, who had agreed to make the sausages for our German joint. Well, if Chuck Sanders could find someone to make his authentic sausages, then certainly I could suss out the bread source.

In between my bread excursions and staff interviewing, making pre-staffing schedules at the office, and making sample batches of German potato salad in the test kitchen, Chuck would roll into the office, suit-wearing and stogie ash a-falling, and say to me, "Come along." On one such tag-along episode, he deposited me into the kitchen at the Munich Festhaus near one of the fair entrances, which appeared to be open already, even though the fair around it was still a construction site. I learned later that Chuck and the Festhaus owner had become friends, traveling to fairs and running restaurants together over the years. Tossed into a kitchen of scowling men, me not saying much as usual, but comfortable enough to turn sausages on the massive griddle, I dished sauerkraut onto oval plates until it was time to learn the secret of the sauerkraut—which apparently was why I was there.

It's all in the "tea," said the German owner-chef-friend of my boss in an accent that made me think of concentration camps, but he was willing to

hand over secrets to a harmless-looking girl. This tea was a brew of hot water
steeped with juniper berries, bay leaf, thyme, and caraway. The metric cans of
German-imported kraut were drained (not washed) and cooked with bacon
and onion; the strained tea was added and the kraut cooked until tender. Here
at the Munich Festhaus, a 100-gallon stock pot held the booty, and I had to
get on a step stool to stir it with a giant paddle.

I learned to cook German food in this way. I also learned the marinating
and braising of sauerbraten from a woman in East Vancouver from whom
we'd be ordering our pastries. She had a tall forehead and a jutted-out jaw;
we'll call her Frieda. Frieda also shared the secret to preparing red cabbage
(diced apple). Thanks to Frieda, I was able to formulate standard recipes in
our test kitchen for every item on our German menu. Meanwhile I picked
up bread rolls here and there, most of them moldering at the bottom of my
backpack, not always seeing Chuck, then too shy to approach him when I
did. Finally, I took a bread original from that first sausage restaurant to Frieda
and asked if she could replicate it larger, and with more substance. She did,
and our sandwich bread supplier was confirmed.

I had a partner in crime in the adventures leading up to the opening day
of Expo. A local Vancouver man named Michael had been hired as director
of operations; our preopening goals overlapped, and I helped him gain what
little insight I knew about Chuck. Evenings, Michael and I started to go to a
West End pub (where you could drink beer or cider without eating) to compare notes, Michael focusing on the money and front staffing issues, while I
planned recipes and interviewed my own staff. Michael's mentor was Chuck's
brother, Dick, a voice of practicality in all things money, ice cream, and Belgian waffles, these two latter mainstays of the fair to be served out of the Swiss
deli joint, F-11 (or was it F-8?). When you're daunted by such large tasks as
I was—all these different restaurants, menus, scheduling, recipes, food cost,
staff, food quality, et cetera—you need to know your limitations. So I relied
on Michael and Dick regarding issues concerning money, ice cream, and waffles, and throughout the fair drew a line around myself to preserve my sanity
by saying, "I don't do money," or "I don't do ice cream," when asked by a
counter girl to count her bank or fetch more chocolate ice cream.

Michael was a second-generation German, his parents having immi-
grated to British Columbia before he was born. I easily succumbed to his

advances—what else was there to do? This man, un-folksy, businesslike, and recently divorced with two young girls, was the farthest from my type, but the fair was our commonality, our reason to coexist. Thereafter, Sunday evenings it was dinner at his parents' house to drink beer with his dad in special German beer glasses and talk to his sweet mother about whatever meat she'd been braising on her little stove all day. German immigrants were plentiful in Vancouver, so I secretly commended Chuck on his quest for authenticity with the German food. And I did like the sausages. Now, with those World's Fairs years long behind me, once a year or so, usually at Christmas, I put out a spread of traditional German meats and sausages—and yes, even sauerkraut and German potato salad—which I buy from our local German deli.

The transportation and communication theme of the Vancouver World's Fair made for a stark comparison to the watery and baroque world of the New Orleans Expo '84. Vancouver's fair sprawled over 173 acres, compared to New Orleans's 84 acres, and shimmered in a world of sleek modernity, even with its nod to the past with tall ships, antique autos, and steam engines juxtaposed with space ships, an Omnimax theater, and other futuristic endeavors. Each area of the fair was a colored zone, such as purple or red—a very uncreative way to designate fair areas, for in New Orleans, neighborhoods such as Bayou Plaza, Watergarden, Italian Village, Fulton Street, Festival Park, and Riverfront had populated the fair. Each colored zone at Expo '86 had corresponding round beds of colored tulip blossoms, which were pleasant to look at, but the whole effect was too clean for me, too Disneyesque, charmless. Even the mascot lacked imagination: Expo Ernie, a life-size robot, hobbled around the colored zones, compared to the rambunctious pelican, Seemore D. Fair, who drunkenly cruised the neighborhoods along the Mississippi River. Every night at the official closing time of ten, when the parade snaked around Expo '86 and fireworks exploded and the theme song "Something's Happening Here" blasted out of the loudspeakers all over the fair, I'd think: Nothing's happening here.

And the food? Well, the spicy smells that had coddled my psyche in New Orleans were lacking in Vancouver, whose Expo claim to fame was McBarge, a McDonald's on a boat. There were some renowned fancy restaurants in and around Expo '86, with oversized plates of undersized food, but I missed red beans and rice in a Styrofoam bowl with andouille sausage, missed relaxing on a barstool in a dark bar after a day at the fair, missed the upbeat horns of jazz music seemingly always playing in the background.

The fact was that about halfway through the fair, no longer distracted by opening pressures or missing the warm sun and swaying palms of Maui, I missed New Orleans. I wanted to go back. And what was Armand up to? I wondered.

From the F-49 kitchen supervisors' journal:

Tuesday, July 29. Attendance: 148,409

"$25,361.00 Record day! The grill? Whoever closed left a mess!" *Chef*

"Last 2 fryers had gas left on. Please keep potato skins in freezer at all times." *Laurie*

Friday, August 1. Attendance: 127,793

"Terry didn't show up or phone. Michael went and got lettuce. Ron was not on the grill. Only Gary on the line. We had one person in each area and managed to make it thru. Chili was made but we need to add three cans of beans! The new guy on the grill is great, works hard and learns fast, what more could you ask?" *Robert*

"That he learns how to pick up a (cleaning) towel every so often . . ." *Chef*

Wednesday, August 6. Attendance: 153,256

"1 full box of hot dogs left to thaw by sink at 4 p.m. yet in the walk-in there was 4 full hotel trays (plus 2 in grill fridge). Had to order deep fryer cleaner. Birthday cake in walk-in for Chuck Sanders. (Will want around 6 p.m.) Fryers 2 & 3 should have been changed but no oil in storeroom. Funnel cakes fryer left empty so Jim could check for leakage. Again, out of alfalpha (sp?)" *Laurie*

"Alfalfa." *Chef*

"Record day! $30,111.59!" *Chef*

Friday, August 22. Attendance: 132,888

"Jim Bryce walked out @ 10pm. I don't think he wants to work anymore. Gary sick today—nobody to cover Jim's night shift. We will manage somehow." *Laurie*

Thursday, August 28. Attendance: 120,365

"Kim (the smart one) was seen outside smooching with Chris the donut guy!" *Chef*

Wednesday, September 17. Attendance: 140,219

"Fun-Fun-Fun. I love the broiler yeah, yeah. ☺" *Robert*

"Don't have fun, work. Grills not clean. Grill shelves dirty. Line refer dirty. Dish station filthy. Grill utensils not rinsed. Wrong hotel pans in grill table." *Chef.*

Saturday, September 20. Attendance: 200,412

"37.3K. Record again!" *Chef*

Tuesday, September 23. Attendance: 175,080

"Watch potato chip portions! Saturday almost twice as many chips used for only $1000 more business. Bad ketchup bottle found —watch busboys!" *Chef*

"Al Peralla cannot work 'til 4 Tuesday (only 'til 3)." *Robert*

Thursday, September 25. Attendance: 136,150

"The dish pit is a pit. Corn doggers are slobs. So are busboys when they can't wash ketchup bucket and spigot. Everything else peachy keen." *Chef*

"Chili fixings and soup are in reach-in. Fay was a-flipping so was big bob. Hope corn doggers were better." *Robert*

Tuesday, September 30. Attendance: 128,541

"Who is the Curly Q fry box culprit? Soggy boxes out back by freezer doesn't make grandma happy in the morning." *Chef*

"Please remind the grillers to empty the yuk-catcher on the right under the vents. This seems to need to be done 2-3 times daily." *Laurie*

"Watch Ron!!" *Chef*

"The Curly Q would belong to Mike V." *Robert*

F-49 was the biggest restaurant, with the highest profit to lose or gain, so I spent most of my time there. It was the first place I hit in the morning, doing my little-mouse snoops through each of the stations, making any notes in the supervisor's journal, before hopping on my ten-speed and riding around the service road to our other restaurants to check out the previous night's closing, inventory, prep, staffing or other personal conflicts. I found that the human factor was the most challenging thing about upper management. All else could be solved with standardizations and directives, but trying to get minimum-wage workers to follow these standards, and trying to prevent middle-management chefs' egos from destroying the fragile equilibrium of things, were the constants of my days. And some of my chefs were older than me, making the ego dance between them and myself all the more tricky. I put everything on Chuck and made like I was simply there to help achieve his standards, which actually was true. I had had many condescending managers in my time, and I was not about to be one of those.

So although I was bored sometimes, riding around the service road in my chef whites to supervise each cog of the great food-o-rama that I oversaw, daydreaming of gas lamps, the smells of brown roux, the embrace of Armand (that asshole), and a kitchen of my own someday in an old house Uptown, I knew fully that this was a great experience for my resume. I could do anything now.

Vancouver is a beautiful city, with enormous smoky-colored mountains jutting up from the Pacific and also from the land to the east, but as with people, beauty is only skin-deep. I could never feel the substance of the place, couldn't get to know it on my single weekly day off on my bicycle and camera expeditions around the city. The city and its residents were simply too well adjusted and happy for me to relate to them.

Michael and I, with our mutual goals of running high-volume restaurants for Chuck Sanders, had mistaken our work-related goals for relationship material and moved into a West End apartment high-rise with a view of the Pacific inlet, which threw upon us the most beautiful russet-orange to pink sunsets. We weren't there much, so it was mostly a crash pad, but I did dunk my little toe into domesticity by managing the laundry tasks and cooking a few German-inspired meals for him. While waiting for the laundry to spin downstairs, I'd gaze out the sliding glass door at the dusking day, thinking of Hawaii, of New Orleans, of my career, and there was still a black thing lurking somewhere not quite out of sight, teasing me on my periphery. Boredom seeped in through the focused realm of my work. My job—the great distraction—did not distract me from myself enough.

Sometimes on days off I'd bike over to the Aquabus, which floated across False Creek to Granville Island, home of an airy public market. Here I found pink peppercorns, local cream, fresh shrimp, and spinach, a meal born in my head to give me something to do later when Michael came home. Granville Market was as beautiful as Pike's Market in Seattle, only smaller, and I could walk it for hours, a loner taking in the colors and smells of fresh produce, fish, flowers, cheeses, pastas, and meats and the bustle of smiling vendors and customers. I talked Michael into leaving the fair early a few times so we could sit out on the deck and eat Caesar salads and drink Chardonnay, something I wasn't comfortable doing alone. Had there been a bar at Granville Market, or a pub with windows, I would've spent all my days off there, probably not feeling alone at all.

As the fair trekked onward toward fall, summer's long sunny days were swallowed by cold gray rain, which limited my day-off biking excursions. Once, determined to get away from the fair and the empty apartment, I suited up in sweats and rain gear, got on my bike, and rode to nearby Stanley Park, a 1,000-acre park that famously borders ocean and mountains. Car rides through it in the spring had graced us with endless vistas of greenery, colorful wildflowers, beaches, biking, and hiking paths. Its beauty had even broken through my aura of negativity, so one September afternoon I decided to check it out via bicycle, rain or shine.

And on this damp and cold excursion among wilting wildflowers and spongy grass, the point was proven to me: I was miserable. What was I doing here anyway? And why was I living with Michael, who spent more time working than even I did, and who spent all his free time in pubs with his buddies—Chuck Sanders's appointed "restaurant consultants"—none of whom I thought was worth a damn? (One consultant brought in a fake mayonnaise product that tasted like sugar paste, in order to save a penny on every sandwich.) Thank God the fair was almost over.

But then what?

Thursday, October 2. Attendance: 127,226. 11 more scheduling days

"Fay can't work past 3 because she has another job that she is starting and she has her orientation to attend." *Laurie*

"It's O.K. she doesn't work anyway." *Anonymous*

"Watch Ron!!" *Chef*

"Who killed the great alligators of Vancouver?" *Anonymous*

Friday, October 3. Attendance: 167,045. 10 more days

"Everything seemed to go well. Lots of soup and shit. Used the crinkly beets on the condo bar." *Laurie*

"We used the corn on the condo." *Robert*

"Watch Ron!" *Chef*

Sunday, October 5. Attendance: 225,232. 8 more days

"Only 7 more sleeps at Camp Patch. OH, is that bakery out in Surrey? The Bindy was sure dumb. Don't know if you'll get it." *Robert*

Tuesday, October 7. Attendance: 177,526. 6 more days

"Laurie—get 2 jars of m. cherries from F-9. Run outs: sml. milks, strawberries, OJ. The price of cucumbers is going down and the price of green peppers going up so, make sure two pans of cukes and only one of green peppers go out on the condiment bar for the remainder of the fair. Dalvin-John Blais is in at 5 p.m. to help you anywhere necessary. My suggestion is on the line and have someone halfway intelligent like David B. help on the grill . . ." *Chef*

Wednesday, October 8. Attendance: 183,586. 5 more days

"Chili stuff and soup in reach-in." *Dalvin*

"Well let's hope that'll do. Banana splits seem to be selling well. Ran out again. We have been running short on oil." *Laurie*

Thursday. October 9. Attendance: 190,740. 4 more days

"Fay will 'work' morning 8 a.m. Ran out dinner rolls Wed and Thurs." *Chef*

"Everything was peachy keener." *Dalvin*

"Watch Ron." *Chef*

Friday, October 10. Attendance: 235,190. 3 more days

"Prospective run lows: O-rings, sugar packets." *Chef*

Saturday, October 11. Attendance: 256,535. 2 more days

"Prospective run lows: tomatoes. Use leftover tortillas for bar." *Chef*

Sunday, October 12.

341,086!!

Monday, October 13. LAST DAY OF FAIR

"Put all remaining food in walk-ins. Remove all garbage from restaurant. Pull all employee passes. Count all linen. Drain deep fryers. Possible run lows: Coffee (borrow?). Diced onions (dice some). Don't open new case of potato salad. Thank you all . . ." *Chef*

CHAPTER 18

DO YOU KNOW WHAT
IT MEANS TO MISS
NEW ORLEANS

EXPO '86 ENDED WITH A FIZZLE. There was no great move planned, no great chef's position waiting for me somewhere, nothing to look forward to except that the long, pounding Expo days were over. Chuck Sanders, for the press I'm certain, swore his loyalty to Canada (Vancouver specifically), bought a house, and set down roots in the form of three small restaurants in Fantasy Garden World, a small botanical garden/amusement park centered among stone buildings built to resemble those of the Middle Ages.

Despite my misgivings about our relationship, Michael and I had a beach wedding on Maui and a short, teary-eyed honeymoon of island-hopping (my heart filled with angst, I know now), and then there I was at Fantasy Gardens, setting up and running Chuck's little restaurants serving German, Swiss, and British pub food. Cooking nothing food for very few people in a nothing place, and married. Had we really done that? When Michael and I arrived at the stone buildings of Fantasy Gardens every morning, a sense of dread coalesced in my stomach like rendered fat. Greeted by Vancouver's overly cheerful spring blue sky, a Dutch windmill, and yellow and pink tulips lining the cobblestone path of the shopping area, I was reminded of dusty plastic flowers at Kmart. Fantasy Gardens was not *my* fantasy! Michael wanted to stick with Chuck Sanders because he wanted to work Expo '88 in Australia. For me, thoughts of where I'd be in two years were beyond my thinking capacity, like embarking on a lesson in advanced Chinese. On some sort of daydreaming autopilot, I endured the spring and summer toiling in those little kitchens, and on cool nights I sat with Michael and his pals, staring off into smoky darkness inside Vancouver pubs. But when the air became infused with autumn chill and the multicolored heads of those too-cheerful tulips had drooped toward the dirt, my ever-growing boredom and dread fiercely took hold and began shaking me. No more pickled herring and sausages. I needed a dose of New Orleans, or I would go insane.

• • •

"Look at those poor Black kids playing ball—see, those are *projects*!" A big-headed bald man sitting in front of me on the bus on I-10 heading into the city spit out these words like a spider had been on his tongue. "Over there, see? Not even grass to play on!" he said to his wife. A montage of seedy motels, car lots, gas stations, convenience stores, and low brick buildings of various function whizzed by the bus's large windows; this could be anywhere, really. But New Orleans East is the lead-in to all things great, and excitement was building in me like a symphony reaching for crescendo, in spite of the big-headed man's nasty narrative.

When the bus hefted itself onto I-10's on-ramp and the stark white crosses of marble tombs came into view, the man said to his wife, "Oh my Lord, will you look at that! They can't even bury their dead properly in this godforsaken place!" He was referring to the great, aboveground cemeteries where Dona and I had spent many afternoons looking at the cities of the dead through our sepia-filtered Minoltas. I refrained from knocking the guy in the head, instead thinking of all that I would do this month, alone in my favorite city—which had scorned me—with my mountain bike and my cameras. Finally, freedom!

Chrissy Hynde of the Pretenders had sung it so truly: "There's a thin line between love and hate." I considered the city's majestic beauty and historical panache; its crime, poverty, and apathy; the way it had turned away from me, an outsider, a girl; and how hard it was to move up the kitchen ranks. New Orleans strummed a part of me never before touched, made me *feel* something: fear, thrill, want, curiosity, passion. I hungered for these feelings now; I craved them. I needed to feel alive.

It had been the same with Armand, a love so passionate and needy, fulfilling and responsive. I had loved him so yet hated his indifference, arrogance, and narcissism, the way he pulled me down with his self-destructive ways. A year on Maui and a year in Vancouver and I was still down in the hole where I'd followed him, stunned, turned against so-called love, marrying Michael because of some bizarre obligation I'd concocted. Not sure I wanted to even get out of the pit, for down there with my lonely and longing self, I was able to feel. Like a neglected child who acts out to get the negative attention she needs to replace no attention at all, I preferred negative feelings to no feelings.

Nearing downtown, century-old brick facades and parallel lines of gas lamps welcomed me with memories. I could taste spicy gumbo washed down with a cold draft beer; I could see the street musicians and barroom characters who were only blocks away now. "Ugh!" the man uttered to his wife, loud enough for the entire bus to hear. "And look at all those crumbling buildings! These people"—he clicked his tongue—"why can't they clean this place up?"

Falling into the vast pillow of freedom ahead, thirty days to hang around and capture this life in pictures on a budget of twenty dollars a day, I tuned out his words, thinking instead of where to look for cheap accommodations, where to have my first beer, which happy hours to frequent for free food, where to find a cheap darkroom to rent.

My heart skipped a beat when the bus coughed to a stop at Canal and Bourbon. The door flopped open and the hot October wind carried in a scent of gas lamp, feet, and stale beer. The man said to his wife, "God, I hate this place," and I wanted to say, "Go the hell home then."

The cheapest place to rent I found perusing the *Times-Picayune* was an un-air-conditioned attic room with a bed and a sink in the Irish Channel. The neighborhood was dark and remote, and the room smelled like old mattress, new paint, and rotted wood, a place, I envisioned, where an old man would go to shoot heroin. It had a bad vibe. I knew from nearly four years living in New Orleans that some old structures, like my old apartment on St. Peter Street, have that. You walk in and want to walk right out. Like whatever bad or nasty thing that had happened there was still going on in some other dimension, or the past was still alive, or maybe some people, like me, are too damn sensitive. After two nights of restless hot sleep dreaming of serial killers, I began searching for another place that wouldn't cast a gloom over my days. Serendipitously, on the third night sitting in the Que Sera bar on St. Charles Avenue, I mentioned my plight to a couple who told me about a lady who owned a big house farther up the streetcar line, and rented rooms by the week or month for cheap.

Next morning I exited the streetcar under the dappled light of a great oak canopy at St. Charles and Napoleon, walked two blocks, and stood in front of the house the couple had told me about. With peeling white paint, milky windows, and rotting fascia, it sat festering among the more stately Garden District beauties. The house and its associated outbuildings, which all appeared to be connected, took up half a city block, possibly the entire block, since I couldn't see past its many roof lines and small porches. I found an iron gate along the side of the property and pushed it open. An old woman wearing a thin housedress, bent over a half dozen or so flat-headed mewling cats, bolted upright when she heard the rusty scratch of the gate.

"I-I-I was told you rent rooms?" I hoped I wasn't mistaken with wrong information, and was worried I had wandered into the wrong compound.

The cats scattered like marbles. The woman nodded and made a motion with her head for me to follow her inside and up a mahogany stairway, whose unkempt wood creaked under each purposeful step. On the third floor was a giant room, dusty, with vaulted ceilings and more unmaintained hardwood, connected to other rooms that appeared to go on as far as the house had seemed to. My heart fell, knowing I did not need—nor could I afford—this much space.

"Three hunert dollars fo' de month," the woman said in a country Southern accent, as if reading my mind. "An' fifty for de bed."

I became jittery with relief. At $75.00 a week, I *could* afford it. "Fifty for the bed?" I had to ask.

"State law. Sanitize bed between lodgings. Fo' bedbugs."

And a clean bed. What more could I ask?

Well, I had hoped to run into Armand. I visualized him at every street corner I rode by, in every bar I went to. But I knew he was gone; I had received his one letter when I was on Maui and he'd moved to Waveland, full-time at the Yacht Club I was certain, and that was too far to ride on my bike.

So I took the city into my veins, looking at its ancient buildings through my Minolta's viewfinder by day, processing it with chemicals at night in a rented darkroom Uptown, living the beat of it with free happy-hour food and cheap drinks, conversations with characters in bars. I sunk into Anne Rice's *The Feast of All Saints*, walking the French Quarter streets with my nose in the book, imagining the 1840s New Orleans presented on the pages. I was happy in this temporary reprieve from the rest of my life, enjoyed my alone-ness where I was free to fully feel all my angst, want, and dread. I wondered what I seemed like to others, this girl alone on her trip. Did I seem odd? Or was I just another dysfunctional thread in the great tapestry of the city? Did I fit right in, with all these people who were like me in a way, searching, scarred by something, not able to find out what had done the scarring? Some people, however, the ones sitting on a barstool gazing at their drink defeatedly, had stopped searching. Would that ever be me?

I spent days exploring the tiny crowded French Quarter streets, photographing old Black artists selling their wares in Jackson Square, stopping into Maspero's for a bowl of gumbo and a beer. I watched people leaving Arnaud's, the Court of Two Sisters, and Antoine's, with bellies full and pockets light. I listened to stories from people who had never been outside Louisiana or New Orleans for that matter, and I envied them in a way—to have such a simple goal as just waking up every day loving where they were. The way I felt now, in my short, lovely limbo.

Other days I stayed Uptown, rode through the Garden District photographing well-preserved historic mansions, or exploring the small antique and junk stores of Magazine Street, or riding upriver as far as I could until October's relentless heat forced me back Uptown into an air-conditioned barroom.

I wandered the old World's Fair site, which had been turned into a riverfront shopping mecca. I watched tourists buy purple, green, and gold Mardi Gras trinkets, porcelain masks, Saints memorabilia. The food court there was good, and it was three bucks to fill up on a spicy bowl of gumbo or crawfish étouffée. Even fast food in New Orleans is good.

The blissful rhythm of my days changed one night, sitting in Cooter Brown's at the river's bend, where it was two bucks for boudin. I'd just gotten off the phone with Michael, who reminded me to call Albert for Chuck Sanders. Albert—whom I'd never met—had been the company accountant during Expo '84, and Chuck had entrusted some stored items with him and needed them shipped up to Vancouver. It turned out that this jolly guy sitting next to me at the bar, who seemed very un-accountant-like and whose conversation was very much like that of a childhood pal, turned out to be Expo '84 Albert.

"Well," he announced, once realizing who I was, "buy the Expo chef a shot of Jägermeister!" The bartender set the chilled shots before us. To my look of shock after our mutual introduction, Albert said, "Don't worry; I shipped the Expo stuff up last week. So you don't have to call me. Cheers! Do you like road trips?"

"I love road trips."

"Y'ever been to the Tabasco Factory on Avery Island?"

I took advantage of the odd synchronicity. The calmness of my quietly drawn-out days morphed into adventurous day trips into Acadiana with loads of alcohol, LSD, and Cajun music blasting from Albert's car stereo. We were two merry pranksters exploring the terrain, me with cameras, Albert always planning our next swamp romp. He was a relentless party hound, a big lovable squish toy of a man, always laughing, not taking anything seriously, which contrasted with my way-too-serious attitude about everything. I laughed frequently and dove right into a short love affair with this man, his lifestyle of who-the-fuck-cares-about-anything satiating a hungry part of my soul.

We made love in a swamp, ate artichoke pizza on Magazine Street, took a day trip to the fishing village of Delacroix, where we smoked a joint, blasted Dylan's "Tangled Up in Blue," and screamed out the lyrics about a fishing boat in Delacroix while gazing out at the muddy horizon. We watched the New Orleans Saints, football being one of Albert's many passions. He taught me how to watch his bedraggled team play the game and I learned all the terms, the plays, the scoring, and even this was fun. Everything was fun. I was a girl who badly needed fun.

When the month was nearly over and Michael was heading down for my last two days to check out the city that had the heart of his wife, Albert and I parted over Jägermeister shots at Cooter Brown's. Where it began, it would end. Outside under the watchful eye of a full moon, I hugged and kissed the irresponsible kid of a man goodbye, told him I loved him, and, teary-eyed, mounted my bike and rode back to my rambling rented flat above the flat-headed cats. The next day Michael would be there. I would show him the city. And convince him we had to move to New Orleans.

CHAPTER 19

THE LAND DOWN UNDER

MICHAEL WAS RELENTLESS in his goal to work for Chuck Sanders the following year at the World's Fair in Brisbane. Conversely, I wanted to settle down, in New Orleans preferably, and do what a twenty-seven-year-old is supposed to do, like have kids, I thought. I wanted to resume my career, my life. The two fairs I'd worked had given me the experience needed to blast through the restraints that had previously held me back, and I was ready to test the culinary waters with my new resume. Michael promised that after the Australian World's Fair, we would move to New Orleans. But what to do in the meantime?

After a few miserable weeks in Vancouver nursing my post–New Orleans emotional hangover, and staying far away from Fantasy Garden World, I flew to Maui. Fine, we would go to Australia, but Hawaii is on the way and if I was going to lie around and be miserable for five months, it may as well be at the beach, and in a country where I could find work. I moved in with Mom at Waipuilani, printed up consulting business cards, and sucked in my nervous guts to cold-call local restaurants for a little freelance work. I landed a few menu-costing gigs for some Kihei restaurants, and relieved chefs on their days off for others. In between odd shifts, I watched the Saints get into the playoffs for the first time. These games broadcasted at 7 a.m. in Hawaii, so I awoke early on game mornings, pulled a beer from Mom's refrigerator, sat on my bed in front of a small TV, and called Albert collect so we could watch the game together. By eleven, with a thick beer buzz, I'd climb under the covers and go back to sleep.

Michael came to Maui for Christmas—a disjointed time, when I was an actor onstage with no Saints games, no morning beers, all of us fake smiles and nods, slipping into my familiar groove of childhood with everybody acting like everything was fine when it wasn't. Grandmother and Mom were experts at this, and I was an A student of dysfunction. Then Michael left for Australia in January to work on start-up procedures with Chuck and Dick Sanders, and I resumed my beer-in-bed-sitting, collect-calling Albert, freelance cooking shifts, and sleeping faceup on the beach.

In early March of 1988, via a long-distance telephone call with Michael, I got the summons from Chuck Sanders: They were ready for me in Australia.

After the thirteen-hour flight (I'd skipped over a day to get there), when I looked up from the tarmac at the Southern Hemisphere's blue cotton candy sky, an electric energy recharged my batteries. I was a star in the Martian Chronicles, for I had traveled far and this new land had a different, friendly, exciting, and adventurous feel to it. The canary-yellow sun cast upon me such a comforting grace, previous tensions evaporated like hour-old sweat. I walked into Michael's arms buzzing with instant love for the place. I had just landed on Mars!

The galactic aspect of things carried into each new hour of those early days before Expo '88 fired itself up. Many subtle things were simultaneously confusing and amusing, and these newfound little mysteries were a feather's gentle tickle to lift my spirits.

Michael and I were sharing a large apartment with Greg—Chuck's nephew, the Waffle King—and Ed, another manager hired to work with Michael. The spacious apartment had a balcony that overlooked the blue-gray Brisbane River and the fair site, which was still under construction and racing against the clock to open on time. The things one normally sets up when moving into a new place confounded us all: Where's the lint catcher in the dryer? (Turns out it's behind the dryer.) How do you set the clock on the stove? (We never figured this one out.) Is that thing that looks like R2-D2 from *Star Wars* a coffee maker? (And where's the instruction booklet?)

The first few times I flushed the toilet, I looked into the bowl to see if the water whirlpooled to the left instead of the right. A button on top of the commode was the flushing apparatus, so the water just sucked downward. I looked into sinks then, to experience this wonder of the Southern Hemisphere, but I couldn't tell if the water swirled in the other direction or not.

The first few nights, Michael, Ed, Greg, and I ate out at pubs in downtown Brisbane, where oddly, giant steaks were considered pub grub. Nowhere within walking distance could I buy ground coffee, juice, or toothpaste, so on Thursday, the only weeknight that stores were open, I embarked upon the excursion of grocery shopping. Not yet ready to drive the company van on the wrong side of the narrow streets, I took a cab, which pulled into a circular drive in front of a large building in a nearby suburb, the closest grocery store to downtown Brisbane. "This is the grocery store?" I asked the cabbie. "Yeah, ma'am," he said in that wonderful Aussie accent. I paid him, stepped out onto the sidewalk, and stood alone and bewildered as the cabbie drove off.

First of all, it didn't look like a grocery store. The building's windowless, concrete facade resembled the back side of an office building. And . . . where was the door? I wondered, if only briefly, that maybe the Aussies weren't as friendly as they seemed and this cabbie had just played a horrible joke on me, stranding me somewhere, and there was no phone at the apartment to reach anyone. Where was I, and how would I get back?

I spotted a single solid door at the far end of the building and relief propelled me to it, where I opened it to find a cubby with a single elevator. Inside the elevator car I pushed the button for the top floor, figuring I'd try out each floor before panicking. At the fourth floor the doors opened into pink leggings and the stationary bikes of a health club. I poked the button to immediately close the elevator doors. On the third floor the elevator doors opened to the clatter and bustle of a large grocery store.

Finding the door to the store was only the first act of confusion on this adventure. All logic self-destructed as I wandered the aisles looking for things that were supposed to be in certain places—rice near pasta, orange juice in the freezer section, milk near cheese—but these ingrained juxtapositions of American life weren't so in this place. Rice was in the meat department; there was no such thing as orange juice concentrate in this citrus-producing region of Australia; milk and cheese resided in opposite ends of the store. It was funny, really, making my mind do somersaults like this, and I giggled up and down the aisles as if a test mouse in a maze. I finally exited with a grocery cart full of bagged supplies—including lots of lamb because it was cheaper than chicken (and if the guys didn't like lamb, too bad).

· · ·

Walking from the apartment to the pub with Michael on our first night in Brisbane, *sceep-sceep-sceep!* noises echoed ominously above us in the trees as we passed through a tiny park along the Brisbane River.

"What's that?!" I began walking faster to avoid whatever lurked above.

"Monkeys," said Michael, deadpan.

Sceep-sceep-sceep!

"There are *monkeys* here? I never read anything li—"

From the curl on Michael's lips, I saw I'd been had.

"You! Those aren't monkeys. What are they?" I stopped, cocking my left ear toward the stand of trees we'd just passed under.

"They're bats."

Sceep-sceep-sceep!

I would have thought he was joking again, but I saw the giant arc of a black creature rise above one tree and land on another.

Definitely not a monkey. But . . . bats? *Sceep!*

In the distractingly strange and wonderful world of wrongly arranged grocery stores, gourmet food courts, fall weather in March, multitudinous pubs, left-side driving, flying bats, and lovable Aussies, the fair—and my job—were gearing up.

And I had competition.

Sanders International Ventures, now Brisfair, had gone big for this fair. We had the entire Boardwalk Restaurants venue, consisting of T-49, "Food on the Walk," a sprawling open-air food court supported by a central kitchen producing Greek, Chinese, Italian (there's that pizza again), Belgian, and Tex-Mex cuisines along with ice cream, waffles, and fresh fruit serving stations; S-4, "The Ultimate Buffet"; T-4 upstairs, "Top O' the Walk," where sit-down dining would feature Queensland beef, seafood, and tropical fruit crepes; and T-6, "The Cock and Bull," a burger bar and fried chicken joint. These were my four restaurants for which to test menus, formulate bulk recipes, hire staff, and run, once the fair opened its gates.

But there was one more establishment at the other end of the fair: The Americana Food Village was also emerging from construction dust. The building style was reminiscent of the European Village at Expo '84 but featured seven regions of American food, including Texas barbecue, New York deli, Polynesian, and yes, Creole and Cajun. This restaurant had been given to an Australian-by-marriage from Canada named Mark Dunn, a former hotel sous chef with a Northern Hemisphere–style ego—the likes of which I hadn't at all missed so far, being in the friendly Aussie world of smiles, winks, and nods.

How could a Canadian know how to prepare American food anyway? Did Chuck give me the Boardwalk because it was bigger and I had more experience? That must have been it. But I was the one who had cooked a New Orleans dinner at Chuck's house in Vancouver, not this Australian-dwelling Canadian know-it-all. In the test kitchen, I had already begun formulating the high-volume recipes for the seasoning mixes and American dishes when Mark Dunn arrived on the scene to spend most of his time cultivating his ego through his endless conversations with local suppliers and newly hired cook-helpers.

Creole seasoning by the kilo, shrimp Creole and gumbo by the liter, jambalaya measured out by kilos of rice and liters of shrimp stock, coconut shrimp garnished with a sauce of orange marmalade, lime, and cilantro, techniques for slow-roasting Hawaiian *kalua* pork. For all these items, I buzzed about the kitchen, tasted, wrote down measurements, costed the ingredients, calculated and costed the portion, and then followed recipes, tweaked until perfect in taste, ease of production, and value.

Looking back, I suppose maybe, just maybe Mark Dunn was a little intimidated by my fair experience and my silent and formidable relationship with the big man Chuck. I now know that's how many men act, even some women: When their egos are threatened, they overcompensate by becoming dickheads. And although comfortable in my tasks in the test kitchen, I was still insecure about my lack of formal training, which apparently Mark Dunn had, and my fragile psyche fell down a notch each time he criticized or tried to one-up me. Which appeared to be his mission each day.

"You should always mix your cornstarch and water with your fingers, not a whip, to avoid lumps," he said over my shoulder at the stove one morning while I was thickening a batch of teriyaki sauce, a simple recipe I'd learned from Roy at the Mana Kai, and which had never contained lumps.

I wanted to say something derogatory about cooking school, remembering when CIA grad Chris at Arnaud's got thrown out of the kitchen for putting the omelet under the broiler, but instead replied with, "Are the J-crumbs here for the shrimp?"

"I called my supplier. They'll be here by ten."

My supplier.

We were preparing the Polynesian menu items, which meant that I was doing most of the food for the afternoon tasting while Mark Dunn focused on staffing and other organizational tasks of getting his operation ready— when he wasn't instructing me how to thicken a sauce.

Other tasks were ongoing in the test kitchen, like finding the right hot dog. The Australian hot dog was a limp little red-dye-number-something wiener with gray guts and a taste reminiscent of orange peels. This would not do for the Chicago-style hot dog, and it had already been determined that neither Hebrew National nor Nathan's would be able to export volumes of their dogs to Australia on such short notice. So we had to teach a local company how to make an American hot dog.

Daily, the samples rolled in from different meat suppliers. I directed the size, color, and cost, knowing exactly what Chuck wanted there, and let Mark Dunn ramble on with *his* suppliers about flavor—tubified meat scraps not being my bailiwick. Besides, the culinary school grad needed something to do besides bother me.

Sometimes in the test kitchen world of competitive egos and my lack of quick comebacks to Mark Dunn's subtle digs, I would catch a break. Chuck Sanders never played favorites with either of his two chefs; he simply said what he thought at all times. But at one afternoon tasting, Chuck had great praise for whichever one of his chefs came up with slicing the green onions on a bias.

That would be me. It was almost silly, his reverence for the little green things sprinkled upon the shrimp stir-fry on his plate, but I basked in every minute of his rare gush of praise.

"Who thought of this?" he said at first, holding up a forked glossy shrimp, two delicate hollow scallion ovals stuck to it like little green remora. Mark and I froze, each thinking, *Uh-oh, what'd I do?*

"W–hat?" I asked with some hesitation.

"The green onions! Cut on an angle like this—these are so, so classy, they give the dish an elegant flair. Who thought of this?"

I hadn't *thought* of it really; sometimes I do nice-looking things like slice green onions on a bias. Or had I picked that up from a sushi bar somewhere? "I did," I said proudly.

Chuck looked at the shrimp again before shoving it into his mouth. "I want all the green onions for the Polynesian menu cut this way. It's genius."

And what I wanted to say to Mark Dunn was, "Ha!"

Running the Boardwalk Restaurants would turn out to have some advantages over the Americana Food Village. Instead of managing one joint, I'd have chefs under me to manage my four restaurants. I was upper management, responsible for hiring middle chefs to carry out the ways of Chuck Sanders and my own for a smooth and profitable fair.

Laurie, my star at F-4 burgers in Vancouver, came over to run Food on the Walk. Her boyfriend, Don, would manage the night prep and receiving crew. I hired an Aussie named Murray to run the buffet restaurant. Andrew, an Aussie with fine dining experience, would be chef at Top O' the Walk. A Canadian named Stephen who had managed the Unicorn Pub at Vancouver's fair would run the Cock and Bull. Rumor had it there was a cluster of Canadians, of which Stephen was one, who had been brought over by the Irish Rovers Unicorn Pub and dumped when that company pulled out of their concession at the last minute. Chuck heard the rumor and sent Michael after the group of fair-seasoned Canadian managers to scoop them up before they returned to Canada. I got Stephen.

The days leading up to the fair's opening were full of work and adventure, while my ragtag crew of chefs built their kitchens with staff that I interviewed and screened for them. At banquet tables pushed together in the test kitchen, we commiserated over staff selections: "Ron has fine dining experience and he's English," I said to Andrew, passing the employment application to him. Andrew had collected a crew of young Brits—Pommies—on temporary visas and many knew each other. So most English applicants I handed over to Andrew. To Stephen I said, "Al's coming over from the Chick-Inn downtown, could be your fryer guy." To Laurie I gave young and obedient ones, to run the food court windows at T-49. Murray hired cronies from a previous job of his, running each by me for a stamp of approval. Mark Dunn interviewed his own staff, he and I finishing up the last few volume recipes and hot dog selections between applicants.

We built our crews by day and went to the pub at night. Nights in Brisbane were crisp; my skin read the temperature to be in the sixties, since my brain couldn't compute the Celsius readings and the fact that it was autumn in March. Nights walking to the pub, my neck tilted back, looking at the strange stars decorating the sky, I could barely contain my excitement at this experience I was blessed with.

The newly restored Ship Inn had opened early on the site, a perfect spot for fair management to continue their planning over a few pints of Castlemaine Four-X beer. Everything was coming together: staffing, food, menus, schedules, recipes, and training. Chuck Sanders didn't bother us much. He'd hired all the Chinese cooks for the Chinese section of T-49 and put Michael in charge of hiring Don's midnight crew, but otherwise, my four chefs and I and Mark Dunn (who demurred a bit once I had Andrew, Stephen, Murray, and Laurie as my minions) were left on our own to pull things together in the kitchens.

Here in Australia, my tissue-thin marriage to Michael was overshadowed by the hustle and bustle of pre-Expo work. As we had in Vancouver, he and I mostly talked about work, aspired to improve Chuck's systems, and prided ourselves in being his dream team. But there was this business-oriented life with Michael, and then there was the fun of hanging out with my own kind, my chefs, a group in which Michael did not belong. Our separation started gradually, with my preference to stay within my group, then ratcheted up notch by notch as the fair gained momentum.

As I walked the site wearing a hard hat, the vision of what was to come became more evident each day, as workmen toiled under the kiss of the fall sun, round-the-clock toward April 30, when the festivities would begin. The theme of Expo '88 was "Leisure in the Age of Technology," and from the edge of the Brisbane River rose a ninety-eight-acre sun-sail-covered extravaganza of international pavilions, featuring some countries that hadn't been at the previous two fairs. Fiji, Vanuatu, and Tonga were set in the Pacific Village's tropical growth, where shirtless natives put the finishing touches on the traditional woven roofs of their hut-style pavilions. This area reminded me of Hawaii, which added to the thrill of the fair's progress. New Zealand had a huge presence here, so did England. Japan was surrounded by serene gardens calling up grade-school field trips at Oahu's green and misted Valley of the Temples. The Munich Haus was anchored at the opposite end of the site from the Boardwalk Restaurants, and I was thankful for the lack of German food on all my menus. Excitement built in me on these dusty excursions around the site, not only for the great tasks ahead but also for the collective giddiness felt all over Brisbane. "Oh, you're here for Expo," a waitress would say to Michael and me at a local pub, flashing us a proud smile.

The laid-back Aussies, the sunny clear days, the upward sweeping sail-like images all around the fair, the four restaurants I'd soon be running, and the fact I still couldn't set the clock on the stove . . . there was no time for my usual longings to permeate the dreamlike aura of this place. Armand receded into memory. Albert was like a childhood buddy outgrown and left in the old neighborhood. Michael felt like part of my job. I had two new lovers now: Australia, and my job as executive chef. For now, I had arrived.

CHAPTER 20

TOGETHER WE'LL SHOW THE WORLD: WORLD EXPO '88

AT 6 A.M. I'M IN THE T-49 WALK-IN, half a pint of TruMoo chocolate milk in one hand and a prep sheet and pen in the other. I have floated on to the Boardwalk in the dark, the sun just now a suggestion in the humid cool air. I'd been awakened at 3:14 a.m. by my beeper, whose little red screen broadcasted to my bleary eyes, *Dale drunk, sent home. Will be short on prep.* This prompted me to fumble for the phone and call Robert, my ex-con night shift supervisor, who'd taken Don's place when Don split up with Laurie and quit.

"Be sure to get all pasta cooked, need the stove clear in the morning," I told him. "I'll be there early, need a little more shut-eye." I fell back into the pillows of my empty bed in my new apartment, for Michael and I have also split up.

At seven Laurie arrives. I fill her in and she calls in extra forces to make up for last night's staff shortage. At eight the cooks show up: Aussies, Pommies, and Kiwis, this local slang making my crew sound like a fruit basket. The sun is now full bore in the Brisbane blue sky, its lemony light blazing on the empty boardwalk like a spotlight.

With the hub of the Boardwalk Restaurants, T-49, now coordinated, I venture over to the buffet to check on Murray and his crew. His kitchen usually smells like curry, Murray's well-received Australian answer for left-overs. All leftovers funnel to Murray's kitchen and his job is to repurpose them into something luscious for the buffet. Sometimes with mixed results.

"Morning, Chef!" says Murray brightly.

"Smells good in here, Chef!"

"Thanks, Chef!"

I scan the kitchen prep and back door areas. "Appears the cleaning check-list is working?"

Murray, a round young man, looks down at first, his scolding earlier in the fair for not supervising his closing crew having apparently scarred his ego for life. "Yes, Chef."

"You need anything?" I head for his walk-in for a quick mental inventory.

"No, Chef."

Then I take a brief cruise through the Cock and Bull, now run by for-mer Chick-Inn cook Al; Canadian Stephen has been moved out of my ruling realm to Mark Dunn's kitchen. Al, like Stephen, needs little supervision or guidance, and the chicken and burger joint runs like a top.

"Need anything, Al?"

"All good, Chef."

Upstairs at T-4, Andrew nurses a hangover with coffee and a salad at his desk in the rear corner of the kitchen. He and Stephen went on somewhere from the Plough last night and I don't want to know. At the top of the stairs I say, "Chef!"

"Chef," he responds adoringly, as he looks downward at his untouched salad, then over to his singing cooks.

The Pommies are prepping at two stainless steel tables pushed together in the center of the kitchen. With a cutting board in front of each of them, they are singing Motown, their staccato knife-chopping creating a unified drum-beat to their harmonies. Discovering that London-dwellers have a thing for Motown is just another absurdity that makes me love Australia. And because of the singing Pommies, Andrew's kitchen always gets an A for morale. They look up when I breeze past toward the walk-in cooler. "Hey, Chef," "Hey, Chef," "Hey, Chef . . ." they each say in turn, as if a rehearsed part of their chorus. The Pommies, a calm, happy, and focused bunch. A contrast to the stressed-out Andrew.

Andrew's walk-in is empty, not restocked from the downstairs main unit, the first task of all my chefs in the morning. "Andrew!" I yell from the cave-like chill.

"I know, Chef . . ."

"Get it together, man; you'll overwork your happy staff, sending them downstairs for everything." I'm in his office now, glowering at him.

He only nods.

"Delegate if you can't do it. W-who do you want to delegate to?"

"I'll take care of it," he says, and rises from his chair. "Paul?" he yells toward the singing group. I go over to the cooking line to make sure the croutons have been baked with butter and herbs, not fried in the deep fryer as has been done on occasion.

Back downstairs at T-49 I cruise the stations, entering at Belgian Waffle with a nod, stopping in Tex-Mex to check the hand-rolled enchiladas, scanning the fruit salad cutters in the fruit station, avoiding the ice cream station (remember, I don't do ice cream), lifting the metal lids from Italian sauces in Italy's steam table. "Hi, Maria," I say to the Italian woman Chuck found to work Italy. Maria has the Italian mamma look he wanted, and Laurie and I taught her to cook. We're proud of our protégé, for she can work circles around many of the other cooks. Right now she's all set, stocked, and ready, and helping the Chinese cooks cut vegetables, looking like the novelty she is to them. Behind Maria, a double conveyor oven cranks out garlic bread and soon it will crank out pizzas for the day rush. Unwanted memories of Expo '84's pizza station flood in every time I pass through this pizza station: Jimmy James's thumb squirting blood, the frequently missing Willie, perpetual holes in pizza dough, the hole in my heart that has never been filled. In fact, I don't even eat pizza anymore.

Walking behind the Chinese cooks—because they are pretty much self-supervised and create no drama whatsoever—I'm in Greece, a station that attracts much drama, or creates it, I can't be sure which. Laurie is here, lips clenched, shoving over the young Kiwi who is obviously late (just now tying his apron) while she hefts the spiked meat onto the vertical gyro grill. "You need to get this going first thing, ay? Go get the salad mix, stock your salad fridge. Don't be late anymore—"

"You need anything, Laurie?"

"Check the guys in Burgers, I—" Shaking her head, she turns on the grill and the meat begins to rotate.

"On my way." I look at my watch: 9:40. Twenty minutes 'til showtime, not enough time for the gyro meat to cook. "Any sliced meat left from last night?"

"Oh! Not sure yet." She rummages through the under-counter refrigerator and hauls out a one-third-sized pan of last night's sliced gyro meat.

"Give it to Maria to heat. I'll check Burgers."

Laurie nods and we take off in opposite directions.

At 9:45 the opening music starts, and my stomach acids respond to the great rush of music and song: "It's gonna be great and I just can't wait . . . we'll show the world, together we'll show the world . . ." Many of us can't help but mouth the words to the fair's theme song by now, every morning hearing this woman sing how great it's going to be. If we don't run out of food, that is.

Just after 10 a.m., all gates have opened and tens of thousands of people rush in on all sides of the fair, Expo passes and money in hands, ready to explore the mini-world. And many of these people are, well, hungry. "Don't these people eat breakfast?" I say to Laurie, both of us back in the Greek station to make sure the moody little Kiwi can handle a six-hour rush. The previously serene view of the empty sun-bathed Boardwalk and Brisbane River beyond is now filled with bobbing heads of those lining up for ice cream, waffles, fruit, or burgers, usually the first stations to get a pre-lunch hit.

At 11 a.m. I do a post-opening check-in at the other restaurants. By noon the Boardwalk is packed, lines are everywhere, and food is flying out of service windows and kitchens in all four restaurants and I roam a figure-eight throughout all of them: an arc through the semicircular T-49, through the Ultimate Buffet on to Cock and Bull and up the stairs to T-4, checking, tasting, helping, quashing little fires before they become big ones. At 1:10 I pull my beeper off my belt loop to read, *T4 needs tomatoes . . .* I know where there are extra tomatoes. I hustle over to Murray's kitchen, snag a box from the walk-in, heft the case above my head to avoid hitting the crowd, and head up the rear steps of T-4 to save the day.

At 2 p.m. I'm sheltered away in the T-49 mini-cave of an office, checking the schedule, when manager John the Greek (grinning, always flirtatious) tells me there's someone at the fruit salad station to see me. A tall man in a gray business suit stands on the other side of the counter carrying a briefcase—an alarming sight, actually. But he introduces himself as Mr. So-and-So from the Queensland Pavilion and he's heard I have pins to trade. Do I have extras of Vanuatu or the French Pavilion? I ask what he has to offer, dash back to the office to get my booty (pinned onto a cloth rice sack and rolled up) and we strike a deal right there over chopped melon and strawberries. I trade him one 1986 Expo Ernie pin for an extra Fiji and an opening day Singapore, and we trade some other minor 1988 pins. I guess I'm sought-out in the Expo pin-trading world: "Go see that little girl chef on the Boardwalk; she's collected pins from three fairs and has some real rare ones."

At 2:30 the avalanche of food out the door slows and breaks begin. Michael comes around carrying his Maxwell Smart–sized portable phone and collects the cashier's banks. Michael handles mostly the Americana now, and Dick Sanders the Boardwalk—Chuck's strategy of peacekeeping after his two top executives split up over the Cock and Bull Canadian, Stephen (me), and an accounting girl in the office (Michael). We nod at each other and get on with our tasks. I do a post-lunch rush figure-eight check through all the restaurants, then meet smiling Stephen, who's walked over from the Americana, his new cooking post with new boss Mark Dunn, to join me for coffee at a Boardwalk table and compare notes about our days.

The supercharged air calms while we sit in our bubble, and we are immune to the order-calling, pan-clanking mechanics of the machine we help to propel throughout the day and night. In the protective aura of each other, we chitchat, nod, and grin. A hint of something in our futures hangs between us, like a tease. Then we stand, the sun casting an angelic sheen to our starchy whites; I take the cups, we smile, mini-bow, and walk away from each other to our respective dragon-slaying stations on opposite ends of the fair.

At 3:30 the Boardwalk Restaurants are staffed, stocked, and prepping for the night, and now is my opportunity to get away if I can. On good days I have an hour to wander through the international pavilions, walk the silent Japanese Gardens, explore the Pacific Village, take photographs, search for new pin releases at pavilion gift shops. My favorite find is a little wine bar nestled between the New South Wales and Victoria pavilions. Falling into its cellar-like atmosphere is the relief I need from the cacophonous and pounding Expo workaday. In the welcoming dark, a two-dollar glass of white wine from the currently un-exported South Australia wine regions is my salvation. I sit with a glass of Sauvignon Blanc and gaze behind the bar into the pastel poster of New South Wales vineyards, fortifying myself for the next six hours.

One evening I take my break late and detour through the Japan Pavilion, since the line is short. Stepping into a cocoon of lute music and giant screens of falling cherry blossoms is too much for me, the contrast to my exhaustive day so great. I push a button on a smaller screen on the wall, calling up a scene of people lounging in outdoor hot springs. Snow falls into the hot water, as steam rises from it and a geisha-type girl arrives with a platter of sushi for the naked water-dwellers. Way too much. I dash back to the Boardwalk, do a figure-eight through all the restaurants, leave instructions for all, change out of my whites, and hail a cab to drop me at the nearest sushi bar in Brisbane.

You'd expect that sushi in Australia should be awesome, being so much closer to Japan, and in my experience this is precisely so. On that evening I belly up to the sushi bar with a nod to the cutter, and I order miso soup and sake from the Japanese waitress. Feeling like I've been poked full of holes to let the tension out, my deflated self orders hamachi, saba, ikura (with quail egg), toro, and ika. The sushi cutter, I learn through his broken Australian-accented English, has been here only a few months. When I tell him I'm from Hawaii, he beams at me. As I'm finishing up my sake and digesting my fresh meal, my stress-releasing holes all closed up, my new cutter friend puts up a finger, signaling me to wait, and says, "I make for you, a spec-i-al-ity."

He pulls a little slab of hamachi from the refrigerated case in front of him and expertly slices off a quarter-inch piece of the creamy white meat. He cuts a scallion into thin rounds, then begins to mash the fish and onion into a paste with the tip of his knife. Reforming the puree over the rice, he garnishes my dessert with slivers of more scallion and some radish sprouts. Melt-in-your-mouth exquisite. My pager is quiet in my purse, my brain on a temporary pause. I may be thinking a little of my future: of an impending divorce, of a union with Stephen. I order another sake. I do not go back to work on this night.

On another night after a wine bar break, on my return approach to the Boardwalk, I see Dick Sanders leaning on the railing, looking at the Brisbane River, pensive as usual. I join him for a check-in and for any words of wisdom he may impart. And there are some on this day, sort of. Regarding the recent concentration of daily health inspections due to an outbreak of *E. coli* at an unrelated restaurant across the fair (resulting in very bad press), all Expo restaurants have been required to purchase disposable rubber gloves by the truckload and enforce absurd glove-wearing rules. Gloves must be thrown away after touching one kind of food, then replaced with a fresh pair. The math of this, with one hundred cooks going through multiple pairs of gloves per day at so much per glove, gets way too close to infinity. Dick tells me that last night he went into the men's restroom and one of my Chinese cooks dashed in wearing his gloves, took a whiz, washed his gloved hands, and returned to the kitchen.

"Well, he washed his hands," I joke.

"Yes, but . . ." says Dick, in his usually serious tone, but I see his mouth turn up slightly.

"Okay, I'll take care of it."

The 5 to 6 p.m. pre-dinner-rush routine is the same as the 10 to 11 a.m. pre-lunch-rush routine: I figure-eight through the restaurants, checking on the evening staff, food pars, schedules, sales numbers, steam tables, attitudes. The sky purples over the river. The dinner rush hits.

Chuck Sanders strolls through T-49 around seven; he's carrying a package of disposable oval plates. I continue my station checks and when I'm back near Italy again, he calls me over.

He has laid out on the counter two of the oval plates, which I now see are tri-compartmentalized. On one plate's large section, fettuccini Alfredo has been dished up and on the other, spaghetti with meatballs. Each plate has a hunk of garlic bread in another compartment. The third compartment is empty.

"Do you think," Chuck asks, "if we put something else on this plate, say, Jell-O for example, we can charge $7.45 for it?"

I look up at the menu board on the wall, which lists the pasta and garlic bread combinations at $6.25. *Jell-O?* Yuck. I look at the plates for a moment, as if contemplating the question but actually mustering my confidence to tell him the truth, not what he wants to hear. The wine makes my face flush, but I knuckle under and speak. "I-I think you'd be insulting their intelligence. Who even likes Jell-O? W-why don't you just raise the price to $6.95 and d-don't change anything." My heart is pounding, having essentially told off my boss. I dash off to monitor the dinner rush. (The next day the prices on the menu board are changed to $6.95.)

It's now 7:30 p.m., and time to eat. Having only nibbled all day, I ask the Chinese cooks, who all have charming Australian accents, for half an order of shrimp stir-fry, which is seared and tossed with a clank-a-clank of metal spatula against metal wok. Eating in the cave-office, my back to the door, I review the inventory sheets of all walk-ins and storage rooms and begin calling in orders that will arrive between midnight and six. For an hour I sit and plan the next day's deliveries and prep lists, consider the schedule, and make any necessary changes, for there is staff attrition: disappearances, jail visits, stressed-out cooks who can't take the pressure of hashing out food for eight hours solid.

At eight o'clock I make another sweep through the kitchens, most of which are winding down. Upstairs T-4 is still backed up on the sauté line; sheet pan trays of pre-sautéed barramundi fillets are waiting to be fast-fired with a serving of Moreton Bay bugs, a lobster-like crustacean endearingly called "bug meat" by the Aussies. I make some dessert crepes in the open display kitchen and help Pommie Paul expedite orders through the pickup window. At nine it's one last rummage through the walk-ins, confirming I've ordered everything required for the next day's rushes. At nine forty-five music starts up, blasting through giant invisible speakers to announce the closing parade that passes in front of the Boardwalk, and I stop to watch it. A lighted Qantas airplane, an articulated float of giant bugs, and a bright white-winged unicorn roll by on invisible wheels, with satin-skirted dancers juggling lighted balls moving and jiving to the musical backdrop of Michael Jackson's "Enjoy Yourself."

Parade over, the theme song starts up again, and the Boardwalk swells with people viewing the fireworks and laser light show over the river. The last ice cream cone has been sold, cash register banks have been collected by Dick Sanders and whisked off somewhere, the pizza oven has made its last creaky rotation for the day, and closing and cleaning checklists are monitored.

Then it's back to the Plough or the Ship, where Stephen, grinning at me, will meet us Boardwalk chefs for drinks and gossip, all of us unwinding as much as we can before it's time to return to another day, where fairgoers have little idea about what goes on behind the scenes to produce their hot dog, plate of stir-fry, slice of pizza, or sautéed barramundi with bug meat.

CHAPTER 21

GOING WALKABOUT: A TRAVELOGUE CHAPTER

STANDING IN CHEF ANDREW'S SUNNY KITCHEN in suburban Brisbane, I ask him about his heritage. He's twenty-four, and like many Aussies his age, he owns his home and has a good education from the impeccable Queensland public school system. "Ah, fuck de English! Dey couldn't put us down; dey gave us this beautiful country anyhow." He shrugs, as if shrugging off his ancestry of bread thieves and murderers.

It was 1787 when the British government started a colony in Australia as one of their many efforts to populate the world. Only Australia was 10,000 miles away, a remote outpost, practically another planet, and, therefore, a jail. More than 160,000 criminals and convicts were exiled into dystopia and ignored. This was my kind of place!

"And now the Brits come here on holiday," I say, "and you have a kitchen full of them at T-4."

"Yeah, no biggie," says Andrew. He scoops up three cans of Four-X beer from a shelf in the vintage yellow Frigidaire and we walk out down the back porch steps to the yard, where Stephen is sunning himself in a plastic lawn chair.

I have stumbled into a comfortable groove with these chefs, these friends, amid the magical sunshine and cool eeriness of Australia. It all makes me feel so special, as if no one else gets to have all this fun, all this friendship, all these *experiences*. And to think I hadn't wanted to come and work this fair; I'd had notions of suburban child-rearing or some such bullshit. My life right then was incredibly fulfilling, fun, and thrilling. I was the luckiest girl in the world.

Moreton Bay, Stradbroke Island, Mooloolaba, Sunshine Coast, Colored Sands, Gold Coast, Jondaryan Woolshed, Brisbane River Cruise, Lone Pine Koala Sanctuary, Castlemaine Four-X pubs aplenty—these were day and overnight trips Stephen and I enjoyed on our weekly coordinated mutual day off. While he seemed content to toodle around Brisbane, I was a maniac with a map, a mission, and a newfound appreciation of driving on the left with the boss's car. Exploration was my salvation from the endless workdays, and what better place to explore than this warm and friendly land Down Under? On days off Stephen and I were "Off—off like a bucket of prawns in the sun," for places for beer, breathtaking sights, and good food.

Brisbane proper had to be explored first, of course. Early on in the fair, and in our courtship, we took the Brisbane River Cruise, which drifted up (or was it down?) river to a remote enclave away from the city where the city bats slept by day, clustered high up in the gum trees like stringers of fish. It was like Transylvania, I thought, looking up at the sticky white hides, their smoky gray-black exteriors hidden under sleep-closed wings. Every few seconds a bat would drift from one tree to the next and rehook himself to another slumbering cluster. Hmm . . . a bad dream? Does his sleep-mate have bad breath? It was eerie and quiet and the thought *of all these bats* flying around the city at night, well.

The river cruise ended at a kangaroo sanctuary and this destination proved to be amusing and adorable, the friendly marsupials lolling about, ready to become part of a hammy photo. Look, Ma! I struck a pose behind an oblivious mama with a baby hanging from her pouch—a photo I did send home to Mom.

Exploring with Stephen meant exploring with a man amenable to all my whims, one who apparently was not at all bothered by my inner control freak. During those long-ago days I'd spent with Armand, I had been the follower, the student, and he the teacher, leader, and planner of events. With Michael we were equal, and he didn't do much of anything, so my explorations of

Vancouver were on my own. But I was Stephen's boss, so when it came to excursion planning I took charge of my precious day off, and Stephen was a willing accomplice. Exploring new places was better than anything I'd experienced before, and my excitement was boundless. It was good to have company driving on the wrong side of the road.

And then there was the food. John the Greek, T-49's day manager, was part of an extended Greek family and one of his so-called uncles owned Café Paradise in Paddington, an adjacent Brisbane burb. Café Paradise was BYOB—a category of ethnic restaurant that proved always to have excellent food at affordable prices. You could gorge for less than ten bucks, including a tip. Many BYO nights involved a big table with our Canadian and Aussie Expo compatriots, bringing vodka, beer, and wine. At Café Paradise we would find ourselves at a family table out on the stone patio, tummies full of taramasalata, smoked octopus, lamb kebabs, and bathtub ouzo made by someone's so-called grandpa, tossing cheap clay plates at the outdoor fireplace. This—getting drunk and throwing plates—I was told was a Greek tradition. Nowhere since have I had Greek food that good.

Indulgence in the affordable ethnic BYOs sometimes was supplanted by a venture to an upscale seafood restaurant, for all seafood restaurants were upscale in Brisbane. Rambling wooden seafood houses on the river lit with neon or hotel seafood buffets welcomed us with Australian shrimp, fresh oysters on the half shell, sautéed fillets of barramundi (the local fish), and Moreton Bay bugs drenched in butter and lemon. These were splurge nights with lots of Australian wine and a big dinner bill to split among us.

It felt as though nothing was expected of me on these food and drink fests except to have fun, talk when I wanted to, observe a lot, drink a lot, and pay my portion of the bill. I was the executive chef, after all, and I was dating the popular Stephen. I felt equal to everybody for a change, not the insecure and stuttering teen sitting on the beach outside the Rusty Harpoon aching to fit in somewhere. I was now twenty-seven years old and I'd found a place to fit in: in a foreign country, with three nationalities of restaurant workers prone to drug abuse and alcoholism. I fit here just fine.

Stephen and I alternated our overnight adventures between the Gold Coast to the south of Brisbane—more populated, and the place for surfing—and the Sunshine Coast to the north. The Sunshine Coast was rural, crafty, and funky, and my favorite of the two. We were more apt to find a cheaper little motel near the two-lane main street in Coolum Beach or Sunshine Beach, where quaint craft shops and BYO restaurants awaited our perusing. The Sunshine Coast is where I first discovered Chefwear in a local shop, a stylish combo of white wraparound chef pants and a coat with faux buttons and a high collar. When I tried it on in the curtained changing room, I saw that I was a chef with a *figure*—a new and slim figure I liked very much, after a stress-induced weight drop from opening the restaurants, drinking, and infidelity. I purchased a size small right away, with visions of introducing this new line of chef's uniforms in the US. I would become rich! Of course, Chefwear and many copycats have since been introduced in the States, unfortunately not by me. But I saw them first.

On one trip we headed farther up the coast, because I'd been lured by a brochure for a place called Noosa Heads and its remote, colored sands. Here we overnighted at the Jolly Jumbuck Homestead, and the next morning we left at dawn in a jalopy that drove us and a handful of other tourists along miles of deserted beach, only accessible by four-wheel drive. The white sands and aqua South Pacific Ocean were separated from civilization by cliffs of what looked like red-and-pink rock but were really made of ancient, talc-like sand. Stephen and I had a beach lunch, swam in the cool salty waves, climbed the sandy cliffs, saw a family of spotted stingrays in a lagoon, and explored a beached barge-wreck called the Cherry Venture. We were silent all day, so stunned by the pristine beauty and our luck to have experienced it. The beauty and excitement of this place lulled us both into a dreamlike state. Which surely was true love, wasn't it?

On another such excursion filled with beauty, we were sitting in the sun at an outdoor mustard-colored Four-X pub overlooking the blue waves of Stradbroke Island, where we'd seen surfing porpoises during a morning walk. The pints of Four-X were cold, the wind soft on our skin, and Stephen looked at me with an uncharacteristic seriousness and asked, "So, what are you doing the rest of your life?"

So this was it, then. Not the whirlwind rush of Armand, not the dead dullness of Michael. A man who respected me and my whims. A man who would do what I wanted. Who would leave Canada for New Orleans. A fellow cook. A man with a sense of humor, who liked to have fun. A man who would need a Green Card. A man who loved Australia like I did. A man who liked to party. A handsome, boyish-looking man. A pal.

So my response that day, my shoulders burnt from blazing Southern Hemisphere sun, and thinking that Michael had simply been my vehicle to get to Australia to meet Stephen, was this: "Guess I'm divorcing Michael."

Dining in the little restaurants along the Sunshine Coast always highlighted our beach excursions. The most memorable meal was an appetizer of goat cheese wrapped in large lime leaves, then grilled over a wood fire. Sitting on a small deck under the kiss of a fuchsia dusk, sunburned shoulders cooling in the breeze, we opened the packets of lightly charred lime leaf to find inside gifts of soft, warm cheese. The smoky hint of lime was so intriguing I felt like I knew nothing at all about food as I ate it, which impressed me immensely. I took a menu from this sunny little place for my collection and it was as beautiful as that appetizer: rolled-up parchment with a satin ribbon and fancy calligraphy introducing the menu items. (Several years ago, unfortunately, tired of ferrying around from move to move a huge accordion file of menus, including the Marketplace's—Beef Wellington: $9.00—from 1977, I tossed them out, figuring I would never need them for anything, right? Of course there was no way of knowing at the time that I was going to write this book.)

In Queensland you can see a pub from a mile away, because in and around Brisbane anyway they all have the same paint job: Castlemaine Four-X mustard yellow slashed with four blood-red Xs. Farther out into the country, Foster's had obviously sanctioned some paint jobs because occasionally a pub had blue, white, and red paint. At first, the Aussie hotels and package stores excited me. Two-story wooden structures sometimes still advertised rooms upstairs; reminiscent of Wild West cattle-rustling, they were old and dusty with a bartender to match. Eager for some history and good storytelling, I'd belly up to the bar. With my two Minoltas, I took pictures of these pubs inside and out, stopping the car for a picture and a pint every time I saw a Four-X pub in a remote town, on an empty road, or on a beach. "I'm working on a photo essay of Australian bars," I told Stephen, who would nod, smile, and take a gulp of his pint.

As similar as they were on the outside, they were similar on the inside, too. Once I had the pictures arranged in my album, this was obvious. (Fortunately, I still have these pictures.) It's as if one bar followed us around: always the same paint on the outside, same architecture, same warped bar top, same craggy bartender, same drunk old man sitting on a lone stool, same working men sitting at a round table, slamming down shots and speaking in drunken Aussie rhyming slang. "Young an' frisky on the Cain and Able"—whiskey is on the table. That one was translated for me once, so I get it, sort of. And we'd say "hit the frog and toad" when we meant hit the road. But when the barflies were going at rhyming slang full tilt, I understood not a word; they may as well have been speaking Gaelic.

What we Northern Hemisphere dwellers know as summer months merging into fall, July and August in Brisbane were chilly winter months merging into spring. As October approached, the fair plowed onward toward its conclusion. The camaraderie cultivated between Stephen and the rest of his Canadian merry managers and Andrew and his Pommie crew, and the fact that the two men were best drinking friends or best pals or whatever bromance had formed between them, created a sense of family of which I was comfortably a part. Our friendships and seemingly familial fun—dining, drinking, throwing plates at Paradise Cafe, day-tripping—were all doomed of course, for soon the fair would end, the Pommies would return to England, the Canadians back to Canada, and the rest of us would disperse. This fact put a needy edge to our bliss, because permanence was not part of this gig and we all feared the end of it, especially me, since these happy, frazzled people were my first true tribe. Desperate to make the most of our time together, drinking and copulation accelerated among the cooks and managers, and the closer we got to the fair's end, the more teary faces arrived at work each day. Since I was everybody's boss and knew that we all needed one last blast together, I took it upon myself to plan a post-fair trip where we all could eat, drink, cry, explore, and consider our next moves, without the interruption of work.

Oz-Oasis Resorts was a big affordable campsite with permanent six-people tents in the coastal town of MacKay, about six hundred miles north of Brisbane. The town is about halfway up the east coast to Cairns and the Great Barrier Reef, where Stephen and I planned to venture to after ten days in the tent village. When I'd selected Oz-Oasis, I had no idea November would bring a muggy ninety degrees and that residing in bright orange-and-green tents with no circulation would amplify this to a hundred degrees—no wonder it was cheap!

So we only slept in the tents, or ran inside them for cover each afternoon when the sky swelled with bruised, humidity-filled clouds that exploded onto our bathing-suited, beer-filled selves. "Great idea, Chef!" became the laughing mantra, to which I responded, "I'm a chef, not a travel agent."

But life at Oz was just what we all needed after the daily freight train of Expo. Fifteen of us were scattered through three tents arranged in a cluster, so we had our own village. We rose early each day, drank cold beer and sat in the sun, swam in the pool and in the ocean, played board games in the open-air clubhouse, and took day trips around MacKay on rented mopeds. Couples had sprouted up among us: Canadian Lynn and Andrew, Canadian Paula and Pommie Paul, me and Stephen of course, and there were others, Pommie cooks and their girl pals, sometimes two couples breaking off to moped or ride horses, other times girls only going off together. I did not participate in these female excursions, being more comfortable hanging back with the guys. (Besides, I couldn't see putting on makeup in the heat, and didn't own any anyway.) We grilled out, sprayed our bare skin for mozzies (mosquitoes), and turned in late, long after the sun's heat left the village.

The long days in our tent village had rhythm, but after a few days I got bored with the aimless drinking that masked our communal angst about the future. I kept this notion to myself, that all this drinking was an excuse. If I'd been writing back then, I would have been doing it to ease the transition between ferociously employed and aimlessly unemployed. Being a rock-solid, income-producing workaholic hurled into the paper-white future of nothing-ness carried too much fear to bear.

So one morning, leaving Stephen and Andrew in their beach chairs with an ice chest of Four-X between them—"downing tinnies," as they say—I went into town and bought a fishing pole and some tackle. I needed something, and fishing, I believed, would satisfy it. The tent village Oz was surrounded by water, the Coral Sea and a sea-filled lagoon or river—not sure what official name it bore—an ever-contracting and expanding body of water that snaked behind our tents.

The thing I needed—time to consider what to do next—was satisfied greatly by rising at 7 a.m., while the other tents vibrated with snores, and hurling my baited line out into the watery, lagoon-ish thing. Bedecked in cap and anti-sun wear to ward off the blazing rays, I stood alone on the muddy shore, my pole anchoring me to the earth, absorbing MacKay's pristine colors and smells. I wished I could do this forever. Why did I need a job anyway? Why couldn't I just fish? Why couldn't I stay here and fish? (And never catch any fish, apparently.) Where were we going, Stephen and I? We'd agreed on New Orleans, ultimately, and that I looked forward to—I thought. I'd have to get my divorce over with eventually. But Stephen and I also wanted to stay in Australia longer, wanted our work visas renewed by a company that might want us. But who? Where? We were culinary orphans in this great land. The sparkling Coral Sea, the air singing hollow with quiet, save for bug hums and a few chirps in the distance, mangroves creeping along the muddy shore and the tide rushing out drastically—this serene setting was oblivious to the answers for my future, but soothing just the same.

In an hour the lagoon emptied, leaving a muddy track of itself. Fishing gear stowed in the tent, face flushed with sun and sweat and salt, I pulled a can of wet Four-X from the ice chest next to Andrew while he and Stephen hawed-hawed in drunken camaraderie.

I got a tide schedule and tried fishing during incoming tide, then outgoing tide, each little fishing venture fun and satisfying in a way but rendering no fish. Finally I got frustrated at being fishless and went to the office/country store to get some pointers. There on the bulletin board above the front desk was a small ad: "Fishing Excursions with Dave," with a picture of a small boat and a phone number. I called it, got the info, and went back to the tents to make a managerial announcement.

Two days later, eight of us, after splitting the half-day fishing fee and wearing panty hose to ward off jellyfish stings, as we'd been instructed, piled into Dave the Schoolteacher's twenty-two-foot boat. We'd driven in his Jeep, towing the boat into mud flats, where he said we had four hours to fish and return to the Jeep or the tide would come in and wash it away.

First stop, Eimeo Beach, "to pump for yabbies," he yelled above the motor to us. The air was hot, like cruising over water in an oven, but still salty and exciting. Minutes later, Dave beached the boat and pulled what looked like a bicycle pump and three small plastic baskets from behind his seat. The baskets had waist belts attached and one of these he handed to me, another to Andrew, and the other to Paul. Dave was already wearing his. I put on the belt basket and waited to see what came next.

At Eimeo Beach the tide had recently gone out and there were tide puddles in the fine, mud-like sand. Dave primed the pump in the air with a few quick motions, then jammed it into one of the sand puddles. The pump made a sucking noise, and then Dave shot its contents onto the drier sand, yelling, "Grab 'em!" as a dozen clear shrimp-like things with legs and snapping pinchers scrambled about. Now, I can grab a live shrimp from a bait bucket and skewer it onto my hook—but these things looked like inch-long cockroach larvae with pinchers. I held back at first, but knew that I, the one who had spearheaded this excursion, and who now wore a basket at my hip into which these pinching things would reside until fishing time, would have to stop acting like a girl and get into the fray.

On Dave's second release of the pump, I scrabbled on the sand, catching two yabbies, which tickled my palm before I jammed them into my basket. They clicked and clacked their angry pinchers once caged in the plastic on my hip, which made me feel like a cave person. And so it went on, pawing in the muck, the unsettling tickle on the palm, the knowledge that this was only half of it. We'd be fishing soon, and the yabby grab would continue, this time from the basket, and what would the things look like once speared with a hook? I looked at my watch: 9 a.m. A beer sounded good right about now.

Our baskets full of crabbing yabbies, we were off to Green Island. Now, there is fishing—what I had been doing all week—and there is catching, which is what we did that day. I'm certain we'd crossed into a time warp at uninhabited Green Island, where eucalyptus scrub gave way to powder-white sands decorated with silver driftwood, which gave way to an aqua ocean so plentiful with squirming whiting, we could have probably caught them with our hands and skipped that whole unpleasant yabby thing. We were cavemen: no rush of cars in our lives, no concern of jobs or money, each of us hauling up our catch with a yelp of pleasure, filling buckets, our skin toasting red in the golden sun. Once I pulled in something heavier than a whiting and braced myself to see what came in on my line. It was a spiny, toothy puffer fish, with puckered-up lips. Fish with lips tend to creep me out, so Dave de-hooked it for me and tossed it back into the waves to scare something smaller than a human.

When it was time to motor the boat back to the Jeep before high tide, we had nearly fifty whiting. Whiting are small and bony fish, but we had so many, and I had a crew of chefs ready to do my bidding. That night back at Camp Oz, downing tinnies aplenty around the giant grill, the Pommies deboned our fish on picnic tables, Lynn and Paula made salad, and I grilled. As I stood over the grill full of crackling little fish fillets, my head flush with beer and a day of sun, anchored in the present sweet hot air of Camp Oz with my mates, the angst of my future culinary endeavors subsided. Slightly.

After ten days at Oz the gang departed separately, with the plan to meet back in Brisbane for Christmas. Stephen and I headed northward to pursue jobs, to the heart of the Great Barrier Reef. Noel, former manager at T-4, was now managing a resort up there and we hoped he could help us. So off we went, renting a beat-up car and stopping for a night in the rain forest at the Kookilldoo Inn, where curious brown wallabies watched us eat dinner on the patio and shiny black bugs the size of silver dollars flew in through our open windows at night. We could've made a fortune selling window screens in that town.

Mission Beach was our stopping point the next day: a beach village reminiscent of pictures I'd seen of an uninhabited Waikiki in the forties, with its deserted palm-lined sandy beaches and groves of blooming plumeria trees. It appeared to be populated by only a few Aboriginals and some hippies. We drank in the generic Four-X pub, ate average Italian food in the local BYO, and the breezes that night were a degree cooler and salty, minus the black bugs, so we slept better there than we had in Kookilldoo.

In Cairns the next day, we rented a room at a charmless but bright motel and set off to find Noel, and hopefully jobs. Find him we did. But Noel was the assistant manager of resort operations and primarily managed the boat excursions out to the Great Barrier Reef, so a free snorkel dive turned out to be the only thing on our agenda, a consolation prize for our trek to the great hot north.

The shallow reef dive out in the middle of the ocean amid mountains of coral and Day-Glo tropical fish was thrilling, the Great Barrier Reef being one of the Seven Natural Wonders of the World and all. But as I kicked around with my fins, viewing the scene before me in the cold water, a pit formed in my stomach. My mind tallied the next few weeks like a ticker-tape machine. Three weeks until Christmas. New Year's in Sydney. First week of 1989 on Maui. Then off to New Orleans to find work. A school of thumb-sized cobalt-blue fish darted by and my thoughts paused for a split second. Stephen was treading water, looking down at a gray grouper in a deeper crevasse, the fish looking up at him. I had missed New Orleans since the day I'd moved away three years ago, but now those days of jambalaya, gumbo, Cajun music, and ancient architecture seemed so foreign. Was it wrong somehow to go back? Back in time? Why didn't I just move on? Why couldn't we stay here?

Stephen and I followed the group of snorkelers to where some underwater pointing and abovewater exclaiming distracted me. We swam up to the leg-waggling crowd to see a four-foot-long shark swimming slowly around a castle of maroon-and-tan coral, its grayness a dull contrast to the day's colorful show. Stephen and I looked at each other through our watery masks, blinking in communication: "Back to the boat for us!" We jettisoned off, mutually completing our snorkel dive.

As I was flying out of Sydney a month later, sadness hung over me like a weighted blanket. The Aussies had made me feel at home in their world, this perfect mix of tropical paradise and city, of mixed cultures and quirkiness. And I'd only made a dent traveling in Queensland; what about the Nullarbor—the single road across the Outback toward Ayers Rock and Perth? What about the other states: Tasmania, Victoria, New South Wales, and Western Australia with all that desert, rain forest, beach, fishing, sheep farms, wine country, and a plethora of generic pubs? And the food—I could live off giant steaks, barramundi, oysters, Moreton Bay bugs, and fresh tropical produce. I'd even learned to navigate the grocery stores. I'd miss Oz rock and roll, John Farnham, Jimmy Barnes, Men at Work, Crowded House, all those cassettes that got much road play in the boss's car during our day-off excursions. I knew how to drive left now too, so how would I navigate the right side again, back in the States? Nearly a year ago I'd arrived in this country married to one Canadian and I was now leaving with another, each of us bringing back a little piece of Australia in our hearts. Returning to the States would bring me closer to what I had avoided during my year in the Land Down Under: my insatiable quest for something I could not name, the hole in my heart where Armand had once been, my infidelities, my fears about where I would wind up. Eventually I would apply for residency in Australia and be denied. Somehow I knew flying out that day, seeing the gentle arc of the Brisbane River receding in the plane's window, that this experience was over and that I'd never be back. But it turned out I'd need these kind memories in the days to come.

CHAPTER 22

THE WORLD'S LUCKIEST FISHING VILLAGE

WITH THREE YEARS OF WACKY-PACED, high-volume, multicuisine management of World's Fair concessions under my belt, I was now ready to tuck into the serenity of a small or midsize fine-dining establishment. To manage a staff of, say, ten, rather than a hundred. To actually cook some things, make soups and sauces again, specials. To have food suppliers arrive in the daylight hours to show me products and gossip about my competition. To manage a kitchen that actually closed after the last meal out, allowing me nights of uninterrupted sleep. I wanted this, and felt I had earned this right. I deserved a dream chef's job. After all, I had some training, some talent, and now loads of experience orchestrating kitchens.

But New Orleans? I guess that city just doesn't like me. Or maybe I should blame the oil bust of 1987, which broke the city with high unemployment and rose its already high poverty like bread dough in the summer. The city certainly *looked* down and out when Stephen and I arrived in January of 1989. But beyond the sun-bleached, rusted street signs, perpetual potholes of the below-sea-level streets, and people loitering on street corners was the colorful, musical, culinary-inspired city that I loved. So many memories popped up in the muck of my psyche and dropped down again—the tumultuous and angst-filled ones with Armand, the fun times with Arthur.

Stephen and I rented an upstairs apartment in a big old house carved up into a fourplex Uptown on Plum Street, and every morning I combed the *Times Picayune* for chef's jobs. Only there weren't any. I didn't find this discouraging at first because good chef's positions are like buried treasure; there are hints and rumors passed around by word of mouth, and finding the job requires some sleuthing, especially if you're an outsider. So I went into the restaurants and hotels that advertised for cooks and inquired about higher-level positions. I took the streetcar and hoofed it to all midsize and large restaurants, the ones that weren't too historically embroiled in their history, anyway. I knew from my years cooking in New Orleans that these establishments would certainly shun the nonindigenous White female. Meanwhile, Stephen, a Canadian without a Green Card and unable to work legally, spent days sitting on our secondhand bed and watching daytime television on a newly purchased small black-and-white TV.

Each afternoon I arrived home at the apartment a little more beaten down. I worked at polishing my demeanor, minimizing my stutter, and putting forth my professionalism, and I believed myself to come across as sincere and knowledgeable. But still there were no jobs for me. I tried the hotels, the big chain restaurants, each day widening the net. Our savings were dwindling fast.

At first, when I believed a good-paying job waited right around a corner, I bought my favorite foods and cooked dinner in our small kitchen: rabbit Mangani, shrimp Creole, wild mushroom, and brie omelets. Stephen seemed unfazed by my feasts, which I interpreted as being unappreciative of my tasty meals, and small spats ensued. Later—much later—I would come to see the dull-brained alcoholic languishing inside this sweet man, one more step toward learning how common this was in the restaurant gene pool.

When the savings were half sucked away by rent and my nightly cooking endeavors, Stephen and I fed ourselves at happy hours. There were several bars within walking distance that laid out free food from five to seven. Meatballs, teriyaki chicken wings, chips, and queso dip at Bruno's or Hillary's, where flashes of my Armand-wounded self would saunter into my rum-soaked brain, or we'd take the streetcar down to Que Sera on St. Charles for three-for-one drinks and mingle with Jägermeister-marinated college kids.

Mardi Gras came early that year, a welcome interruption to the job search. Early February ushered in a cold front that swooped down from the north. For the day out walking, parade-viewing, bead-catching, humanity-observing, and of course drinking, we needed to be warm, or at least as warm as we could be. I'd heard that if you wrapped your toes with plastic wrap, it would keep your body heat in and keep the toes from freezing, so Stephen and I did this before applying layers of clothing, tucking small bottles of rum into our pockets, and setting out for Magazine Street. The temperature hovered in the high thirties and I did not at all feel festive. My toes froze anyway, and were black-and-blue from lack of circulation when I removed the sticky plastic wrap in the men's room at Le Bon Temp (too long a line at the women's room). The day, unlike past Mardi Gras parade days of laughter and partying, was miserable—and maybe I should've taken it as a sign. But I got a lot of beads. I got drunk. I froze.

By the end of February I was hitting up the newsstand for copies of newspapers from Texas, Florida, Georgia, and the Carolinas. I mailed out resumes. I succumbed to some jittery interviews over the phone. One human resource interviewer from a resort hotel in South Carolina said I sounded "interesting" and would keep my resume on file. "I *am* interesting, so why can't I get a job?" I yelled at the phone after hanging up. I looked at Stephen, who was sitting cross-legged on the bed drinking a beer. He shrugged.

Finally, in early March, a chef's job appeared in the *Times Picayune*. A resort property in Destin, Florida, a coastal panhandle town a five-hour drive away, was advertising for a chef. After nearly three months holed up in New Orleans, getting poorer by the day, a beach town sounded really good.

Destin was a little town airbrushed on the edge of the turquoise Gulf of Mexico. (At least that's how it was back then, not the big, sprawling, unruly Destin of today.) When Stephen and I first cruised over the little hump bridge in March of 1989, a grinning cobia painted on a sign welcomed us to the "World's Luckiest Fishing Village," and the expanse of whiter-than-white sand made our hearts pop. Pelicans dipped around us. Wooden shops and shacks hugged the harbor's edge. Who needed New Orleans, anyway? I could live in Florida. Dona and I had been on our way to Florida when we wound up in New Orleans—so long ago—and now New Orleans would be how I wound up in Florida.

Chef Michael Pollick, while touring me around the beachy town during our interview, told me Destin had more restaurants per capita than any other city in the country. I got the job and a new hometown. "Look at all these restaurants!" I said to Stephen as we drove through Destin to Sandestin Beach Resort, our temporary condo digs until we found an apartment.

Restaurant chef at Babe's Seafood House in Sandestin was not the ultimate chef's position, but I needed a job and once again—you'd think I would have learned by now—I needed a way out of New Orleans. Babe's was the black sheep of the trio of Sandestin Beach Resort's restaurants, the other two the well-run Harry T's in town and the fine-dining Elephant Walk across Highway 98 on the insanely turquoise Gulf. Babe's was Florida fried seafood, and like the Mana Kai it served breakfast daily, requiring supervision of that first early shift. Babe's was Friday night seafood buffets, grilled amberjack burgers, and a staff that included many Black women from DeFuniak Springs who'd quit pulling chicken parts at the poultry factory to drive out to the beach and move up the labor ladder. Babe's was food for Midwesterners, and I was introduced to the term "snowbird" for those tourists from the north who came to avoid the cold, and who were typically retired from something—penny-pinchers with mediocre taste buds.

I shared the kitchen with Omar the banquet chef, a man infamous for sitting in our shared office sharpening pencils while the rest of the kitchen went crazy, and for searing his steaks on the big broiler early in the afternoon for a dinner banquet hours later. This created fodder for my cooks: "It's already 10 a.m., better get those hot-boxes fired up for the party at seven!" Or, "Get those steaks on, can't have any rare meat around!" Omar, a hunk of Egyptian descent, I figured must have chauvinism attached to every bone in his body, so I played to his professional sensibilities to create a coalition with him. As much as I thought he should be more hands-on in the kitchen, and wondered why he needed all those sharpened pencils anyway, and wanted to tell him that starting steaks that early for a seven o'clock banquet was food heresy, I only smiled at my cooks' criticisms of Chef Omar. I might need Omar's help someday, and it was best that we played for the same team.

I put a New Orleans slant on my new Babe's menu, all approved by executive chef Michael Pollick. Seafood gumbo, shrimp Creole, and seafood-stuffed eggplant with shrimp sauce (dialing down the spices for those sensitive Midwestern palates) were all added to the usual snowbird fare of fried items, steamed lobster tail, New England clam chowder, and prime rib. The seafood was different here than in New Orleans but equally as plentiful. Fresh fish with strange names rolled in the back door daily: wahoo, which upon inspection I recognized as ono; triggerfish was *humu humu nuku nuku apua'a*, a fish we hadn't eaten in Hawaii, but okay, I'd sauté up the slender little fillets. We also had flounder, snapper, grouper, cobia, trout, Gulf shrimp, oysters, and loads of wormy amberjack, a large bottom-feeding fish. As I cut the amberjack slabs into steaks and pulled out the long white worms, I could not fathom why people ate such a trash fish. "Look, Martha," the snowbird husband says, "I'm eating fresh fish in Florida!" "Dude!" says the fisherman. "I'm gonna catch me a shark with this big wormy bait!"

Once the thrill of our move had settled into reality and I had time to think about where I was, I wanted Mike Pollick's job. I felt overqualified for the likes of Babe's Seafood House and the Sandestin Resort hierarchy. At World's Fairs, it had been boss man Chuck Sanders, then me, no one in between. Here there was Peter Bos, the owner, and below him a democratic and corporate bureaucracy of administrative offices and middle management, then the corporate chef, Mike Pollick, and then me, along with the chef of Harry T's (who, I noted, drove a black convertible Mustang), and the new chef at the fine-dining Elephant Walk, whose job I also coveted. So I was just "that girl cooking fried fish and bland gumbo over at Babe's for the snow-birds." My ego curled at the edges like dried-out mollusk.

You hear an old song on the radio, and whether you liked that song or not when it first became popular, that era of your life rushes in as soon as you hear the first strums of the intro. Maybe it's "Stayin' Alive" by the Bee Gees, even if you just couldn't imagine going to see *Saturday Night Fever* because you thought men in stacked heels were gross. But you're hearing it now and you sink back and enjoy it, think about what you were doing while your friends were dressing for disco. *Ah, yes, those were the days, my friend*, you think fondly. And this is how it is with my Babe's Seafood house memories: They roll in and tug at my older self, calling me back into the past like an old pop song. The job was merely average, Destin outstanding. I divorced Michael that year and married Stephen on the beach, witnessed by three strangers in chef's coats. We lived across the street from the blue, blue Gulf in a rented town house for $425 per month. We paddled on the Blackwater River, fishing under the bridge for flounder.

That summer, I took charge of my mom when she was diagnosed with a second round of throat cancer and I insisted she move from Hawaii to Destin for her chemo and radiation. She packed up the condo, tossed her belongings in boxes and mailed them book-rate to Destin, and left nineteen-year-old Christopher to fend for himself on Maui. When I picked her up from the tiny Fort Walton Beach Airport and saw the alien bulge on her neck, I felt a knife twist in my gut, and fear grabbed away any words I should've said. For the week leading up to her hospital stay, we did not talk about her mortality. We did not talk about what my stepdad had done to me throughout my childhood. I did not ask her if she had known and chose to ignore it, or if she was just blissfully stupid. We didn't talk about my grandmother's emotional abuse of me, while my mother had been elsewhere. All these things flooded into my brain and heart on a therapist's couch years later, and I wished I could reel back to that week my mom and I were eating grouper sandwiches on the beach in Destin, and that we could have talked about it.

Then, after her week of treatments in the hospital and a tracheotomy, I held her while a liter of blood gushed from a hole in her throat, leaving a gruesome trail of blood in our town house. I zombied through the arrangements: calling Uncle Jack for money, flying Christopher out from Hawaii, arranging the cremation. Christopher and I scattered her ashes into the Gulf across the street, where I'd been married two months before, and each of us tossed out a single red rose and said our silent prayers. This brother I hardly knew, and with few life skills taught to him, would now be in my emotional care. At work, I produced Friday seafood buffets for a record 600 people. After work I drove home along the dark beach highway with a strong margarita in a plastic cup on the seat between my legs, yelling at her spirit, "I know you're there, talk to me!" Once home, I sat on the cool white sand across the street and stared at the moon piercing a hole into the silver Gulf. I went into town late to pick up Stephen from his job at Pier 98. We drank at their bar. Back home on the sand and hypnotized by the waves, I thought about what was lacking in my life—my fifty-year-old mother, now dead; a mediocre job; a marriage that was already becoming unsatisfying. I needed to do something. I had fallen from the throne, then crashed into myself. What to do? There was only one way to break the monotony.

CHAPTER 23

A FLORIDA WALKABOUT

I TOOK OFF IN A RENTED CAR on a sunny July morning, a Jimmy
Buffett cassette whirring in a boom box on the passenger seat and an ice chest
of beer and my fishing tackle in the back. I had no destination; I just knew a
beach or an island waited for me somewhere east of Destin, and it was time to
explore Florida. Alone. Stephen waved me off without a care.

Tiny post offices, dusty hardware stores, and beach shacks blurred by.
These were the Gulf towns with names like Seagrove Beach and Inlet Beach.
Salt and freshly caught fish perfumed the air rushing in through my open
window, and I inhaled this sweet air as greedily as I had at the Ala Wai Yacht
Harbor when I was six. I passed through pink and tacky Panama City and
drove through Tyndall Air Force Base, the two-lane Highway 98 dwarfed by
Australian pines on both sides. The pines were tall and pencil-straight as if an
invisible hand had reached from the sky and pulled them from the earth. The
vision of my bled-out mother hung on, and the dull ache of her loss persisted
and would persist for years. I drove for two hours, and although the funky
beachiness of it all was interesting, my Shangri-La had not appeared.

"Off to See the Lizard" serenaded me as I began to doubt there was anything illuminating out there for me. The Japanese call a sudden illumination
satori; Jack Kerouac defined *satori* as "a kick in the eye" and used it in his book
Satori in Paris, about bumming around France for ten days with no apparent

aim. Since reading Kerouac's book, I'd felt a trip was required for my version of the *satori*: a trip in search of that kick in the eye. But so far, nothing had kicked me in the eye.

Doubts about my escape-hatch road trip disintegrated when I burst through the pine forest to see the road narrowing along a shallow bay framed by bait shops and piles of spent oyster shells. Slowly, I drove through the quaint tourist meccas of Mexico Beach and Port St. Joe, then a stretch of pine and palm forest, then past seafood houses with faded stenciled names on cracked concrete walls. A familiar feeling comforted me, of being out in the world by myself, lonely but content, a comfort zone I needed to be in, a reprieve. Little houses in pristine beach towns sat unencumbered by dinosaur statues, water parks, bikini shops, or condo furniture stores common in the Redneck Riviera part of the coast where I lived.

The road continued to curve around a bay, then deposited me in a town bejeweled by buildings so old, it looked as though Uptown New Orleans had been chiseled up and dropped here by the water. The buildings sported dormers, sloping front porches, rows of tiny windows underlined by boxes with fluttering red impatiens. Here, in this half-mile stretch of road, were all the things I loved: seafood, rural simplicity, history, beauty. And surely there would be true salvation: oysters and beer.

The historic town of Apalachicola is part of the so-called Forgotten Coast, but it's not forgotten so much as it's a secret—*my secret*, so don't go building condos there. This is the town where ice was invented, where logging and cotton made history at its docks, and where oyster harvesting occurs for much of the South—a Gulf and river port town basking architecturally in its colorful history. That day, parking my rented car in front of a dusty antique store, I knew I'd found *it*, and believed that my mother, knowing what her daughter needed, had somehow found this place for me.

Ultimately wanting sand between my toes, I was directed by the proprietor of the antique store, a lady with spun-gold hair, to drive over that bridge—she pointed to *that* bridge—and go over another bridge in Eastpoint to St. George Island. An *island*, how good that sounded! Windows down, salt air rushing in at me, I drove over that bridge, my heart floating in my chest.

The four-mile bridge from Eastpoint to St. George spanned a bay dotted with skiffs of single oyster cullers poking the murky bottom with sticks.

When a dolphin on a sign welcomed me to St. George Island, I pulled a can of beer from the melting ice in the back. I was ready to explore.

At one end of the twenty-eight-mile-long St. George Island is a state park and at the other, a gated plantation of homes. But in the middle, white sandy beaches etch one side of the island and a mangroved bay laps at the other. Water and sand are everywhere, divided by this narrow island of scrub. I saw pastel-colored wooden houses scattered among the white dunes like so much flotsam. The houses, with wraparound galleries, towered on stilts, protecting them from floods and increasing their views of both beach and bay. The more humble homes squatted on sandy yards (built pre-1980, I guessed). None of the houses had landscaping, and the terrain was consistent all over the island: patches of white sand showing through the beachy scrub, a smattering of pine trees. In some areas, dunes were forming where the scrub had blown away and small white hills had been carved up from the earth by the wind. I was giddy, satisfied, my pores and lungs intoxicated by the boat-smell air and the vision of it all.

I drove east toward the state park and slowed to watch dolphins frolicking in the Gulf, and slowed even more to allow a sand-dusted, Frisbee-size turtle to cross the empty road. The only other movement besides the turtle was a truck with a sign out front advertising Dale's Fresh Seafood, and a smiling toothless guy—presumably Dale—sitting in the truck behind a slide-up window. A handwritten sign said, "Apalachicola Oysters, Bay Scallops, Grouper, Gulf Shrimp," and I wanted to buy them all and become a squatter in one of the empty homes, and fire up a stove.

Instead I booked a room at the stately St. George Inn and went fishing under the Apalachicola Bay Bridge. And, as things were going well now, I hooked a flounder near a bridge piling, put him in the pickle bucket I'd brought, and returned to the inn and asked the proprietor to cook him for me later.

Everything was perfect. The aimless drive, this pot-of-gold island at the end of my excursion, the hooked flounder flopping at the end of my pole. My world began to open up, my sights not so constricted anymore. Hope for the future. Maybe we'd buy a house here someday. Where would I work? I picked up real estate brochures in the inn's lobby, kindling for this dream.

Of course I noted the island's bars on my initial tour. The "inland" Harry A's, which I'd walked past on my way to the bait shop for shrimp, I planned to visit after dinner. For post-fishing, post-shower, and pre-sunset libations, I walked past Dale's now-empty spot over toward the beach, where a little wooden tavern sat some steps above a clearing of sand and scrub. Inside, I ordered a draft in a plastic cup. The smoky bar had a single pool table, and two guys wearing cutoff shorts, T-shirts, and fishing caps were smacking around balls with their cues. Behind them a wall of sliding glass doors opened onto a wooden walk, leading down to the sand. Hand-shading the sun from my eyes, I stepped out and looked over the pearl-white beach to the Gulf as if on a ship's bow, Columbus in search of land, Marisa in search of her satori. Below me more steps straddled a dune, then gave way to a wooden walkway over the sand, ending at another little square of railed deck where three people sat laughing, drinking from cans of Budweiser.

A waitress, a fisherman, a biker, not people from the stilt houses but people from "in town"—Apalachicola—here to catch the sunset. I settled in with them and quietly watched the sky turn from a crisp lemon yellow to a russet orange. After the sun had set, we remained in the silvering dusk. Then something surprising happened. It would still seem surprising to me the next day, hungover and driving back home, and for years afterward. The incongruity of the small event, in 1989 small-town Florida, where culinary delights peak at fried chicken and oysters on the half shell. Where grocery store takeouts were of the potato salad variety. Where the closest Asian food was two and a half hours away in Tallahassee. Maybe this bewilderment was my satori kick in the eye; in my depressed state, the smallest oddball occurrence could brighten the big nasty world.

The square of wood where we were sitting shook and my three new acquaintances looked up to greet a woman walking toward us with some "heys" and "there you ares!" The approaching silhouette, in cutoff shorts and with uncombed hair swishing at her waist, carried a huge round platter wrapped with plastic wrap. Rice Krispies Treats? No. Barbecue? No. Finger sandwiches? No.

The Apalachicola waitress girl leaned over to me, Budweiser on her breath, and asked, "Y'all want some sushi?" Sushi? Had someone made sushi? Driven it from Tallahassee? The surprise of this culinary offering mystified me and I declined, retreating into my shell to watch the darkening sky swallow what was left of the day.

The trip to Apalachicola did end. Back in my life in Destin, nothing had changed. And I had only changed so much as to have had a little rest, a fresh flounder dinner, the dream of owning a solitary house on a sand dune, and some good times talking to strangers. Babe's Seafood House, Stephen, the ache in me over my dead mother—my life was still indifferent. I still missed New Orleans, Australia, and Hawaii. I still wanted a real chef's job. All of these things I thought about as I sifted through Mom's boxes of belongings, which had begun to arrive from Maui after her death. Polaroids, old calendars, birthday cards (from me), mementos, contents of junk drawers swooped into boxes with a sweep of my mom's arm. Then, one night going through her things, staring into a Polaroid of her standing in the distance from five-year-old me, an aloof and awkward mother (why wasn't she hugging me?), a flash of brilliance, instant and fast like lightning, hit me, that which would plug my emotional holes.

I had the conversation with Stephen on our newly bought, Sears-credit, floral couch in our living room. Across the street, waves hushed along the sand at Henderson Beach as if listening. When the words of my sudden parental urge coupled with financial apprehensions (he still with no Green Card, me the only breadwinner) tumbled from my lips, he was so gung-ho for the getting-pregnant idea, I'm thankful for him still. He became uncharacteristically animated and excited. "Of course the time is right. If you wait for the time to be righter, it may never happen. Nothing is ever perfect. You want to get pregnant now? Let's do it!"

I was pregnant the following month. I found out after I took Stephen to experience St. George Island—where the magic obviously happened.

At eight months, I was a stick body carrying a watermelon. I wore stretchy maternity jeans to work and sat on a stool commanding my forces while picking shells from crabmeat. I mostly ate brownies and Shaklee protein drinks. At the local bar I ate frozen yogurt and played pool with Stephen. I still tanned in my bikini. I never felt more beautiful. On Memorial Day Weekend, the kickoff to the tourist season, stuck in traffic on the bridge heading to Fort Walton Beach Hospital, Saramaile (*sara-miley*) Christine was ready to make her entrance into my world.

Now I had another designation besides struggling chef: I was a *mother*. And I planned to be a damned good one.

CHAPTER 24

WASTING AWAY IN MARGARITAVILLE

IT IS OBVIOUS I LIKE BARS. I especially like Florida bars. Old and funky ones. I made a stab at writing a book once about these disappearing staples of Florida culture called *Tiki Bars, Chickee Bars and Fish Camps: The Real Florida*. I traveled around the state—as much as I could, having a real job and all—with an entourage of friends who clearly thought my mission was a worthy one. "Yes," they said, "we want to help you do market research!" I even came up with a pen name: "Chickie LeBarre." I believe the seed for this passion started in Destin, at a place called the Boathouse.

The Boathouse bar sits at the edge of Destin Harbor. Its name was apt, as it had been a boathouse for a single boat, so it was a small structure whose narrow balcony jutted over the water. Wooden and slanty, this shanty was our small family's destination on Mondays off for afternoon longnecks and a couple dozen Apalachicola oysters while taking in the bustle of boaters and jet-skiers powering in from the shimmering waters of Destin Harbor and Holiday Island beyond. On the tiny wood table, Daughter's baby bottle stood beacon-like between our sweating longnecks, and Stephen and I would pass our baby between us. She was not at all fussy. How could she be? This was paradise. Florida-style tomato-based seafood gumbo boiled in a big pot on a butane burner outside behind the bar's tiny kitchen, a small electric piano was set up inside for sunset music, and dollar bills hung from the low rafters and flapped in the salty breeze. Each person walking into the Boathouse, whether local or otherwise, would suddenly get a look of relief on their face, for the place had that effect on a person.

Eight years later I found myself back in Destin on business—I was by then living in Sarasota and designing and installing commercial kitchens, and we were building some retirement home kitchens north of town—and I returned to the Boathouse, eager to settle into the relaxing atmosphere of the place once again. Late in the afternoon on a Friday, bikers on loud hogs rolled up and parked symmetrically, and inside, the place pulsated with humanity. Something was different on this trip; new planks had been applied here and there, and from the barmaid I learned that the Boathouse had slid into the harbor during Hurricane Opal in '95. Devoted patrons dove in to retrieve the debris, and donations were made to replace what was unsalvageable. In a labor of love, the barflies rebuilt their bar. A kitchen had been added and now the gumbo simmered behind walls, a move to please the local health officials.

That weekend I patronized the Boathouse a few times. I went at night once, when the band was Southern rock and redneck ladies danced on the picnic tables inside and strung their bras from the rafters. I was really impressed! The following year I brought Daughter to Destin for her spring break, and when we returned to Sarasota for her middle-school art project she was to draw a picture of her vacation. There, on her big sheet of art paper, was my red Nissan 240SX, pulled up to the Boathouse on the water, motorcycles parked symmetrically out front. A proud parental moment for sure.

But that came later. When we still lived in Destin, some Monday afternoons Stephen and I went farther into the harbor's hub to the giant tiki hut of AJ's. AJ's had a huge upper deck overlooking rows and rows of charter boat slips. Late afternoons, the boats returned with mounds of red snapper, pompano, and flounder, the catches of the day displayed above the boats' marquees by ramming hooked nails through the fishes' eyeballs. Fishy and salty aromas emanated upward toward the deck while we sunned our faces in the afternoon sky and drank several shaken salty margaritas. These afternoons, through scent and brain buzz, I was back again at the Ala Wai Yacht Harbor as a barefoot little girl. The memory was vague and soothing, only the tiniest part of me wondering about my mother's days on the boat, her relationship with my stepdad, and her bloody exit from this world. There was a disconnect in my brain, not able to ask myself the question that would taunt me for many more years before I finally turned around and gave it recognition: Had my mother known her husband was molesting me and just ignored it? Or had she been conveniently ignorant of this fact? This black banner of confusion flapped in the distant breeze of the all-consuming and comforting new motherhood, where I was grounded for now.

Daughter was a little barfly in her portable carrier—the "joyride"— which Stephen proudly carried, swinging his new joy like a precious purse. I have pictures to prove this: new father in beach shorts and flip-flops, wide grin carved into his tan face, as he gazed adoringly at our prize. Every Monday afternoon's routine included one or more bar explorations and some food. Oysters at the Boathouse or at Goatfeathers at Santa Rosa Beach, fried grouper sandwiches at Gilligan's, boiled Gulf shrimp at AJ's. Shuffled between sitters all week, she was content to sleep through loud music and that was fine with us. Stephen and I were restaurateurs; we didn't watch TV or garden or do anything besides work, and on our mutual day off, we patronized restaurants instead of working in them.

That summer I was to turn thirty. With a year-old marriage, a three-month-old baby girl, a dead mother, and a dying career, I needed to dress up and go dancing, like the old days in Australia. So we arranged our first evening-time sitter. I'd worked that day and came home to a blissfully quiet husband. I put on a dress—a rarity for me—and painted on makeup, another rarity. We had a dinner reservation at a romantic spot on the harbor, and I was all a-chatter about leaving my twenties behind and embarking on the rest of my life. In the boxes that had arrived after Mom's death I'd found a Polaroid of her posing in a green dress on her thirtieth birthday, brown hair combed long to her waist, cat-eye glasses and bright red lips, posing sideways-sexy, her hands on her thighs as if she'd just sculpted them down her curvy body. I had Stephen get the camera, and I posed in my black dress (always slimming) the same way. Both these pictures mirror themselves in a photo album now.

At the restaurant, Stephen remained quiet. He ordered a scotch, and I a glass of wine. I chattered on, wondering if he was happy for me: I was moving on! I had come out of my funk! I was a proud mother! I loved him! Look at the pictures of Mom and me at thirty! When the meals came I ordered a second glass of wine, and he perked up. Wearing a lazy lower lip, reminiscent of Armand's on his drunkest days, and his head herky-jerky on his neck like a bobblehead doll's, he said, "We should just order a bottle."

Acid dripped into my stomach then, as disappointment and angst raced through my veins. Because a part of me knew if he drank more—which obviously he was going to do—he would not go dancing. "B-but I want to go dancing after d-dinner," I stammered.

"I don't want to go dancing," he said with a scowl.

I glowered at him. I put on the most hurt face I could. Tears came, which made him angrier. A passive-aggressive remark erupted from me as I paid the bill: "I'll just go by myself then." This caused my stomach to soar with nervousness like I was a kid again, asked to read in front of the class. When we headed outside into the beachy night, I forced out another anger-fueled statement: "I'll drop you at home." As my stomach fell off a cliff, I gasped an inhale.

"Just let's pick her up and go home," Stephen commanded, in a voice that didn't take me seriously.

"Wow! What a great birthday! Maybe I'll turn thirty again next year and we can try again!"

He slammed the car door.

I slammed the car door and rattled the keys into the ignition. I took a deep breath to energize the courage to yell out, "You're fucking up *my* b-birthday, and you're mad at *me*?"

His eyes were fiery beads in the dark. "I don't want to talk about this," he spat. His tone reminded me of Armand's dark side. It made me so uncomfortable and afraid that I stifled my anger.

Our sitter peered through a crack in the door, then swung it open when she saw us. "Wow, you're early," she said.

"We're just tired," I lied, my face tight with determination not to cry. On this night of my thirtieth birthday, I'd received an invisible, unwrapped gift: self-preservation. Some may call it stupidity or weakness. But this night signaled the start of my conditioning: To avoid the feelings of confusion, of sadness and inadequacy, and to tamp down the pure rage that burned inside me, I knew now not to ignite Stephen's fuse. Aside from a handful of explosions on my part—a can of baby formula flung through a glass window, an empty vodka bottle hurled at the side of the shed—for the next ten years I was a picture of a calm, accepting wife.

CHAPTER 25

GO SOUTH, YOUNG WOMAN

DESTIN WAS A TEASE. If you're going to live in Florida, you need to live farther south, among palm trees and balmy weather, in the land of Jimmy Buffett. Of course this notion turned out to be dead wrong, and I've been trying to get back up to the Redneck Riviera for years. But back then I took North Florida's lack of palm tree–infused paradise as an excuse—after slinging snowbird fare at Babe's for almost two years—to move on, to move south.

And there was my job, listed in the *Tampa Tribune*: "Needed: Fine Dining Restaurant Chef on Longboat Key, in Sarasota." A town about an hour south of Tampa. For the interview I rented a car and drove eight hours of freeway and was put up at the Wellesley Inn on US 41. That evening I drove around Sarasota and tried to catch the vibe of the place, which I couldn't, really. It wasn't like when Stephen and I first drove over the bridge to Destin and our hearts bloomed with love for the little beach town on the water. But I ignored the fact that the bay lined with queen palms looked contrived, and that I couldn't find a bar I felt comfortable going into; I wanted this job. I was hopeful that this could be *the* chef's job.

The next day I drove out to Longboat Key, to the blinking yellow light at Avenue of the Flowers, where the velvet and chandeliered Plaza Restaurant sat behind a Publix grocery store. I interviewed with General Manager Randy Ellis, who said the restaurant had fine and contemporary food but had had a consistency problem, and needed someone to straighten things out. Since Longboat Key was populated by mostly upscale condos, which emptied out during the summer, the Plaza was off the beaten track and needed to be a destination in order to be successful. I was all over that. I must have impressed Randy with my talk about standardized recipes and the food I'd offer based on all my travels, for I was invited back the following week—this time with Stephen and Daughter—for dinner, whereby I offered my critiques on the food and the service, and proceeded to land the job.

This was December, when we drove from Destin to Sarasota for the weekend interview. We'd driven all day Friday, and our dinner at the Plaza was the next night. Tired and hungry, we checked in at Howard Johnson's on US 41, then went off to find a bite to eat.

I knew I would get the Plaza job and that this town would be our new home, and I needed a really adventurous, fine, fun dinner to solidify this place for me. So we drove south on Tamiami Trail, which runs parallel to the Gulf, Stephen pointing to every chain restaurant and dim-looking steakhouse. "I want to go to an interesting restaurant!" I insisted. I was adamant that it was important to find something special in our new hometown. Stephen was hungry and probably drunk. "Let's just eat," he said. The tension in the car made Daughter begin to cry. Fortunately, I was driving, and able to control things to my way of thinking and finally, *finally* after about six miles of stop-and-go driving, the road darkened a bit and a hulking wooden building loomed before us with a neon sign saying, "Fast Eddie's: Warm Beer Lousy Food."

I pulled into the parking lot. Stephen scowled at me. Daughter stopped crying.

When we walked into the loud restaurant, Stephen made a comment along the lines of, "So this was worth that drive?" I ignored him. Once seated, we had smoked mullet dip and fried fish and it was all okay, probably not worth the drive with a cranky child, but here we were.

"I'm sorry," I finally said, once we got Daughter quieted with some food, and beers were in front of us. "I guess I'm just excited about the move and this new town. I just need to find the feel of it, I guess."

Stephen shrugged and took a drink of beer. At least he was no longer agitated.

• • •

The Plaza Restaurant was everything I dreamed of: a skittish staff of male cooks I had to encourage, a fine wine list, tuxedoed waiters, a young Swiss pastry chef, stores of the freshest gourmet ingredients, edible flowers and fresh herbs, a pasta maker, happy food suppliers rolling in the back door to show me their wares. First order of the day, the menu. It was big and heavy and expensive. I ran it for the month of January, considered to be in season, but began to plan a lighter version for the spring and summer months.

Sarasota has theater, arts, and all that upper-crust stuff to fill the evenings of the wealthy who make their seasonal homes there, and the Plaza Restaurant needed to be part of these nightly forays, not just a place to dine for special occasions. So I created the pre-theater dinner menu of smaller portions of homemade saffron ravioli stuffed with seafood mousse, black olive pasta with shrimp and herbed goat cheese, grilled sea scallops on angel hair with shiitake and mango-ginger butter. I also promoted the ordering of appetizers for an entrée by including a glass of wine in the price: escargots with braised leeks baked in filo dough, grilled duck sausage on wilted spinach, grilled shrimp salad with tomato vinaigrette. Why did going out to dinner need to involve an appetizer, a salad, and an entrée? It was just too much food! (There wasn't much time for this lighter fare to catch on, but twenty years later there are small bites and happy-hour food all over Sarasota's fancier restaurants . . . I was way ahead of my time.)

The Plaza served dinner and private parties only, no breakfast or lunch to distract me from my culinary tasks. The kitchen was clean, the restaurant dim and elegant. Finally, I had landed. Stephen, fully Green-Carded now, got a job cooking lunch and dinner for the Limerick Junction in downtown Sarasota, an Irish bar with a vintage dinner theater upstairs. Between our schedules, each day we tag-teamed Daughter to and from babysitters recommended to us on the other side of town. We rented a house; then with part of the proceeds from selling the Maui condo we bought a house, and we got comfortable in Sarasota. Then, after the season, in April, the Plaza Restaurant closed its doors.

It wasn't my fault, Randy told me. The Graham Group, who also owned the wildly popular Marina Jack's on the harborfront, had given the Plaza several years to get off the ground, and the location was just bad. Had Randy known this had been the plan, he wouldn't have advertised for a new chef, or moved me to Sarasota.

Randy was being moved over to Marina Jack's and he offered me a position there. But they had a chef already, and I said no thanks to this consolation prize.

I was crushed and tired. Tired of proving myself. Tired of ferrying my daughter all over town. Tired of the business. Tired of never getting a fucking break. The Plaza closing made me face the damn restaurant business that had raised me and yell out: "Oh yeah? Well you just see what I'm going to do!" I had money still from the condo sale. So what does a down-and-out chef do in a new town with money and a nagging maternal instinct? I enrolled in real estate school and got a part-time line cook job for some extra cash. I was going to learn something new and get the hell out of the business. It was a decision that came to me in a dream, then stayed with me all the next day as I inventoried the Plaza's food for delivery to Marina Jack's. I had had it.

Michael's on East was advertising for a dinner sauté cook. Michael of the Klauber family owned the place, which had a sterling reputation, as did the other restaurant and resort holdings of the elder Klauber, namely the Colony Beach and Tennis Club on Longboat Key. Michael's on East was just south of downtown, not far from our house, and when I went in and applied, the world suddenly got very small. As I stood in Michael's office, there on his wall hung a picture of him shaking hands with Archie Casbarian of Arnaud's fame in New Orleans. The guy I told off, then got fired by, years earlier.

"Oh!" Michael exclaimed upon reading my resume. "You worked for Archie."

"Yes, I did," I said, demurely as possible. *Please don't check that reference*, I thought.

"He mentored me in college, a great guy."

"Oh, yes," I lied. "I loved cooking in New Orleans. H-how long were you there?" An expert redirect, and I commended myself for it.

"So, you're actually a chef." Still scrutinizing my resume. "Why are you applying for this job?"

And so on.

He liked my answers, so there I was, working for his sloppy chef, commanding the dinner line once I learned the ropes from the grill guys, making specials, piling up the mise en place in my prep refrigerator for 200 covers a night, afterward scrubbing down the line with hot soapy water, then a cold beer next door at Bennigan's with my hard-drinking compatriots. No kitchen management required. It was kind of fun, this going back to my roots, but I'd outgrown it somehow; the kitchen felt like an outdated toy. I'd loved it once, so kept it around for posterity, but I was thirty-one and I had a daughter at home, and a nagging desire to do *something else*.

Being a real estate agent was another thing entirely. I did sell two houses. But as I began to realize getting my license was only a small part of the uphill battle to become successful at the house-selling game, especially if you're shy around strangers and you *stutter*.

Then there was a $9,000 tax bill from the sale of my condo. This actually saved me from deciding if the Realtor life was truly for me. A Kihei accountant had set up my condo as an investment property, and there was a huge profit in the sale of it after my mom died. After six months of playing with food at Michael's on East and driving around looking at houses—actually thinking I could get out of The Business—I was back earning a consistent income in order to pay off my tax bill. The restaurant business obviously had not taken my desertion threat seriously.

Tournament Players Club (or TPC) is one of many golf and country clubs in Sarasota. In fact, country clubs are part of the Southwest Florida landscape, and they were what had turned me off about this part of the state in the first place. They're everywhere, in all their sterile, white-bread glory. It may be many a Northerner's dream to retire to a stucco Mediterranean Revival house in a gated community with a view of man-made ponds and green turf dotted with old men in white shorts putting a ball around, and this is their right—as it is my right to hopefully retire someday to a fishing dock with a pole, a bucket of live shrimp, and a six-pack of cold stuff. But these clubs are a *culture* in Florida, and they are *everywhere*. And a lot of the Northern club-goers simply march to a different beat than I do. Or maybe it's the other way around.

All this I figured out as clubhouse chef of TPC, where cooking for people I couldn't relate to seemed odd to me. Everyone likes good food, and on this level I could relate; whether it was a midweek taco buffet, a BLT or Reuben lunch plate, or a fine dinner party for two dozen, I did my best to please the golfers and their golfing wives. Besides, a clubhouse job wasn't so bad, with dinner only a few nights a week, lunch six days, Sunday brunch, some parties and golf functions. The kitchen was closed on Mondays, so I was guaranteed at least one day off and no late nights to caress a Myers's and grapefruit to calm my adrenaline. It appeared to be the perfect chef's job for a parent, so I settled in, in spite of what would become my nemesis: the waitstaff.

In New Orleans, waiting tables can be a high-paying profession. Even though waiters don't start in the kitchen as they do in France, good service is revered, and most waiters do well by their cooks and chefs. At the Mana Kai on Maui, waiters were needier, knowing that in order to pay for their beach-bum lifestyle they needed to put forth a certain amount of professionalism. At Babe's in Destin, professionalism was a bit looser, but Southern hospi-tality and general Redneck Riviera friendliness prevailed. At the Plaza, the waiters had been very professional, older men—lifers in the business—and many were also chefs. So when I first encountered the whiny young women at TPC who treated my kitchen staff like unwanted stepchildren, my inner bitch emerged with both fists swinging.

"I *said,* this BLT is for Mr. Cardinal and he doesn't want mayonnaise!" This from Diane, after sticking her exploratory fingers into the sandwich, slamming the plate back down on the stainless steel pass shelf and scowling at Bert, my big, Black, soft-spoken salad man trainee, who looked bewildered.

"Diane!" I yelled from the hot line, where I was giving Eddie a break on the grill. "We're not psychic here; put 'special instructions' on the ticket!"

"Well, I *told* him!" Hands on hips, mother-style.

"Diane! Don't argue and *don't* talk to my cooks. Put-it-on-the-ticket!" I emphasized this point by banging the metal spatula on the pass shelf, creating a reverberating echo to my words.

I later got scolded by upper management for yelling at the waitstaff, for not being diplomatic, for what—not having parenting skills at work? I saved these for my well-behaved daughter, who needed less maternal manipulation than this batch of nagging, moody servers.

The resentment between cooks and servers was huge. My cooks toiled long hours in a hot kitchen for seven bucks an hour. These ladies twirled around the dining room serving old men for a few hours, made their demands on my staff, then left with a pocket full of money, while we still had another shift ahead of us. Also, our small kitchen had apparently been designed for the lunch trade only, to supplement a main clubhouse, which had closed a few years ago, leaving all food service operations the responsibility of our tiny ship. On busy nights this was a difficult endeavor with our limited prep and food-storage space.

There was no winning this war with waitresses. A crying server in the general manager's office got the chef—me—in trouble. Those girls pushed my anger buttons regularly. One Wednesday night, our busiest dinner night in our ill-equipped kitchen, Diane came back to the line holding two bowls of seafood gumbo, chock-a-block with expensive seafood and shellfish. She had dredged the soup-well like a bottom-feeding shrimp boat, and was saying the customers complained that the soup wasn't hot enough. "Okay, just a minute," I said upon hearing her predicament, for I was head down and working the middle, plating up a large table. Once the food was in the window, I looked up for the bowls of soup, expecting them to be sitting in the window for my saucepan or microwave. But the bowls full of expensive crab, fish, and shrimp were nowhere.

"Diane, where's the gumbo?" Aggravation was building in my voice.

She looked at me questioningly and with a slight shrug said, "Well I tossed them out."

At that point I let loose with flying invectives, screaming about food cost and server stupidity, banging my spatula loudly on the stainless steel. The cooks kept their heads down and focused hard on the food to avoid my tirade, and Diane started crying. Eventually the dining room manager escorted her back out to the dining room while I prematurely eighty-sixed the gumbo, and I heated every dinner plate to singe-the-fingers temperature on Diane's subsequent tables. The next day I was called into the club manager's office.

"Are you some kind of an anomaly?" Mr. General Manager said to me after a brief pause when I entered his office for my managerial scolding. Through the picture window behind his desk, the golf course looked like a fake scenery poster in an old movie.

"What do you mean?" I'd never heard this phrase before to refer to a person.

Mr. General Manager, a balding, serious man, rose from his chair and came around the large wooden desk to face me where I stood leaning against his credenza. "Oh, I mean it in a good way. You're just outside the norm of most people. You have high expectations and you expect people will be the same way."

To which I stared at him. I hadn't expected a character analysis.

"I understand your frustration about the staff," he went on, "but you have to understand, people aren't like you."

"So, I'm to assume everyone's a dipshit? And manage that way? I can't do that. I-I had too many condescending bosses in my day. I can't—"

"I don't mean that exactly. You just need to be more patient."

Diane, dear, please don't throw out my expensive soup that I took two days to make, that wastes my time and my food cost, I thought. "Be more patient. While all that money goes down the drain?"

"Diane is having a talking-to also."

Kids in the schoolyard. "I see."

And so, after eighteen years in the kitchen trenches in Portland, New Orleans, Hawaii, Vancouver, and Australia, cooking everything from German to Creole food, managing a hundred chefs and cooks, I was now a BLT-making babysitter.

How much longer could I do this?

CHAPTER 26

A CHEF, A MOM, AND THE TRAVELING BLUES

"WHERE WE GOING T'DAY, MOMMY?" Daughter looks up eagerly from her bowl of blended Cheerios and Froot Loops. It's Monday, my day off. Stephen is at work, so it's just the two of us.

"Oh, how about beach, then Cha-Cha Coconuts?"

She nods emphatically, her mouth full of tan and colorful Os. She knows that after beach, she'll get pushed around St. Armand's Circle in her stroller, window-shopping. Then we'll sit at an outdoor table at Cha-Cha Coconuts, while her mom has a beer. We'll share an order of spiced fries, and chat up tourist couples with kids at nearby tables. My daughter, the socialite.

I love every minute of my day off. The leisure of drinking coffee in the morning and reading the paper like a normal person, instead of rolling out of bed into chef's whites, then dashing off to hole up in a kitchen all day, putting out emotional fires and not seeing the sun. On my day off the world is wide open before me, welcoming, the healing warmth of the sun reminding me of all that I am missing in life.

Daughter is the great companion. Sometimes on a day off, I bike downtown to antique stores with my toddler strapped into the seat behind me. Eventually, we'll start fishing together; first, she'll have a Mickey Mouse pole, then a real one, and she'll catch real fish, as long as I bait her hook for her. I take her to restaurants, outdoor patio places where I can have a beer and she can wander within my sight. The days with my daughter make the rest of them tolerable, those six days when I can't wait for Sunday afternoon, after slinging poached eggs for golfers, when Stephen wanders into the kitchen with Daughter on his hip, my girl eager to be plied with deviled eggs and chocolate mousse, me eager to begin my night and day off.

After a year at the club, I had earned a paid week off. This was a first for me, and I researched the best trip for my limited funds, since I was still paying down my tax bill. After two years of domesticity and attempting to hold my tongue at ditzy waitresses, I needed to go exploring. It was an unspoken thing between Stephen and me, that he would stay home and work while Daughter and I would take a trip. South America seemed close enough, and I hit the travel guides to learn that for the money and the short week, a cruise would take us more places. And a cruise ship seemed to be the most comfortable option for traveling with a three-year-old. I set aside all my negative stereotypes about cruises as the Walmarts of the travel world and scooped up the cheapest five-day fare I could find.

South from Sarasota we drove one sunny June Saturday morning to spend the night and most of Sunday in Miami before the ocean liner *Britanis* pulled out of the Port of Miami Sunday afternoon. Daughter bounced in her seat as we drove. Her thrill of seeing unknown places and going on a trip with Mom kindled my own bubbling excitement. We were two birds flying high above the stagnating workaday world. We were free!

South Beach in 1993 hadn't hit its full boom yet; hotels were cheap, though painted up nicely thanks to Michael Mann's stage setting for *Miami Vice*, and the place was relatively quiet in the early summer heat. I had booked a room for fifty-five bucks in a Deco hotel, its name long forgotten. The open-air lobby was mirrored along one long wall with a shiny marble floor reflecting the cool pink-and-black decor. Always a fan of art deco, I gazed at all the retro glamour. Then Daughter tugged at my shirt. "Mommy! Mom! Mom!" I pulled my eyes from the cool surroundings and looked down at her. "Yes, dear?"

"But Mom, where's *your ami*?"

"My what?" My *ami*? *Myami!* And after a long hard laugh, which appeared to insult her, I knew that on this trip I would be truly blessed, that I'd see things from an entirely different perspective than my previous explorations.

That night at a restaurant's front deck along Collins Avenue, we split a bowl of linguine tossed with garlic and smoked chicken. I sipped a glass of Chardonnay across from my little lady date dolled up in a dress. We watched the sun set with an explosion of pinks and oranges over the Atlantic and chattered on about what we would be seeing over the next five days. My three-year-old, an elegant and outspoken companion.

Traveling with a small child, no matter how well behaved and classy the kid, can have trying moments, however. After a blissed-out Sunday at the Miami Seaquarium, watching dolphins dance and twist in the air, at 4 p.m., it was time to board the ship, and Daughter went into devil-hell mode. She needed a nap, a kid luxury that would not be allowed on this trip, and as I pulled my screaming kid up the ship's metal steps by her arm, people looked at us with horror. *Wait until I tell your ami about this!*

"Oh, she'll be okay, once she gets her nap," I equivocated toward concerned stares.

Once checked into our tiny, cave-like room, sufficient only for sleeping, I coaxed her up to the gift shop and bribed her with a coloring book and a package of overpriced felt pens decorated with safari animals. We sat on deck while the boat pulled away from the dock, she coloring with jutted-out chin, me promising that we would have a good time as long as she was a good girl.

Dressing up for dinner and talking to our table-mates over the huge array of ocean-liner food overwhelmed both of us, and Daughter settled into a sleep-depraved buzz, a smile plastered on her face in between yawns. She was highly overstimulated by the food, the Caribbean waiters doting on her, and the ship's gentle rocking, but she hung in until I let her climb into her lower bunk that first night, where she passed out from exhaustion.

We stopped a few hours in Key West the next afternoon and explored the streets, gift shops, and vintage houses on a rented bicycle, which is the best mode of transportation when Daughter wants to be carried and Mother wants to cover as much territory as possible. The bike ride was leisurely, the photo moments perfect, and I had yet to regret not bringing her stroller.

On the boat we gorged on three meals a day and all-you-can-eat midnight buffets, and I drank responsibly and lounged like a useless sloth, while the old cruise ship bounded toward Cozumel. From my collection of maps I knew we would be cruising right past Cuba, a place of mystery I wanted to glimpse, even if from a distance, but I was told by a uniformed steward that our passing of Havana would occur late at night, while we all slept.

And slept we did that night, until we hit rough water and the ship rolled over high swells, then crashed down and then arced up to crash down again. My stomach woke me first, the roller-coaster ride thankfully disrupting my line-cooking dreams, which recently had morphed into Marisa-at-fifty nightmares, still wearing checked pants and a bulky coat, twirling gray hair under the hat, putting baking soda into green beans like the old washed-up chef at the Portland Golf Club. A thump and a peep bolted me upright, and I looked over the side of my bunk to see the bottoms of Daughter's feet above her bed. Her torso had slipped from the bunk, and she'd caught herself on the floor in a groggy handstand, appearing to be still asleep. I climbed down the steps and rearranged her, quieting my giggles so as not to wake her.

Finally, we were in Mexico. Cozumel was the first day, big and touristy and dusty with tequila-saturated Midwesterners singing along to the Mexican music at Carlos'n Charlie's. There were many streets to walk and Tecate beers to drink at cafés, but Daughter wasn't up for walking. So the first half of the day in Cozumel, my back aching from carrying her, I wandered into shops, searching my dormant Spanish to ask where I could buy a *coche de bebe*. Finally, settled into an overpriced collapsible stroller and comforted by a colorful Mexican blanket in summer's scorched air, my daughter slept while girls in embroidered white dresses raced by us on bike taxis, and aromas from food vendors made my mouth water. We were fed plenty on the boat, but I stopped for Tecates here and there, taking in the sights and sounds needily, loving the limbo of travel, wondering why I had to ever go home.

Playa del Carmen the next day was a lovely place, although it sat in the ruins of the future with the giant white ship floating offshore like a sinister beacon, its insides spilling out people flashing greenbacks and trouncing all over the quaintness of the yet-to-be-spoiled village. The town's innocence and beautiful beaches strummed a sad note in me, and I wished I'd gotten there some other way than via the looming white eyesore marring the horizon. Daughter and I swam in the cool turquoise water, then sat at a small, open concrete bar on the sand where I spoke Spanish to a young fisherman who had caught the shark whose jaw hung from twine above the rear counter. We shopped among the stalls of trinkets, scarves, and hats, ate chips and salsa at a local restaurant. No one spoke English. I felt anonymous and liked it that way.

The view of endless horizons from the ship, the turquoise ocean at Playa del Carmen, even the muddy port at Cozumel—all signified something I pondered on this trip. The possibilities in life, like the ocean, were vast and endless, the opportunities boundless. So why did I limit myself so? Because of a stutter? Because of a debilitating shyness that I suspected had something to do with my less-than-ideal upbringing? Why hadn't I stayed in college to become a teacher or a journalist? I was smart and had drive, but was paddling in circles in a rowboat instead of commanding a great ship. I couldn't even figure out how to get *on* the great ship of success, fulfillment, happiness, or whatever.

Once home, Sarasota's sunburned air assaulted me, as did Tournament Players Club's smells of overly crisp bacon, floor grease, and bleach. I was dropped right back into the scene with waitresses skittering about with bottles of ketchup drooping from their fingers. Back to cooking for the golfers and golfers' wives again, I felt the depression creep up, silent and slow like a plague. One short week was all I'd gotten to step out of this life. I wanted more.

CHAPTER 27

HOLIDAYS IN THE KITCHEN

HOLIDAYS? WHAT ARE THOSE, when you're a chef? Holidays I have to order more food, make sure everybody shows up for work, and juggle Daughter among sitters who don't mind an extra kid around for family gatherings. Easter we awaken a sleep-deprived, grumpy kid to hunt for eggs at dawn so I can get to work in time to pre-poach three hundred eggs in the thirty-gallon kettle for the golfers' Easter brunch. Christmas Eve I dash by the German deli after work to buy sausages and cold cuts for dinner. Valentine's Day I just plain hate.

But on Thanksgiving, I am determined.

Early Thanksgiving dinners hold the strongest childhood memories for me, if not entirely pleasant. Mom and Grandmother would each nurse a slow buzz throughout the day, making a holiday attempt of being friendly to each other, defying their otherwise jagged relationship. Each would smile defiantly while staking her case on whether or not to put an egg in the family stuffing recipe. For me there was the thrill of scooting my little red stool to the counter and turning the crank on the old metal food grinder; listening to the *pop!* of cranberries for the Jell-O salad; the sound of ice clinking in glasses; butter, garlic, and sausage popping like popcorn in the big pot in the stove; and the sizzling turkey basting in the oven all day—all this stimulation wooing me into the eventual happy turkey coma. Then there would be another spat about

who would make the gravy (I found that if I simply dragged my red stool over
to the stove in defiance of not being part of the gravy ceremony, they'd let me
stir it), more ice clinking in glasses, Stepdad smoking cigarettes in front of the
TV all day, until we'd all sit down to eat. In silence. That was as good as it ever
got with my family—but they were my family, and it meant something to me.

In my heart, Thanksgiving is the most important day. Babe's Seafood
House was closed that first Thanksgiving in Destin with Stephen, and I cooked
up my feast for him. Three months pregnant and not drinking, I replicated
the family meal, right down to the limp frozen green beans with almonds,
and skipped the egg in the stuffing because my loyalties were to my deceased
mother, not my deceased grandmother. We ate and ate and ate until we were
literally rolling on the floor, stuffed and silly.

But at TPC, golfers didn't cook Thanksgiving feasts in their stuccoed
second houses; they went out, and with two-hundred-plus reservations for
turkey night, my staff and I cooked all day to put food out for a Thanksgiving
buffet, the un-holiest of food events. I'd worked Thanksgivings before, at the
Mana Kai, where I left Mom's condo in the morning when the French-cut
green beans were thawing in the sink and came home in time for the comple-
tion of the gravy. In New Orleans I worked some Thanksgivings, and some
I cooked with friends. But now, with my newly acquired motherhood gene,
working on Thanksgiving felt very wrong.

So on Thanksgiving that first year at TPC, I told my cooks, "Dinner at my
house when we're off work." I called the event "Thanksgiving for Orphans"—
for in a way we were all orphans, or we wouldn't be working on this blessed
holiday. There was Steve, my often bullheaded sous chef recently separated
from his family; line cook Eddie, the apartment-down-the-street-from-the-
club-dweller, whose bipolar attitude I always tried to stay on the right side of;
Ron, who was like a father to us, whose wife was spending the holidays with
her family; a seasonal prep girl from Michigan who drove a giant black SUV;
and lovable Fran, a recovering alcoholic whose etched face showed years of
drug and alcohol abuse and who liked, while cooking, to sing Eric Clapton's
song with new lyrics: "I Shot the Sous Chef."

After scrubbing down the kitchen and making off with pans of stuffing
(with egg this time), sliced turkey, and mashed potatoes, by 11 p.m. we all
were gathered around my dining room table (except for Fran, who was hitting

an AA meeting before coming over). The rest of us were heavy drinkers, but I had O-Doul's in the fridge for Fran. Stephen was home from his day at his new cooking job at the Helmsley Sandcastle. Daughter was put down in her fairy princess bed after being picked up at the sitter's. I'd whipped up some shrimp Creole and Lafayette Lettuce—sautéed grated zucchini and yellow squash with garlic, butter, and Creole seasoning—so our food spread wouldn't be a total rehash of our workday. We scraped the TPC leftovers from the hotel pans into mismatched casserole dishes and arranged them on the table as if they were fresh from the oven. We ate, drank wine, made crude jokes, made fun of management, drank more wine, ate pumpkin pie I'd made the day before, and drank some more. A good time was had by all, and Fran drove all the drunks home.

The next morning, those of us at work shared wan, hangover smiles.

Christmas season in Sarasota is the unofficial beginning of tourist season, which hits full tilt in February. Fall is slow and steady while the year-round golfers use up their club minimums on food, but otherwise this is when scheduled hours get cut, staff takes time off, and in the kitchen, cleaning projects take on the importance of the days. As chef, I typically got two days off in the fall, Monday and Tuesday, but sometimes I got called in anyway, for something Steve or Eddie couldn't handle. The work was dull, simple, and the calm before the storm: the holiday banquet season.

Banquets and private parties I knew about peripherally from working with Omar at Babe's. And I know now, as a kitchen designer, that a proper banquet kitchen, in order to handle multiple parties and banquets while simultaneously cranking out the regular dinners, will have a separate banquet line and a separate entrance and exit for the banquet service, and a ton of refrigerated storage for pre-setup salads, desserts, and mountains of food that show up on a Friday for a busy weekend of food production and service.

TPC had none of this. My kitchen had been built as a lunch-only kitchen, to supplement the big Country Club of Sarasota on the course property, which had closed down several years prior for reasons unknown to me. That put the full weight of the entire club on the little satellite kitchen of which I was chef.

Before I realized the scope of the work heading my way that first season— when Peter Savage, the food and beverage manager, would book parties as if I had ten kitchens—I was having fun producing food for small autumn dinner parties for which I controlled the menus. I had time on my hands and time to get creative, and one afternoon found me rolling up sushi for a party of seventeen. It had been something I'd wanted to create: Creole roll with spiced crawfish tails and mullet roe, with the California roll ingredients of avocado and cucumber. I stood on the server side of the cold pickup line, since we had no separate prep area, rolling up the ingredients into rice and dried seaweed with the bamboo roller I'd brought from home. Peter strolled in, asking what the sushi was for. I pointed to the weekly party clipboards above the door of my office across the kitchen. "Tonight's party says 'chef's choice appetizers,' and these are the appetizers."

He seemed rather impressed, actually. But I didn't realize how impressed until a month later, when all seven clipboards were full of booked functions. I had perused nearly all of them, pre-calculating purchasing, prep lists, and scheduling, when I came upon one sit-down dinner menu for a hundred that listed sushi rolls as an appetizer.

"What the fuck!" I exclaimed, standing in front of the clipboard.

"I can't roll sushi for a hundred!" I said to Peter in his windowed office, wanting to gag on the view of the manicured golf course.

"But those were so good when you made them last time," he said.

I wanted to demand that *I* book the parties, and produce my *own* banquet menus, since this affected *me*, right? But I was stuck in this slot of clubhouse chef with preordained clubhouse chef duties, and one of those duties was to simply answer to management. I hated answering to anyone, but this was absurd. I was not making sushi for a hundred golfers. No way.

My food cost was shot that month, having to order California rolls from the local sushi bar, precut with garnish, and pay retail for them. We arranged them on a platter, which, when I looked at the finished product, symbolized all that was wrong with my job.

Another thing disturbing about working the club on the holidays, more so than in other kitchens, was the proximity to and interaction with the dining members who, as I noted before, were a different clientele from my previous norm. At the frequent buffets, old golfer guys wanted to meet the chef, asking their waitress if I'd come out and meet them. Uncomfortable, and hating myself for hating those who appreciated me, smiling and nodding was all I could do, like it was such an honor, yes, such an honor to meet retired you. Once I was invited into the private dining room for an embarrassingly long standing ovation for my New Year's Eve dinner of filet and lobster with bordelaise and roasted red pepper puree, the wives clasping my hands in their own cool wrinkled ones. In the kitchen bubbles of New Orleans and Portland, when you're master of your own universe every day, holidays run past you with little consequence. But those member-golfers and their families for whom I was scooting around to wipe up a food display or refill a hotel pan of taco meat for the Tuesday night buffet, or replace the salad bowl of romaine for the luncheon ladies who are sipping Manhattans at two in the afternoon? Well, all I could see was that smack-dab in front of me, they were having fun.

I watched them get to go out and party and eat, while I, as chef, was fucking working yet again.

CHAPTER 28

FOOD PREJUDICES

I UNDERSTAND WHY some people have prejudices against certain religions or certain ethnic people who happen to be Americans; I don't agree with it, but I understand that narrow-mindedness is an ingrained trait stemming from familial upbringing. Blame the parents. But I do not understand why people say they don't like a food *when they have never tasted it.* How can they know? How can they make such a judgment?

My mom was a clear example. From that early French dinner at Chez Paul's when she'd turned up her nose at escargots, I knew my mom was food-squeamish. Once, years later, when she said to me, "I don't like shrimp," I replied with a question: "Oh, when did you eat shrimp, Mom?" I knew that shrimp was something exotic (even if we were in Hawaii and surrounded by water), and we never had an opportunity to eat it when I was growing up, mostly because of cost.

"I just don't like them."

To which I felt embarrassed. My mom was obviously very narrow-minded—but at least she ate and cooked with onions, while Grandmother did not. Perhaps a childhood barren of onions could have contributed to my mom's lack of adventure.

Later in my upbringing, Mom explained that in the Bible chapter Leviticus, many of the foods she refused to eat were listed as off-limits. So this meant no camel, buzzard, or shellfish, but she did eat pork. My mom was also a bit of a nut.

In the Mana Kai year when I returned to Maui, when Mom was working as a condo cleaner, she took home the food found in the condo refrigerators, and I believe this is how she saw how the other three-quarters lived. I'd find in her refrigerator things like wasabi mustard, zucchini, or a bruised orange, just sitting there next to her usual staples of iceberg lettuce, onions, butter, wheat bread, and bologna. These "unusual" ingredients were waiting for something to happen before the rot settled in.

"Mom, what's with the zucchini?" I'd say, pulling out the carton of orange juice for a rum drink. Her stock of booze was also better now from her cleaning of condos.

"Well, I hate to throw it away . . ."

"Why don't you eat it, then?"

"Well . . ." I believe this was a struggle: She didn't want to say, "I don't like zucchini," because she knew what her daughter the chef would say, so instead she'd say, "I don't know what to do with it."

So a cooking lesson would occur.

Soon Mom was sautéing up disks of zucchini with butter and toasted almonds, steaming broccoli, and emulsifying a butter sauce for mahi-mahi or mako shark. The orange and the wasabi became an orange-wasabi beurre blanc.

My mom became master of the butter sauce.

Then she started calling me to say things like, "Marisa, Star Market had shark on sale and I have some fresh broccoli; how about coming over for dinner?"

She even ate a shrimp at a restaurant on the Big Island when we went to my grandfather's for a small family reunion with Aunt Sandi, Uncle Jack, and Aunt Emily. The platter was being passed around and I was giving her the stink eye, so she buckled under the pressure. I stared at her as she chewed and chewed, her face completely blank, as if not tasting the salty crustacean at all. I thought she felt the pressure from all her immediate family, not just me.

So in my mom's later years (which weren't that late, since she died at fifty), she was able to live a little in the culinary department. I'm glad for that.

On to my kid. Of course, if you force a kid to eat something, they'll hate it forever, and if you deprive a kid of something, they'll love it. This is the delicate balance that Stephen and I maintained throughout Daughter's upbringing. Health was first, but I wasn't growing my own vegetables and pureeing my own baby food like those overly blissed-out-looking women in the pastel parenting magazines. Multitudes of healthy people had been weaned on Gerber's, so this was good enough for my kid too. But I didn't put soda pop into her baby bottle either—which, to my horror, I actually witnessed once at a day care. I'd never consciously thought about candy and soda in my child's life up until then, but I was so appalled by this toddler sucking down carbonated sugar and chemicals that I decided from that point onward that my daughter could try the stuff, but junk food would not be around the house and would not at all be encouraged.

One afternoon, early in Daughter's toddler life, her dad and I were forced to explain why other kids got to consume crap and she did not. It was Christmastime and the day care parents had provided gifts for a grab bag for the kids. When Stephen picked up Daughter, she had in her possession a book that opened to about a dozen rows of Life Savers tubes. She had eaten one full tube of the candy. I'd just gotten home when Stephen flung open the front door with Daughter crying on his hip. In his hand he held the Life Savers book.

"Look at this! Look at this!" he barked. "*Look* what another parent gave *our* child!" He waved the book at me; Daughter cried louder and reached for it. He pulled it from her reach and she shrieked.

"Oh, shit!" I said.

Stephen put Daughter down and she came running to me.

"I want my present!" she cried into my shoulder.

Stephen explained, "I tried to trade it for something else, but they wouldn't let me."

"What's wrong with that place?" I yelled above Daughter's accelerated screaming. "Okay, okay, let me see it."

He handed it over, saying proudly, "Good thing is, I don't think she wants the candy; she just wants the present."

I took the offending book while Daughter, still leaning against me, quieted for a moment, looked up at me, then gazed upon her present as if thinking, *Well, Daddy was mean about it; maybe Mommy will be nicer.*

No, Mommy is just more cunning.

"Hm, I think you're right," I said, agreeing with Stephen. I opened the book and gazed into it adoringly. "Well, it is a pretty book, isn't it? With Santa and his reindeer printed inside?"

Daughter nodded, as I proceeded to remove the tubes of candy from it.

"Honey, this is a lot of candy. I don't think the mom who bought this realized all this candy was in it . . ." (This mom who was just plain fucking stupid and unthinking.) "You know all this candy is bad for your teeth, right?"

Daughter nodded. I handed the candy to Stephen.

"Now we'll keep the candy safe for you, but you can put Polly Pocket in this book. You think she'd like to live in here for Christmas?"

Daughter nodded and I handed the empty book to her.

She never asked about the candy.

The dipshit day care lady got a lecture from me the next day about limiting the gift bag to toys and that believe it or not (although we were apparently a minority), some parents cared about what their kids ate.

One night, sitting at the dinner table, Daughter, at seven years old, proclaimed a sudden dislike of tomatoes. "But you've always eaten tomatoes," I responded, frustrated.

Stephen said, "Eat your tomatoes if you know what's good for you."

"But I don't like them, Daddy."

"Eat them!" Stephen barked.

She began to cry. "I don't like them anymore and my teacher says your taste buds change every seven years." Blubber, blubber, blubber.

"What?" I asked. "That's ridiculous." I was certain I sounded like my grandmother.

After a forced father-daughter tomato-eating episode, with Daughter gagging, she said it was the texture that turned her off. She no longer ate bananas either, or any other fruit for that matter, unless it was in juice form.

Although broccoli had always been okay by her, cauliflower was a little sketchy at first. Probably for the inedible look of it—bland, mealy, resembling albino brains.

"It's just like white broccoli," I said to her one night at the dinner table when she was about three. I popped a forkful in my mouth and winked at her. Her eyes, fixed on me, got very large and then both eyes blinked emphatically. She was trying to wink! Without missing a beat, I popped in another forkful and winked with the other eye. "See, and cauliflower makes you wink!" And with that I had her. She was eating cauliflower and trying to wink, while Stephen held his sides to keep his laughter in.

There are a few things that I prefer not to eat, of course. It's not that I don't like these foods; I just prefer not to eat them.

One of these foods is frog's legs. My mom told me a story of visiting Georgia in her childhood, when the adults went out hunting for frogs. When they returned to the house, she saw them in the kitchen with baskets of croaking amphibians. She said they killed the frogs by way of some game where two relatives sitting across from each other at the Formica kitchen table each held on to a leg, wishbone-style, and split the live frog in two. That was why, she said, she wouldn't eat frog's legs. And I found that to be a *very* good reason.

When I moved to New Orleans and pretty much did all things a Southerner would do, I found myself with a gang of chefs at a catfish restaurant in Mobile, Alabama. The family-style crocks and platters of food came to our big table: Fried pickles, catfish, hush puppies, coleslaw, beans, and frog's legs were passed to each of us. I knew I had to at least try the frog's legs. I could not go through life saying I didn't like something because the generations before me had messed it up. So I took one of the little leggy things and gingerly chewed crispy fried meat from a little bone.

It tasted like chicken. So why not eat chicken, then? (The kind without all the hormones, anyway.) I'd tried a frog leg and I didn't dislike it; I just preferred not to eat it, and still don't.

Despite my love of sushi, sea urchin is another food I don't eat. I tried it at a sushi bar once and found it to be rank and stinky. Perhaps it was rotten? I'll try it again sometime.

As for bugs—I don't think so. Bugs aren't food; they're bugs and should go on eating other bugs or get sprayed with something.

Any food with a higher ratio of profit to wholesomeness, as in fast food? I'd rather starve.

These very strong sentiments about food will last, whether I am a chef or not.

CHAPTER 29

THE COMPETITION

EVER SINCE MY FIRST JOB at the Sea Scoop in Lahaina, something happened to me in kitchens that made me like who I was. This is why throughout my teens and twenties, I endured the long hours of kitchen work and persevered to become chef. In the kitchen, I was confident and passionate. Kitchen life was fun. I related to my peers in the kitchen. There was partying afterward. The camaraderie made me feel whole. Outside my job, I remained weak and insecure. So I stayed inside my job as much as possible.

But at thirty-three, I had a husband and daughter. I no longer partied with my cooks. The premonition (and nightmare) of being fifty and donning an oversize coat and checked pants was a frightening tableau of my future. The problem was that I didn't know what else to do. I was sick of sunless kitchens, even if they had tricked me into being confident. In addition to being overworked and bored, by this time I had a stinking bad attitude—which, in the confident bubble of my kitchen, had translated into cockiness.

One afternoon at the club, Peter Savage came behind the cooking line in his suit and shiny black shoes. I flipped a turkey sandwich over on the griddle. Had I done something wrong? Made a waitress cry? Insulted a guest? Had one of my cooks overcooked a steak?

Peter rustled a paper at me. "I think you should join the American Culinary Federation."

With toasted sandwich balanced on spatula, I pivoted to the cutting board, hacked the sandwich in half at an angle, slid it onto a garnished plate, and put the plate in the heated window. "Lisa! Table ten!" *Tap-tap-tap* went the spatula on the stainless steel overshelf. To Peter, I said, "Join the ACF? Why? To get certified? You know I never have time for that. Chefs who have time for all that shit aren't working hard enough."

"No, not certification," Peter said, backing away as I whooshed sandwich crumbs and lettuce bits from the cutting board with my towel. "There's a Hot Food Competition at the Florida Restaurant Show in two months, and I've signed you up. But you have to be an ACF member to participate."

I stopped, nearly crashing into myself. "You signed me up for a *cooking* competition?"

He smiled his carefree, silly smile. This was something I liked about Peter. He was a person first, my boss second. But how dare he put me into a competitive position without my permission? On the other hand, he must have thought highly of my skills to put me into a competitive situation without my permission. I couldn't do it, though. I was better under pressure at work, not competing with a bunch of culinary coeds. I sighed. "I don't have any formal training, Peter—I'm not suited for that. All those stuffy chef wannabes with their spun sugar and stuffing quails into lambs' asses or whatever. All I ever got from Julia Child was 'Save the liver.'"

"Oh, nonsense. You're a great chef," he said, handing me the application.

I looked down at the papers in my food-stained hands, an ache forming in my stomach at the thought of leaving these kitchen walls to venture "out there."

The competition would be the Mystery Box, where you're handed a box of main-dish meats and you have a half hour to "shop" along tables of various food products already picked over by the other chefs in the competition, then create a four- or five-course menu. Then you have four hours to prepare your entire meal for five judges, then another two hours to serve twelve guests the same menu, who sign up and pay for a chef's table. These people, and others watching the whole affair, select who they think will put out the yummiest meal. You're provided dishes, a refrigerator, an electric stove with oven, and a worktable with some outlets. You're expected to bring all your own cooking utensils, pans, pots, and countertop plug-in equipment.

I tried hard to get out of it. *Who'll watch the kitchen while I'm gone? I can't bake; that leaves me out of it. I'm not qualified. I don't have time to join the ACF. What if they give me something I don't know how to cook? You don't want me to humiliate the club, do you?* But Peter would have none of it. "You'll do fine," he said.

So for two months I attended ACF meetings, read my French cookbooks, and became more and more stressed about the day Peter and I would drive to Orlando, where I would be On. The. Spot. All the while, I wondered why he had such faith in me. Sometimes I tried to focus on that. At home I shared my anxiety with Stephen, who would shrug, smile, and take a pull off his Old Milwaukee.

What I didn't grasp from the vaguely written guidelines (I'd begun to figure out that many chefs and cooks are illiterate, and my inner snob no longer wanted to be associated with this lot) was that I could have an apprentice to help me sling out all the food on the Fateful Day. But I didn't know this, so I slogged on alone, through my lists of things to bring and subconscious breathing exercises. A lone mountain climber preparing for her mission, with no spotter.

On the morning of Fateful Day, with a Black Russian hangover sloshing around my brain from a few medicating nightcaps in the Orlando hotel bar with Peter, I donned my houndstooth chef's pants and white coat, twirled my waist-length hair into a clip, and smooshed a tall toque atop. I then ventured into the predawn to the Convention Center, toward my 5:45 scheduled private slot to receive my Mystery Box.

We chefs received our boxes fifteen minutes apart, so the other contestants were only peripheral, thankfully, while I waited to be handed my goods. It wasn't a box at all but a sheet pan with a giant whole fish on it, which I couldn't identify, and next to the fish, a small package of red meat-something lay like roadkill. "Oh!" I said, faking a smile to hide my embarrassment, looking from the fish to the old chef-judge guy. "Wh-what is it? The fish?"

"Sturgeon."

"Oh, okay. And that?" I pointed to the meat thing.

"Lamb's tenderloin."

"Beautiful," I lied, thinking, *Isn't a real chef supposed to know what the fuck the food is before preparing it?*

I hefted my tray of truly mystery goods to the table I'd been directed to, where a pen and a pad of yellow paper awaited my brilliant menu planning. Leaving the fish and roadkill, I vaulted toward the shopping tables to snatch any food products that would hopefully turn me into a legitimate chef.

I had a lot of improvisational cooking under my belt; I excelled when facing a refrigerator full of odd items, as in Mom's refrigerator full of freebies from condo-cleaning on Maui. But what had kept me up nights leading up to this event was the dessert course. As the old chef's saying goes, "Cooking is an art, baking is a science." In ninth grade I had struggled for my B in physical science.

There were four desserts I could bake without a recipe: chocolate mousse, caramel custard, bread pudding with rum sauce, and cheesecake. The scenarios playing out in my mind during my sleepless nights included, of course, having the ingredients for one of these selections. I even considered a four-course meal without dessert. Who needed dessert anyway? There was an obesity problem in America.

I glanced at the array of picked-over foodstuff on the wooden banquet tables, then began to focus on individual ingredients. Produce rolled around the first table. My brain felt too large for my Black Russian–tightened head. My tongue tasted bitter from the drip coffee I'd had in my room. *Think!* The sturgeon I would treat as a salmon; a fish was just a goddamn fish, after all. I put three Idaho potatoes and a bunch of asparagus into my basket. Where was sturgeon from, anyway? Who cooked this fish? In all my travels, I'd never seen it on a menu. Maybe in Greenland. A bunch of leeks . . . some shallots . . . lemon . . . cantaloupe.

Cantaloupe? "John Cougar Melonsoup," sang a voice in my head, reminding me of what the cooks called the chilled soup we had served at the Plaza Restaurant. The goddess of menu creation was there for me. These ideas certainly weren't coming out of *my* brain. Oh . . . what about that fucking lamb? It had to be a salad. Why not? New Orleans Cajun music spiced up the voice echoing in the cave of my head. Every menu item I'd prepared at every job rushed to my frontal lobe. Was that cheating? "Lamb salad: I'll blacken it, slice it on greens," I thought. I grabbed a package of salad greens, a bunch of green grapes, cherry tomatoes for color.

On to the spices. Pink peppercorns, everything under the sun to make blackening seasoning, horseradish, honey. Then I stopped cold. The Cajun accordion menu maker in my head went silent. There, lying in front of the spices, was a single loaf of white bread. Semisquished, it looked discarded. I snatched it up and the voice in my head operatically sang out, "Bread pudding!"

I finished up at the dairy table, grabbed two cups of brandy and white wine from the cooking liquors, and settled in at my table to write my menu:

Chilled melon soup with pink peppercorn crème fraîche

Blackened lamb salad with white grape vinaigrette

Potato pancake–crusted sturgeon on braised leeks, with horseradish beurre blanc

New Orleans–style bread pudding with orange brandy sauce

I submitted my menu to the judge and with my groceries bounded off to my assigned Station 7.

I filleted the whole fish, my hands shaking like a crack addict's, while a judge came around and checked how clean my cuts were (even pulling the carcass from the trash once to inspect it for waste). Then I cut, mixed, roasted, peeled, baked, braised, and emulsified. Two hours in, Peter showed up, grinning, beer in hand. "How's it going?"

"Yep," I said, not stopping.

"So, *uh*, look over there!"

I looked across the aisle from the cooking stations. The beer garden. Subconsciously I'd seen (and smelled) it, but Peter pointed to a specific booth within the festive arena of hops and grains. A mustard-yellow banner with four giant Xs in bright red glowed like a new sun. Castlemaine Four-X! My favorite beer from Australia!

"My reward when I'm done?"

"I'll bring you two."

"How much more time do I have?"

"Two hours."

"I'm rockin'."

"Good for you. Um . . . apparently you were allowed to have an apprentice," he said, gesturing toward the other chef's stations.

My finger slipped off the button of the food processor containing white grape vinaigrette, and for the first time I looked around at the other cooking stations. In each alcove of two tables and a range, two chef's hats calmly bobbed up and down, compared to my one frantic, spasmodic hat. "Well, fuck!" I said to Peter. "Can *you* be my apprentice? Help me wash pots and serve all this up so I get it out on time?" I'd lose points if I didn't get everything out timely and hot.

He winced. "I'm not a member of the ACF. You'll be okay; you're lightning fast."

I remembered something in the printed guidelines: "Apprentices need to be members of the ACF." My interpretation of that was, "If you're an apprentice chef and want to compete, you have to be a member of the ACF." But apparently they meant, "Yo, dipshit chef! Bring an apprentice to help you, only make sure they're a member too." I jammed my finger on the pulse button until the dressing seeped up from the lid.

Pointing his beer hand at the stovetop, where my bread pudding was cooling, Peter said with both excitement and relief in his voice, "I see you found bread!"

"Hell yeah!" I poured the salad dressing into a small plastic pitcher and shoved it into the refrigerator next to John Cougar Melonsoup. I paused, wiping my hands on my apron, and considered my next batch of tasks as I monitored the braising leeks and beurre blanc reduction on the stove. Next to me, in Station 6, the apprentice had gone off to the community sink to wash pans while a skinny boy-chef stood over plates of cake-like disks, blowtorch in hand, caramel-colored sugar spinning up like hair in the blue flame. I rolled my eyes toward boy-chef for Peter to see, while I stirred the julienned leeks sweating in a saucepan of butter and wine. Peter rolled his eyes too. "I hear that's the chef at Dollywood," he said.

"Ew, that's a place?"

"Yep."

"I feel old," I said, and I kept stirring. I didn't have time to worry about the other competitors. Other than Peter pointing out Chef Dollywood, I was in my own world.

"Well, I'll be off," Peter said, raising his plastic cup of beer. "Good luck."

"Taken."

For two more hours, I multitasked to my personal drumbeat—the food as my muse. I was queen of my stove, oven, prep table, knife. I wasted not a movement to get myself ahead for what would be the biggest challenge: all the dishes of food out on time for the judges, with hot food hot and cold food cold, plate edges wiped clean, the food looking pretty and edible. Searing the lamb and slicing it to order would be the trickiest. Would it slow me down?

It did. The span of time between the melon soup and the blackened lamb salad had the judges scribbling on their points sheets. Then from the fry pan, with hot butter scorching my fingers, I tried to save time by not looking for my spatula (would I get marked down for using my fingers?), arranging the potato-crusted sturgeon onto the heated plates, dished up with a blob of braised leeks in the center and blanched asparagus arranged outward from the leeks like wheel spokes. Atop the fish went the horseradish beurre blanc, and an afterthought of cherry tomato halves between the asparagus spokes, since this fish wasn't pink like salmon and the plate looked too pale. *Bam!* Out went those plates, and a server rushed them off to the judges. Next, the bread pudding. Hot. Sliced. Warm brandy sauce over. Mandarin oranges for color. Then Peter (God love him) was standing there with two ice-cold Four-X beers.

"I did it!" That was all I cared about: I had done it. No real disasters. I knew the food tasted good and looked presentable. And now I had beer! I was ready to clean up and go. But Peter said, "You need to go to the judges now."

"Why?"

"They'll give you your critique."

"Critique" meant "criticism." What would they say—"It sucked"?

Reluctantly I put down my beer, peeled off my apron, and left my station for the first time in four hours. Across the aisle, five judges were perched like royalty above a banquet table. On the table lay the remnants of my meal. I smiled shyly at them.

The main judge, the eldest, the senior, the Food God, spoke. "Nice work, young lady."

Chauvinist.

Next came a blur of comments from four of the five judges, mostly good, about the food's color, texture, and presentation. It was noted that I lost points for the scramble it had taken me to sling out all the food singlehandedly. Which would not have been an issue if these culinary prima donnas had taken a grammar class or two before writing their competition instructions. A fat, gray-haired judge on the end of the table remained silent until we got to the dessert course. Then I saw his badge: Executive Pastry Chef.

"This dessert," the old judge began, "is so beautiful in its simplicity. The perfect comfort food, which conjures up good times, Grandma, and traditions of childhood. Elegantly presented, each serving sliced into three sections to soak up the sauce, and the orange segments were the perfect accompaniment."

Was he shitting me?

"I'm giving this dessert a Gold score. Congratulations."

It was a score that pulled me up into placing fifth out of twelve chefs, even ahead of the sneering, sugar-spinning boy-chef of Dollywood.

Later, I teared up as I stood in line to accept my medal. I knew I had graduated from this stage of my life. I had done it. Not in the way I'd envisioned; I had no restaurant of my own, no real claim to fame. But I'd traveled and I'd run kitchens large and small, with people from all over the country and the world, and now I had this damn silver medal. I was thirty-four and a mother; I was smart, and certainly driven. It was time to move on. Tears spilled from my eyes as my name echoed around the auditorium and I stepped forward. I tried sucking my tears inward, wanting to avoid embarrassment. The executive chef presented me with my medal and said, "You'll be a fine chef someday, young lady." To him, I was simply a young girl climbing the macho culinary ladder. But I knew I'd already reached the top. He draped the medal around my neck, Olympic-style, and I held my breath, wanting to explode into a barrage of tears. Tears of relief. These tears would be the fuel to transport me to my next destination: out of the kitchen.

CHAPTER 30

NEW DESIGNS

THE COMPETITION HAD BEEN in September, and in April of the following year I sat across a mahogany desk from C. J. Fishman, with a portrait of Ronald Reagan looking down at us from his wall. Mr. Fishman was saying, "In order to be as good as a man in business, you need to be twice as smart as a man."

I was wearing a dress purchased at T.J. Maxx, thinking my new Farrah Fawcett haircut was a bad idea and feeling all-around jittery like it was the first day of school. I had hounded this guy for weeks to hire me—to save me from my kitchen job. I'd agonized for months about how to earn a living outside the kitchen. Maybe I could teach? No, not with a stutter. Designing kitchens—yes, I could! TPC's corporate chef told me about this little kitchen design firm in nearby Venice, and stomping my nerves down like so many Medusa curls, I went a-calling, both in person and nervously on the phone, until I got the interview.

In order to be as good as a man in business, you need to be twice as smart as a man.

Smarts I'd always had. It was a bunch of other stuff I lacked: confidence, verbal skills, patience, people skills. This was a sales position. Did I want to lurch out of the kitchen into a pack of hungry wolves? Yes, I had to! Daughter would be five next year, and how would only Mondays off be then?

As I sat for my interview, I hoped my desperation didn't show too much. *Act cool, ferheavensake!* Did Mr. Fishman know I wasn't a Republican? Did he know I stuttered? How could he not notice?

If he knew about either of these things, he didn't let on.

Twice as smart as a man. "Well, that's easy," I said.

Mr. Fishman hired me. Not exactly as a kitchen designer at first, but as a salesperson, cold-calling restaurants and architects to *sell* kitchen equipment and kitchen design.

So in April of 1994 I got out of the kitchen and, on tax day to be exact, began training in all things sales and kitchen equipment. I had stood underneath exhaust hoods for twenty years and now needed to learn how they actually operated. I had also worked around people for twenty years, but I had limited people skills. (Swearing at waitresses was not a skill that counted here.) This undertaking was enormous, but I felt hopeful; like when Grandmother had told me I could not win a race against the neighbor kids because my legs were too short and I won anyway. Something ingrained in my soul persevered in spite of all my embarrassments. I remember Dona (now married to a film editor and living in L.A.) saying with concern when I told her on the phone of my career change, "You're in sales? Are you sure you want to do that?"

Stephen was still cooking for Leona Helmsley at her hotel on Lido Beach and was home some evenings when I arrived with angst-filled chatter about my days. He was usually sitting in a folding chair in our screened Florida room smoking Marlboros and drinking a can of Old Milwaukee (he could drink nearly a case of this crap beer on a day off, but I usually didn't say anything). He'd listen to me and nod—his way of showing encouragement.

Daughter started school, and I signed her up Saturdays at a local dance and performing arts studio. She took to it well and I was a proud mother. Money was tight and the fees were high, but she was focused and she enjoyed it, and performing would become a backdrop to all of her school years.

One night, she was going to sing a solo at the Players Theater. Stephen had the night off and we had the rare family outing. I dressed her up in a powder-blue dress, proud of her on-key voice and her young drive for creativity.

When she was called to come out onto the darkened stage, a mixture of pride and fear washed over me. It wasn't me called onstage to sing a song, so why was *I* nervous? Daughter seemed, unlike her mother, to not have a self-conscious bone in her body, singing at downtown events and festivals with her voice class and volunteering to train for the solos. I felt Stephen's arm tighten next to mine. A normal parental feeling, I supposed.

Then Daughter appeared, spotlight upon her. Her voice teacher played an intro on the piano below the stage. Daughter opened her mouth . . . and nothing came out. Silence. The audience froze. Stephen and I froze. The thought of my mom's dated saying, "You could hear a pin drop," came to mind because you could have heard a pin drop just then, and I wished I could because I really needed to hear something besides nothing.

The piano began again and stopped when she opened her mouth, guppy-like, her voice constricting.

My chest tightened horribly, that familiar feeling of helplessness and fear becoming a physical thing, fouling up my speech, making my face red. How could I help my child not feel this way? Onstage a quiet whimper came from her, but it was the only sound in the theater, goddammit, so it didn't seem so quiet and my face swelled in a big stifled cry, water leaking from my eyes, my hand gripping Stephen's arm, his hand gripping my thigh.

The piano began again. Nothing. A few gasps from the audience.

Liz, one of the voice teachers, appeared at the edge of the stage, arms motioning, coaxing our frightened daughter with smooth words, smiles, nods, cajoles, you-can-do-its. I continued to hold my breath, holding in the avalanche of built-up fear.

But it's what you do, isn't it, when you fear something? To lose the fear, you have to do the thing, until there is no more fear. Only sissies avoid the fear. My daughter is not a sissy. Neither am I. Fearful of things at times, but not a sissy. Which is why, after twenty years in the comfort of the kitchen, I'd decided to give up my comfort zone for something else. I stared fear in the face dead-on and told it, *Move aside, motherfucker, I'm going to the better life on the other side of you.*

Onstage Daughter sniffed up her tears, cleared her throat, and nodded toward Liz—bless that woman's heart. The piano started up again. And then the songbird voice broke the horrible silence and Daughter sang out Annie's "Tomorrow" with all the confidence of a star, her strong, soon-to-be-alto voice filling the theater.

After the song, the clapping and cheering gave way to standing ova-
tions, and Stephen and I joined in, my face wet with tears of pride and relief.
Daughter deserved that ovation, but how many cheering her were actually
thinking, "I wish I had the guts to do that"?

•   •   •

"Can you get me a size six, honey? These are a little baggy." I handed Daughter the slacks and held the dressing room door open a crack to watch her
scuttle over to the sale rack where I had selected them.

A shop attendant went over to her and said something I couldn't hear.
Daughter pointed toward me, the attendant looked over, and I waved and
smiled. *Yes, I do have a personal fashion stylist, what of it?*

"These are both size six, Mommy. I brought you a blue pair too."

I slipped on the black pair and scrutinized myself in the long mirror and
the one behind me. The layer of baby fat that had haunted me during my
twenties and had dropped off during those early stressful days in Australia was
gone forever, thanks to my three-times-a-week exercise classes at the Y. The
slacks were flattering to my short and shapely figure, almost like jeans. But
was this how I wanted to look at my job? Was it the correct image? What *was*
the correct image? Hell if I knew.

"Do these look worky enough to you?" I asked Daughter. I turned side-
ways to see if my tummy looked flat. As if a six-year-old would know, but hey,
feedback was feedback.

She put her forefinger to chin. "Hmm, not sure; you need the top part."

"You're right." I slipped on my T-shirt and we went back to the sale rack
to look for blouses that would look worky with these slacks.

Getting out of the kitchen after twenty years and into a job where people
actually look at you required a few major adjustments.

Wardrobe, of course. At the time of my escape from the kitchen, my closet
contained a pair of faded 501 Levi's from high school, a pair of super-skinny
black jeans from Australia, a denim skirt, some vintage Hawaiian shirts, a
black dress—also purchased in Australia for the after-Expo party—and some
sweatshirts. My dresser drawers were stuffed with shorts, and T-shirts bought
at restaurants and bars: We Install and Service Hangovers . . . The Little Bar,

Fort Walton Beach (my favorite, a faded pink tank I still wear, the bar on the beach long ago blown away by a hurricane); The Crazy Flamingo, Longboat Key; Red Beans and Rice, New Orleans—just to name a few. This was not the wardrobe of a food service consultant, a kitchen designer in training. My years of kitchen globe-trotting hadn't exactly netted me a ton of money for an infusion of office wear into my hippie-chef-day-off collection.

So once every other month, I went shopping for bargain things to add to that first five-day office wear collection that got me started. I really don't like shopping, unless it's for plants or vintage collectibles. Clothes shopping? The brain-sucking atmosphere of malls? No thanks.

But I had my little personal assistant, and we'd make a day of it. Coffee and hot chocolate together at Barney's Coffee. Time to spend with my gal, on actual weekends. Over time I got firm pointers from my little younger generation: "Mom, shoulder pads are so eighties," she'd say, or "That shirt makes you look so frumpy."

Another adjustment was makeup. I never wore makeup as a chef—why bother? I owned a little shadow and mascara for stepping out, barely knowing how to use the stuff, but when you have to present yourself to strangers, to clients and potential clients, the boss, the people in the office, well, you should look like you know how to look nice, like you care about yourself and your job. As Mr. Fishman said, "Perception is everything." There's a lot to hate about that statement, but it is true.

Another big change when I joined the daily workforce was grocery shopping. As a six-day-a-week working chef, grocery shopping involved purchasing twelve-packs of beer and cereal and milk for the kid. Chefs don't cook on their day off, no more than the painter who needs his house painted or the plumber who needs his fixtures replaced. Chefs go out to eat on their day off. Once I was home seven nights a week, cooking for two, sometimes three when Stephen was off from the restaurant, the new requirements were endless: full-blown suburban grocery shopping, cutting coupons from the Sunday paper, wheeling the kid in the shopping cart while she pointed to the lower shelves, returning plastic bags to the store when the cupboard got stuffed with them.

At first there was something blissful about grocery shopping; at thirty-four years old, I had never grocery shopped as a routine. The sit-down planning of the event, all that we would cook and consume in a week's time, and what I'd seen on sale in the paper reminded me of my mom's extensive planning (pencil, paper, coupons) for her trips to Kihei's Foodland, Azeka's, and Star Market. Into Sarasota's Publix or Kash n' Karry Daughter and I would embark, she chattering about what we would do after shopping, me doing shopping-cart demolition derby with the rest of society. I wheeled up and down every aisle, reading labels, not trusting most brand names because Big Food just wanted to throw shit down our gullets at a profit. Daughter sometimes reached out to touch things. "I want to see, Mommy!" I'd tell her, "I don't see eyeballs at the end of your fingertips!" Then our cart would be full and we'd be in line, looking at other people's carts full of soda and frozen packages of premade things, while our cart held vegetables, milk, eggs, whole-grain cereals and bread, packages of fresh meat, beer—all the major food groups. I was still a food snob.

Southwest Florida gets very hot and muggy in the summer and starting around mid-May, it's unbearable. So air-conditioning is *big* here, very big. But in the culinary worlds that Stephen, Daughter, and I had lived in, we paid this no mind. We were seldom home. Why have the air-conditioning jacking up the electric bill all day when we weren't there? We got home late, around ten, had a few beers, stripped off our clothes, and fell into bed, on top of the sheets. Day off? We'd be at the beach, home in the late afternoon, and maybe I'd click the air on to cool the house down for a little TV watching before bed.

We eventually got to know our neighbors across the street, who told us that they would watch our front window when the weather transitioned from pleasant spring to hellacious summer, to see when the window would close. Their air went on by April each year and they were shocked to see the humid summer months slide by with our front window still open. "Look!" Pam from across the street would say to her husband, Dan, peering out their living room window. "Mid-July and finally, they've closed up the house and turned on the air!"

We only had a thirty-five-dollar-a-month electric bill because we also did not have that symbol of suburban living: a dryer. With so few clothes to wash and only once a week, why buy a dryer? We could just hang the clothes in the sun. Rainy August? Hell, hang the clothes dirty and the constant hot rain will wash them (okay, I'm joking with that one). It was a little embarrassing, I must admit, when Pam across the street once offered to put Daughter's damp shirt in her dryer and Daughter said, "Mom, what's a dryer?"

When I joined the regular workday schedule and needed a cool house to paint my face in each morning and hang out in nights at home, our front window was cranked shut by May, like everyone else's on the street. And all the rayon, cotton, and polyester I wore for work needed drying, so we purchased a dryer. The electric bill doubled, while my income had been cut in half.

Another noticeable difference was the number of people roaming around on my weekends off. Where did all these people come from? There had been a certain solitude in having Mondays off, when normal people were all at work. But now, with crowded beaches and stores, instead I basked in the light of two days off with my girl. This time I needed to recuperate from the stressful five days of nervously cold-calling restaurants, making mistakes, and beating myself up for all my inadequacies. But somewhere far away in the vastness of my brain, in the deep subconscious, there was a whisper of a thought that kept me on my path, no matter how horrible of a job I thought I was doing: C. J. Fishman was like Peter Savage, in that he had faith in me when I certainly did not. So I soldiered on, thinking that maybe he knew something about me I didn't know.

Whatever it was that these mentors thought I had, I would certainly need to mine it. For the job was soon to get even harder.

CHAPTER 31

BUSINESS ISN'T HARD, IT'S THE PEOPLE

—C. J. FISHMAN

NO AMOUNT OF STARING through the kitchen window into my once-leafy backyard, cold beer in hand, was going to minimize the stress that was eating my insides out. When the stress animal started chewing away, it was a wonder there was anything left of me to get my ass in to work each day and face whatever discordant music was going on. It didn't matter whether I was on the road cold-calling (Look, Ma, I'm selling toasters!), with stress blocking the speech in my throat, or making any number of mistakes ordering and delivering equipment (Did I measure the space properly? Did I get the voltage right? What about the gas; did I check that? Will the factory ship on time? Will there be freight damage? Will all the parts show up? Will the client like the oven-range-steamer-slicer-toaster after it's in place, or will he say it's not what he wanted?). Always, always, there was the stress.

Work thoughts disintegrated momentarily into my winter-dead yard. This space had been Stephen's realm—mowing, trimming—all to end soon, whenever he finally moved out. By August of 1999, Stephen and I were navigating our divorce while he still lived in the house, trying to survive the civil war of his drunken and my silent marriage of nine years. Somehow, when I finally broke my silence (The hidden vodka bottles! Driving our child around while drunk!), it all went to hell. Or maybe that's when I realized I was in hell.

The bone-like branches of the Florida maple tree swayed in a high wind, shedding dried leaves that floated downward, zigging, zagging, until they fell upon the dried grass like molting feathers. *I should get rid of all that useless grass and weeds,* I thought. In the spring he'd be gone and I'd have the grass ripped out. I'd plant natives, and mulch the rest. I'd sell the lawnmower, tear down the shed, build a tiki bar in its place.

• • •

My persistent pride sometimes prevailed, knocking the work worry down a level or two (only chewing away at my legs sometimes, instead of my insides). After five years of rigorous sink-or-swim training and blind drive, I finally landed the motherlode project. Payoff for all the treachery!

It started with a cold call on an Amish restaurant called Der Dutchman, where I sold them a convection steamer and then micromanaged the purchasing of it, the shipment, delivery, and start-up, until the steamer was in place under the exhaust hood and kicking on with a puff of steam. I then asked the manager, Jeff, if there were any future plans to remodel the otherwise dated-looking kitchen. "Yes," he said. "We own the property on this whole block and we're going to tear this old place down and build a new five-hundred-seat restaurant and bakery."

Determination nudged away my fear of phone stuttering, and I called the main contact in Ohio, got a meeting with him during his next trip to Sarasota, then landed the design portion of the Der Dutchman new kitchen and bakery project.

Designing the kitchens was the best part of my job, and I wished that was all there was to it. For every new kitchen, I visualized every move I, as chef, would make in the space allocated, locating the prep equipment and storage areas within reach, the cooking equipment just a pivot from the chef's counter, studying the menu to make sure the kitchen would crank out the food easily, with minimal steps, adding small touches lacking in many of the kitchens I'd worked in, like spice shelves, pot racks, a rack above prep sinks for colanders-in-reach for draining washed lettuce. The entire flow of the kitchen was so logical, following the food from the back door through its serpentine sweep through storage, prep, production, service, and then dishwashing.

But after the design was done and the client was all smiles, equipment procurement was the next step, which made me a magnet for stress to come after me with fangs bared. Such as that day staring out at my backyard, when I'd trusted the manufacturer's rep and my warehouse guys to the final strapping and transport of a coffin-size rotating rack oven to Der Dutchman, to get it into the building during construction due to its bigger-than-a-standard-door size.

There were a few times when I'd think, *I'm just a girl*. That day was one of them. What did I know about strapping and tying down a thousand-pound piece of cooking equipment into a box truck? Wasn't that what moving people were for? I had my manufacturer's rep there to supervise, and once the oven was forklifted onto the truck, I returned to the office to work on a drawing deadline, knowing full well that I was responsible and that everything that played out was, and would be, my fault.

I knew the rear of the box truck couldn't close due to the size of the oven. I knew my rep would follow behind the truck to Sarasota and would take charge of the offload. I didn't know, until my rep called me afterward—his stupid nervous laughter carving a hole in my stomach—that at the red light in Nokomis the truck braked hard, a strap snapped, and the oven slid out and tilted onto US 41, directly below C. J.'s office window at Fishman & Associates. Traffic whizzed around the thirty-thousand-dollar chunk of stainless steel, now with a dented housing.

As C. J. used to say, "Business isn't hard; it's the people who fuck it up." And like being a chef, I knew that if I wanted everything to be done right, then I couldn't rely on other people. My control-freak self had taken a break and I vowed to never let that happen again.

On the other hand, every week I had two glorious days off to spend with Daughter. Sometimes there were even three-day weekends! We took fishing trips to Captiva Island, Disney trips for her birthday, an airboat ride in the Everglades. The two of us flew to Hawaii in 1997 for my twenty-year high school reunion and she saw my homesick tears. The world was full of possibilities when there was money and some free time. So I trudged onward, through the muck of insecurities, thinking that maybe, just maybe, the muck would clear and I'd arrive confident and happy at my destination, wherever that was.

The dented oven housing got fixed; no one would ever know. But that day and in the ensuing days at the close of 1999, on the precipice of my divorce, the sun was setting on an era of thirty-nine years. A bright new sun was emerging, and I saw something there in front of me, though I wasn't sure what it was. I'd started in therapy that fall in order to navigate the divorce, and found, through the brilliant guidance of the therapist whose name I'd liked in the phone book and had called out of desperation, that the repeated patterns of my life were my own doing. I'd been voiceless and fearful since childhood, and if I wanted a voice, I'd have to go find it.

On January 1, 2000, at Henderson Beach in Destin, where Christopher and I had scattered Mom's ashes eleven years earlier, I stood in the cold at the edge of the frothy Gulf and ceremoniously forgave my mother. The sun came up golden and hard that morning, and with my heart and body buzzing with expectation, I drove off into the new century, in search of my voice.

Stephen and I divorced in March of 2000, and a dead black cat was lying in my driveway when I got home from the courthouse. I would not be deterred. I called a neighbor to dispose of it and convinced my superstitious mind the dead cat was a symbol of my dead past. I was now a single mom with a heavy job, and I had just begun an online writing course. My future lay luminous before me.

CHAPTER 32

THE ART OF
THE ARTICHOKE

"FOOD IS LOVE," my mom used to say. And even though her palate wasn't adventurous and her cooking skills were limited, she prepared meals to the best of her ability and enjoyed a day in the kitchen with her trusty *Joy of Cooking* and some specially purchased ingredients. The great insult was my stepdad's refusal to eat these meals she so lovingly prepared. If it wasn't beef something and potato something, from his black Naugahyde lounger he'd place the dish on the floor for our dogs and countless cats to fight over. Later, during the commercial break, he'd get up to fortify himself with a large bowl of ice cream. His actions on these nights were grounds for murder.

In contrast, my mom and I enjoyed a food ritual together that started when I was very young. Many different gold-flecked Formica kitchen tables are the backdrop to this repeated event, this thing we shared without Grandmother or Stepdad or anyone else. A curious-looking steaming green crown, imparting an earthy aroma, elegantly sat on a dinner plate between us as we took turns peeling off the leaves, dipping them into a soup cup of hot lemon butter, scraping the little bites of meat from the inside edge with our bottom teeth. The closer to the inside of the flowery crown, the sweeter the meat became.

The young me would ask, "Mommy, why are the leaves sweeter on the inside?"

Mom answered, "Because we're getting closer to the heart."

This made sense to me, for I'd learned in Sunday School that God was large enough to fill the world and small enough to fit into your heart. Surely God was inside the artichoke's heart, too.

We eventually would get to the heart, the leaves very thin and meaty around the edge of the artichoke's center jewel. Here, Mom took over, lifting the round stemmed base and scraping the fibrous thorns from its cup with a spoon, careful not to puncture it. She dropped it into the soup cup of butter, sliced it into smiles, and we took turns slowly savoring each buttery bite.

A few times a year we shared an artichoke together, and each time I savored not only the sweet meat of nature's bounty, but also the time spent alone with Mom, that special opportunity to be near her at the table, a rare moment of being on the same level. Excitement built in me whenever I spotted an artichoke in the kitchen, or she told me she'd bought one at the store on sale that day. She wanted to be with me, you see, and this artichoke was her excuse.

A little sadness followed after each eating session, when the artichoke was a pile of spent leaves marked by the imprints of our lower bites. Mom would stand, her aura disappearing into that smoky space of adultness, and clear the dishes. And I'd be alone again.

When I was older, Mom prepared two artichokes, and with a large salad bowl between us for the stripped leaves, we'd talk and talk and talk as we ate, catching up on things, since I was on the go so much. These artichokes and their God-filled hearts briefly brought us together again.

When I left home, I didn't encounter an artichoke until I worked that first summer back on Maui at Longhi's. Artichokes were an appetizer on the menu, served chilled and stuffed with an olive dressing. I thought that was somehow wrong. The artichoke was so delicate and the olives so pungent, so how could that be good? The artichoke is the thing you eat; it isn't the vessel for something else. Later, working for Charlie at Farrago in Portland, fresh artichoke hearts were on the menu and he showed me how to pare down a fresh choke with a sharp knife, a technique I never mastered, my focus instead on all that good stuff—the leaves—going into the trash.

It wasn't until the Columns Hotel with Armand that the artichoke made the leap from childhood ritual to culinary extravaganza. When artichokes were in season in California, cases of twenty-four could be had for less than ten bucks. We'd steam up two cases, have everyone in the kitchen, dishwashers mainly, painstakingly scrape the meat from the leaves with paring knives and, once both cases had been reduced to a bain marie of leaf and heart meat, a puree of artichoke soup was made up and finished with cream, butter, and a hint of nutmeg or mace. It is a wonderful sensation: all the tender artichoke flavor melting in your mouth without the work of peeling down the flower.

It never bothered me, the work of eating a choke, called such by many men in my life who refused to go through the steps to eat an artichoke. Was eating artichokes a girl thing? I wondered.

If I ever ate an artichoke by myself before my daughter was born, I don't remember it, for naturally the most important part of the ritual—the sharing—was missing for me. With Mom gone and me working in restaurants most nights, this probably never occurred. But when I became a mother, a few new things began to happen.

I found myself saying, "Food is love," to my wiggling daughter, as I presented her with a plate of an over-easy egg laid atop a piece of toast that I'd cut up into perfect bite-size squares.

Or, I found myself repeating my mother's words. I had a little cast-iron frying pan that was Mom's, about which she on so many occasions told me while washing it, "You know, Marisa, this pan is older than you. I bought it before you were born," and me saying, "I know, Mom," complete with eye roll. I had this old pan among my other pans and I would say to Daughter, "You know, this pan is older than I am and someday it'll be yours." I thought of every time I stood with Mom at the sink in the stucco house in Kihei, helping her wash three days of dishes, for she liked to store them up that way.

When Daughter was about three, I steamed an artichoke and placed it between us with an empty bowl for the spent stuff and a cup of lemon butter. I'm certain there was a huge smile planted on my face, and this, together with the mysterious delicacy I'd placed between us, surely made her very curious and eager for this thing I was about to show her. My mom had only been gone a few years; Daughter was born just eleven months after Mom's death and now I was the mother. I'd experience the artichoke ritual from another viewpoint.

I believe there is always room for improvement, even for something as great as sharing an artichoke with your loved one. So on nights Daughter and I sat down to partake, I didn't rush off like my mom always had. I didn't want my daughter to feel sadness or any loss after our shared time. This artichoke was the symbol of so many things, good and bad, and I only wanted the good things for her. But I could only control so much, for while the two of us were in the dining room, eating, laughing, and talking about school and such, Stephen was out in the Florida room drinking Old Milwaukee and smoking cigarettes, shortening our marriage and shortening his life, as we would find out in a few years when he was diagnosed with cancer. This certainly attaches itself to Daughter's good artichoke memories, doesn't it?

Daughter and her father were always close. They were adorable together, in fact. And when the divorce thoughts had started to enter my brain, I vowed to make sure their relationship would continue. She stayed with Stephen and his new wife on alternate weekends, and sometimes I mentioned how all her clothes smelled like cigarettes when I picked her up. Daughter made it clear how rude this was. Our broken home was very hard to navigate and I'm not sure I did it that well. Daughter threw herself into musical theater to soothe her depression, and I, trying out new male relationships, was oblivious. And then Stephen was diagnosed with lymphoma.

An angsty teen with a dying father and a mother searching for herself like a teen, Daughter and I still had the ritual of artichokes to bring us together. I'd see perfect pale green plump globes at the store and know buying them would be an opportunity. Daughter would see them in the refrigerator and get excited. We'd schedule an evening when she didn't have rehearsal or a sleepover. Sitting across from each other, dipping the leaves into lemon butter and chatting, we would reground ourselves into each other's lives.

Maybe you just can't have the good stuff without the bad for balance. Maybe the bad stuff just makes the good stuff so much better.

CHAPTER 33

EATING CHICKEN IN THE DOMINICAN REPUBLIC

THE SINGULAR MOST ENJOYABLE ASPECT about my change in career—once I passed through about fifteen years of embarrassment when there wasn't much enjoyable about being insecure, unknowledgeable, and extremely driven—was the opportunity for more travel. Our kitchen design and installation work outside Florida was infrequent, however, and while C. J. Fishman was doing resort kitchens in the Turks and Caicos, I had the excitement of flying up to New Jersey to meet with a client at his restaurant in Livingston. (C. J. did bring back rum for me, though. I didn't bring him anything from New Jersey, except a design contract.)

There was a hospital in Fresno, California, where for the several years' duration of the project C. J. and I would fly the red-eye for an afternoon meeting, go out to dinner, crash at the Hampton Inn, then fly back to Florida the next morning. Dining on those trips consisted of watching sushi going around on a conveyor belt, the novelty of it dulled somewhere in my flight-smacked brain, or sitting in some manly cigar bar with C. J., nearly dozing off after a glass of red wine while he chowed down on a wedge of iceberg lettuce. And the *original* Golden Arches are in Fresno, which rated just under the traveling sushi in my mind.

Then there was my trip to Paris, Texas, to supervise the first of ten equipment installations for a retirement-home client. It was hot. It was also a
version of a dry town, so I spent evenings after long days in the heat in an
Applebee's with a paper ID I'd obtained, giving me permission to drink in the
"dry" town.

So when C. J. and I started courting a company in the Dominican Republic that was looking for a kitchen equipment designer and supplier for San
Juan University, I figured that New Jersey, Fresno, and Paris had simply been
warm-ups to something great. And I, now a fifteen-year veteran of kitchen
design and equipment, keeping my insecurities and stresses hidden away in
that ever-shrinking vault, was ready to charge forward in this new challenge.

On the first trip to the client's office in Santiago, C. J. did the schmooz-
ing (his job as president of the company) and I did the information gathering
(my job as project manager). Once under contract, on the second trip we
were driven down the mountain from Santiago to Bonao to tour an existing
university kitchen (shoddy equipment and over-nickled stainless steel from
China) on our way to San Juan via the capital, Santo Domingo.

From the rear of the SUV it was like watching a movie: narrow roads widening for the rat-scramble of plantain-packed Daihatsus and mini-bomber
scooters piled with families precariously balancing propane tanks on their
laps. This craziness was backdropped by hills fitted with mud-sunk scrap
metal panels and warped boards stacked like Escher boxes, one upon another,
sharing walls and dirt floors. These handmade, forlorn suburbs were a tes-
tament to the country's rampant poverty. The better homes were made of
rough, unpainted concrete with spikes of rusted rebar pointing upward to
the sky. I asked our client, Marcelo, about the rebar and he told me families
expected to add additional floors to their houses when they got more money.
The height of the rebar would be the final height of their home. These unfinished roofs all had black rain barrels installed upon them.

Once we were through the city and its outlying areas, the traffic thinned
and our driver's herky-jerky racing slowed through the towns of Baní and Azua,
where children, teenagers, and women ran up to the SUV, pushing things for
sale: plastic jars of cashews, mangoes, Day-Glo cell-phone covers, a caged par-
akeet. Their dark, eager hands grabbed at our closed windows like giant flies.
Then, as we neared the mountain range that bordered Haiti, checkpoints with

armed militia waved us through with machine guns. Here, C. J. and I did silent double takes in the back seat. Finally, after three and a half hours of lawless, hellacious driving, we were in the mountain town of San Juan de la Maguana to tour our job site.

On my first two trips to the Dominican Republic, I watched the country from the protective bubble of an air-conditioned SUV. I wondered about barefoot kids in dirt lots playing baseball with sticks and bottle caps. Why weren't they in school? Who were the fancy universities for if kids didn't go to school? Our clients were a wealthy family, privileged; perhaps the schools were only for their class. In our nice hotel in Santiago, eating Americanized meals, were we supposed to be concerned about the kids in the dirt lot? These thoughts tamped down the lump of excitement that lived in my throat during my time there.

That first day in San Juan, after our tour of the dusty site, taking measurements for the walk-in cooler, making notes on our blueprints, and stepping over a spaghetti mound of wires, cracked tiles, and dirty concrete that would someday transform into a commercial kitchen, C. J. and I were informed it was time to eat. Finally! My favorite part.

El Espia seemed an odd name for a restaurant, though its wooden sign showing a shadowy face mostly covered by a clandestine hat did conjure up the idea of a spy. When we walked into the unadorned, open-air restaurant, a thin, smiling man raced up to our clients Marcelo and Manuel, Angel the contractor, and our driver, with hugs and handshakes and rocket-speed Spanish. C. J. and I were introduced to the restaurant's owner and we were all led to a large table, with Mr. Owner saying in his rolling Spanish that it was the best table in the house; only the best for us. Or at least, I'm pretty sure that's what he said.

We had El Presidentes all around, except for Marcelo, who ordered a reddish mango juice concoction. Everyone yelled and laughed in Spanish and the menu was in Spanish—a language I loved and had studied for eight years in high school and college, but now the words looked odd to me and the only thing I understood was *pollo* (chicken), and I wanted to know the rest. The newness of this experience reminded me of those thrilling and odd first days in Australia, feeling lucky and blessed and a little bit scared. Who got to do this? I got to! Angel, the job site super sitting next to me, translated the meats for me. *Chiva* is goat, he said, pointing to the paper menu. They had goat? Then I wanted goat! C. J., who usually ordered what I order, and obviously didn't notice the clucking chickens running around in the dirt yard of the restaurant, ordered *pollo*.

Platters of sliced ripe tomato and avocado were passed around and each of our lunch plates came with cups of white rice and a soupy red bean mixture. My goat was stewed and rich, and I mixed rice into it with fervor. The beans were bland, the vegetables just ripened and nubile as if they'd been picked that morning. More El Presidentes all around and soon silliness took over; the owner talked into his watch and wiggled his eyebrows, Marcelo and Angel doing the same. "*El Espia!*" the owner said and whispered into his watch again—was he looking around for spies? Oh, to own a restaurant and have this much fun; I'd never seen anything like it in all my restaurant years. I loved this place!

Eight months later, in February, without C. J. this time, I flew from Miami to Santo Domingo to meet my Orlando-based installation team—Kevin, Keith, and Brandon—to install the equipment at San Juan University. We would be there seven days, two of which would be spent driving up the mountain and back from San Juan, so we had five days to complete our work. There was an episode with the plane when an air-conditioning vent split the ceiling open, when I thought I'd never make it to the D.R. or anywhere but downward to the sharks. We turned around, went back to Miami, and took another plane six hours later. So I was highly frustrated when I arrived in the pitch-black night after what seemed a lifetime in the airport bar, now with few electric lights to lead our way along the dusty streets, *without luggage*, tired, hungry, and led by a non–English-speaking, apish Latin whore-dog (according to my giggling crew, who had spent seven hours with him at the airport) wild-ass driver named John, and nowhere to buy a toothbrush.

"Donde está el hotel?" I managed after we careened around the dark slums of Santo Domingo for a half hour, Spanish rap blasting from the truck's speakers, John with his window down, barking out Spanish to strangers, the street people yelling back somewhat agreeably. Were we *lost*?

With a tongue click he replied, "Oooh, habla español, chiquita?" Or that was the gist of it, anyway. "Un poquito," I replied, presenting to him my thumb and forefinger a half inch apart.

We raced along a seawall, the invisible Caribbean Sea necklaced by a sidewalk scattered with stalls of smoky-smelling meats hanging under yellow lights. "Food! I'm starving!" I said to my crew in the back seat.

Keith, Kevin's son, said, "Ew, I wouldn't eat that."

"What's wrong with street meat?"

A chorus of blahs from the back.

We pulled into a hotel and my heart leaped at the thought of a cool bed, maybe a toothbrush, concierge service. Food maybe? But in the lobby, John and the desk señora bantered a bit and John pulled out his phone and punched buttons, waited, talked, waited, and in ten minutes we were back in the car, careening around again.

What the fuck? Maybe he called Marcelo and the rates were too high?

Finally, around midnight, we pulled down an alley to the Drake Apartahotel, more apartment than hotel. The guy at the desk peered at us suspiciously and no, there were no toothbrushes. I'd learned from John that it was my *maleta* (suitcase) that was lost and I called the airport from the open-air front desk. No one spoke English. I handed the phone and my claim check to John, shrugging.

He rattled off some Spanish and slammed the phone into the receiver. "*Mañana*, Marisa. I call for you. And Marcelo, he be here—*siete y media.*"

Mañana arrived after a tortuous sleep on a lumpy bed, my nose burning from the soapy disinfectant smell of the room. Outside at the desk phone, I spent half an hour on hold with the airport and still had no suitcase. We ate mystery food cooked by three Black ladies on an electric stove on the hotel's small balcony: a root-vegetable mush with oily red onions and fried salami, weak coffee. And we waited, for what I wasn't sure. Surely not my damn suitcase that I believed was lost forever. My frustration at losing part of a workday with all this vague indecision marked me as the high-strung American: My face was rigid and anxious, while my crew smiled and shrugged. At nine, we piled into John's truck, *merengue* music blasting, for the lawless drive up the mountain to San Juan.

I had left the cool February air of Florida wearing a long-sleeved shirt and corduroy slacks but had packed clothes for the Caribbean heat. So when I exited the air-conditioned truck at the job site, still feeling the g-force of highway speed in my head, heat and concrete dust assaulted me like hot lava and I instantly began to sweat. The job site didn't look much different than it had eight months ago, save for the mountains of boxes of kitchen equipment stacked in the dining room, unloaded from shipping containers that had arrived by boat before us. "They said they were ready," I whispered to Kevin, as the four of us wandered the unfinished kitchen, wondering how we were going to get all the equipment uncrated, assembled, and set in place in four and a half days. Marcelo arrived with an entourage of dark-skinned business types, a few of them speaking English, thankfully. "We'll have workers here to help you, Marisa. But first, we need to eat." He said something to John in Spanish, of which I caught two words I recognized: "El Espia."

It was a big lunch at three rectangular tables lined up in the middle of the small dining room, with my team and a dozen or so Spanish-speaking contractors and engineers. Everyone seemed to be an engineer. I reached deep into my brain for some Spanish to attempt some small talk. I ordered *pollo* this time, trying to go easy on my stomach, as my last meal here of *chiva* had backed me up for days. My Metamucil was tucked into my suitcase, which was where, exactly? I passed on the El Presidentes this time, for there was an afternoon of work (I hoped). Beer would come later.

The chicken tasted like chicken—unlike the overly plump, yellow, hormonal, size DD chicken breasts you buy in American grocery stores, which have no flavor at all. Culinary memories rushed in as I feasted on the thin, crispy, boneless breast of yard bird at El Espia. Back in Portland, at Aldo's Restaurant, trays of a dozen boneless breasts would come in fresh, each five-ounce breast to be pounded thin, floured, sautéed in clarified butter, and finished with a classic Marsala sauce or Tuscany sauce with artichoke hearts and cream. At the time it had seemed like nothing really, chicken being the least expensive thing on the menu. But at home when I tried to whip up a little chicken sauté, I had to slice fat strips from the huge chicken breast in order to pound it thinly. And the flavor? None. The chicken at El Espia, though cooked simply with salt, pepper, and oil, was delicious. I vowed, once home, to buy only nonhormonal, nonsteroidal, non–sci-fi-size chicken breasts. We learn things from simpler ways of life.

That afternoon we uncrated kitchen equipment with a dozen eager dark faces who wielded box cutters. Then John took me to La Tienda, since who knew when *mi maleta* would arrive, or if it ever would.

It was a sweet Latin gesture, I thought, when John took my hand and we dashed across the street. Which turned out mainly to keep me from becoming roadkill under roaring scooters and speeding vehicles.

La Tienda was an all-out variety store crammed with goods, open boxes displaying clothes, toiletries, shoes, socks. I selected a small hairbrush, a toothbrush, and a small tube of Crest, a lime-green golf shirt, deodorant, and white ankle socks. John conversed jovially to the people working in the store, as if he knew them. It seemed he knew everybody in this island nation. I was standing in a narrow aisle lined with open boxes of loose underwear, trying to determine if they were boxed by style or size, when John came to check on me.

"Okay?" he asked.

"Si."

He pointed to the wall above one box where a poster of a native-looking woman wearing bikini panties posed against a waterfall. Above another box, a lady wore briefs against the waterfall. "Which one, you?" he asked. I pointed to the bikinis and began rummaging in the appropriate box for a pair that could be a size five.

I'd located a few pairs when I heard "Mareesa!" in a melodic Latin voice. John was at the end of the aisle in front of another box, holding up a pair of thong underwear, making a goo-goo face at me. "Si?"

"No, John." I waggled a blue bikini panty in the air. *Geeze, I'm old enough to be his mother*, I thought.

That first night at dinner, refreshed finally from a shower at Hotel de Maguana and wearing relatively clean clothes, we dined with the entourage of engineers and contractors. There was a lot of waiting at the small hotel bar first, with no clue of a plan, which was to become routine during this week. While waiting to be picked up, I drank three El Presidentes with John and watched an old *Star Trek* episode translated into Spanish, when finally Marcelo arrived to whisk us off to a no-name restaurant where the entourage was waiting for us in a dimly lit dining room off a dark street.

I sat next to Angel, who was enjoying a glass of red wine—an odd juxtaposition, this Latin man swirling the red mixture and tilting it upward toward the yellow bulb glowing in the fake Tiffany lamp above our table.

"Chilean Cabernet," he said. "Very expensive here." Of course I had to have one too. Our meals, it appeared, were all being taken care of by Marcelo.

Our contract stated that the client was to provide only accommodation and transportation, but throughout the week, after Marcelo left for the capital, John plied me and my team with lots of food and drink on his company credit card, even when Kevin and I tried to pay. "My cousin pay. Marcelo, he pay," John would say, with a tone of derision.

So I ordered a glass of Chilean Cabernet and some kind of *pollo* appetizer that sounded interesting, but what arrived was a small plate of fried chicken tenders. Well, I wasn't really that hungry—just ready to pass out from a long day of heat, three El Presidentes, and a glass of Chilean Cabernet. And where was my fucking *maleta*?

At 8:30 Tuesday morning, my crew still waiting downstairs in the dingy cubby of the hotel restaurant after an endless breakfast of coffee brewed one cup at a time and eggs they must have been chasing the chickens around the yard to get, I was pounding on John's hotel room door. *I am the boss, goddammit, and we need to get this show on the road!* "John! Get up!" *God, I really am his mother.* This became the morning routine.

At three o'clock Friday afternoon, our fifth day, my installer Kevin and I were sitting in the open bed of a truck behind the completed kitchen, waiting for a generator to show up from somewhere so we could fire up the walk-in cooler and freezer—an order from the Dominican government—before we were allowed to leave. We were now accustomed to waiting for things—dinner, breakfast, coffee, John, electricians, plumbers—with no exact knowledge of when they would appear. I wasn't feeling tolerant for even more waiting. I was hungry, hungover from all the El Presidentes John had bought us the night before at the bandstand, and tired, because although I'd gone to bed at midnight, the bandstand and all the trucks boom-booming Spanish rap and pop music did not. There were no noise ordinances here. Hot and dirty, tired of the talc-like dust coating my lungs, I wanted food and a beer. We'd been waiting for the generator since two, when we had deemed our work complete; plumbers were now hooking up sinks, the barefoot electrician had straightened up all his wires from the mud puddle on the kitchen floor, the ten-dollar-a-week Haitians were done chiseling out tile to fit the floor troughs, and all our equipment was assembled and level. I wanted to go—somewhere else.

Where were they even going to get a generator, four hours away in Santiago?

Kevin, by nature much calmer than me, and not a drinker so probably feeling rested, shrugged and said doubtfully, "I hope they can find a fifty-amp generator." Kevin had been installing our kitchens since 1999—he'd showed up at the Der Dutchman job with my oven-crashing rep to assemble and install a twenty-three-foot-long dishwasher—and he is a man I respect for his ability to finagle heavy and crated cooking and refrigeration equipment off a semi, bang out freight damage, assemble all the parts and pieces, get equipment through a too-small door and into place in the kitchen, leveled and ready for the plumbers and electricians to do their thing. My job is to hand him parts boxes like a surgeon—*casters, water filter, faucet*—and keep general contractors from messing with his head. Kevin can magically make walls and doors fit his needs, hoist ten-burner ranges through second-story windows, deconstruct a twenty-foot-long stainless steel chef's counter and reconstruct it in place across from the cooking line, and show uninformed electricians how to hook the stuff up so it works, smiling the entire time. And now, to add to his list of can-do things, he can do it in a Spanish-speaking country knowing only one word of the language: "Si."

I dangled my legs off the end of the truck, stretching my hamstrings from standing on concrete all week while I'd kept everyone organized. My frustration with the Dominican laissez-faire attitude regarding my suitcase had energized me to call my office at two bucks a minute and have them work the situation from the American end. It worked; my bag was traced to Haiti, sent back to Miami, and then to Santo Domingo, where it got picked up by courier and driven up the mountain and delivered to me at nine o'clock Tuesday night.

Aside from the weird construction methods, our dining experiences were the most interesting part of our week. Other than at El Espia, service in the Dominican Republic is a very loose concept. The slow service doesn't bother anyone except for us high-strung Americans, trying to complete a massive installation job in five days while mornings the local driver is upstairs snoring off a late night of drinking and whoring about town. Each morning at the hotel, the woman waiting on us seemed to be brewing coffee by the cup in a mysterious place behind the dining room. A kitchen, maybe? Or a porch with residential stoves? "*Negro o con leche?*" She'd take our four coffee orders before toddling off, to return ten minutes later with one cup. God, did I want to buy her a twenty-quart brewer.

One night John drove us up to what looked like someone's house, but it turned out to be an Italian restaurant. We were the only ones there. The waiter wore jeans and knew John, of course, and it looked like the waiter's mother, possibly, standing behind a tiny wood bar backlit through glass shelves of rocks glasses. We drank rum that night and I let John be the macho man and order for me. The menu was Italian translated into Spanish, and I pretty much got the gist of it. John ordered me mushroom ravioli, which was okay. I think the father was cooking.

On another night John went on and on about something called *sancocho* and went about kissing his bouquet of fingers, enticing us, letting us know that we were really going to experience something great. I was having trouble logging on to the internet on my laptop; there was a single spot on the hotel stairs that sometimes got service, and Kevin and I took turns sitting on the step to log on. So I didn't Google this *sancocho* thing John was raving about, and after the cursory wait in the bar after showering, he appeared and drove us to El Espia, where he shrugged off the menus and blurted a long sentence that had the word *sancocho* in it several times. Minutes later—the fastest service of the week—a tureen of bubbling soup arrived with bowls, spoons, and a ladle. It turned out to be the food of the Gods: Pumpkin-y, slightly thick broth, chock-a-block with yucca, potato, carrot, and meats, it was beefy, buttery, spicy, and sweet. We all gorged on several bowls of what I later learned is the national dish of most of the Caribbean islands.

On that Friday when we were waiting for the generator, it was almost five o'clock when we heard the boom-boom of John's truck.

Kevin and I laughed. "Here he comes," I said. "Boom-boom."

With engine running, door open, music still at concert level, John hopped from the cab with arms flailing in rhythm and danced up to where we sat in the truck bed. It made me want to dance, despite my fatigue and frustration.

"We go," he said, motioning toward the truck.

"No, John," I said, "*No está terminado trabajar.*" When he looked confused, I made a phone-to-ear gesture with thumb and pinky and said, "Call Marcelo."

He shrugged and left.

It was so rare in my busy, type-A life that I was just sitting doing nothing, while time spooled away. It was disconcerting and frustrating, which is probably why I was once such an efficient line cook. I could mash all kinds of movements into the tick, tick, tick of time; I could make the tick-ticks fatten and explode with surges of productivity. It was the same with the to-do lists of office and design work, the planning, the organizing, the execution of things, never missing a call, a follow-up, an appointment, or a drawing deadline. Now, there I was, giddy after the experiences of this week, but sitting in the hot dust of nothingness, waiting for something to happen.

I sighed. "I like the chicken here," I said to Kevin, making small talk.

He shrugged. "Keith and I raise our own chickens."

"Really? So you're not subjected to hormonal chickens?"

"Nope, every six months or so we split a shipment of chicks, and once slaughtered, we have chicken in our freezers for the rest of the year."

"Now that's cool."

Then, Kevin told me about his new defeathering machine, much like the potato peeler we had just installed in the kitchen. "Yeah," he said, "you put the chicken into it, it spins around really fast and goes 'squawk, squawk, squawk'"—he made wings with his elbows and rolled his eyes while making the chicken noises—"and it comes out bald."

That was just plain weird and funny.

"Yeah," he said, "the neighbor kids all like to come and watch."

Around 5:30, when we were laughing about the Suessical rhythm of one of the engineers with no ear—punch-drunk, no doubt—we heard tires crunching up the drive. Finally, a truck arrived pulling a trailer with a giant dusty generator on top. Kevin leaped from the flatbed and got to work inspecting the giant generator, and then he was up on a ladder and uncoiling wires from the three condensing units hanging from the side of the building, calling out orders to his crew inside while barefoot Sparky made up makeshift breaker boxes in the dirt below. By 6:30 he'd started up two of the three walk-ins, but the freezer was giving him trouble. Barefoot electrician and Kevin conversed via charades and put wires together, pulled them apart, and tried other wires. At one point one of the engineers went up behind Kevin on the ladder with a camera as he was putting some wires together and a white *flash pop!* froze us spectators and made Kevin whirl around, face stippled with fear and anger. Relieved that it was only a camera flash, but angry at the stupidity of this giggling engineer, Kevin finally got the third walk-in fired up and we left for the hotel to shower and endure an achingly slow and nondescript dinner at the hotel, and a sleepless night crashed into by waves of music spilling from trucks and the bandstand in the adjacent square.

I had hoped for more work in the Dominican Republic. Kevin and I talked about how to make the next job easier; we knew what parts were not available at the local *ferreterias* (hardware stores), so some items I'd order in differently, to include more parts from the factories, and we wouldn't bother lining their floor troughs with stainless steel. We knew what to expect now, knew their levels of expertise on things, knew what their expectations were, and that they didn't look at our blueprints. I planned to bring a suitcase of Louisville Sluggers to give out to the kids in the dirt lots, and only bring carry-on luggage.

But aside from one more trip to start up the equipment in San Juan, when I had a voluptuous-tasting roasted pheasant at El Espia, we didn't get any more jobs there. The Dominican Republic, like my beloved year in Australia, has become a place to visit in my mind, another experience that has contributed to my self-formation. It is also the reason why, when I hear people complain about America, where we have relatively clean running water, customer service, safety regulations, lighted and paved streets you can navigate at night, and coffee makers, I really want to say to them, "Go visit someplace like the Dominican Republic."

CHAPTER 34

WE EAT SWEETBREADS

I WAS STANDING IN THE DRIVEWAY under the searing August sun wearing cotton boxers, a sports bra, bandanna, chill-rag draped across my shoulders, shears held open in my right hand, dumbfounded by my daughter's proclamation: "Mom, I think I want to move to New Orleans."

It was the summer of 2010. Daughter had just pulled up in her Honda, back in Florida and working at Starbucks after a term as a student at Circle in the Square in New York. Before that she'd had an eighteen-year-old's jaunt through Europe, calling from Tuscany to tell me, "Mom! Tuscany is *your* kind of place! I just had the best meal at this little restaurant, a *wooonderful* wine, and this chef from California who is staying at the hostel? He paid for all of us!"

Traveling Europe at eighteen? Talk about making a former globe-trotting mom jealous.

The sun highlighted to golden the dishwater-blonde hair that swished across her shoulders as she expelled a dramatic sigh. "I'm just so tired of applying at all these schools. I want to pick a place to live where I can *feel*, be a part of, then find a school there. New Orleans sounds cool."

I bent to pull a weed from the circle of sunshine mimosa under the great oak too close to the house, my face frozen into a surprise. *New Orleans?* Well, Cajun and jazz music had played in the background of her youth; there was the trip Stephen and I took there when she was seven and was pulled onto the stage by an old Cajun and made to play a washboard; the parties I threw post-divorce and post-chefdom, cooking up in my home kitchen storms of gumbo, jambalaya, rabbit, and blackened fish to form bonds with newfound friends (easy to do through their stomachs). It impressed Daughter's middle-school friends when she'd say, "My mom's having a party; you just *have* to try her jambalaya!" Her childhood was bracketed by framed eighties food festival posters adorning the walls.

Still staring at the unplucked weeds, I imagined my daughter living in the city that owned a fractured little place in my heart. It would be an excuse to travel there more than for the occasional restaurant equipment trade show, or for the one hospital kitchen design I did with C. J., dragging my boss—a willing accomplice—after boardroom design meetings to every rum bar and dive joint on my memory lane.

Weed in hand, I stood with a motherly calm plastered to my face. "Well that's great, dear; there are some good schools there."

As May approached, when the two of us would celebrate her twenty-first birthday apartment-hunting in New Orleans, my excitement was tempered by an odd foreboding. It was as if for twenty years I had put on a show for Daughter, and in New Orleans she would see the dysfunctional person I'd been. Like the child of a prostitute who doesn't relate to what's going on until much later, when she learns her childhood was a lie. I had created a near-perfect upper-middle-class bubble for my daughter: good schools, mall shopping for clothes, dance, voice, and acting classes—what good little Sarasota artsy children should be doing—vacations in Hawaii, Ireland, and Costa Rica, and now a damn expensive college. All of this, I was so proud of—I made her childhood so different from my own.

The single but large blemish on her perfect childhood appeared during the months leading up to the divorce when she was nine. Ten years of my pent-up frustration finally exploded when I'd found the hidden vodka bottles, and Stephen's reaction to my confrontations was a perpetual blank stare. It reminded me too much of the New Orleans/Armand days, and that frustrated girl came raging through my well-honed facade. This stuttering girl, married and knowing better, was still unable to express herself and broke closet doors, dabbled in infidelity, and screamed violently until cops came to the door. Finally, therapy coaxed out the recognition of my childhood abuse and the desperate, fearful child emerged from me slowly, gradually, then turned and waved goodbye.

And now my daughter and I would visit New Orleans. Would that scarred version of myself, the chef girl fighting her way to recognition, be poking her head around the corners of the ancient buildings?

• • •

"Mom. Where are we going?" Daughter asked when I stood up at Community Coffee in the French Quarter—our first stop in the city—and tossed the *Gambit* entertainment magazine on the café table.

"I have an idea, let's go. Hurry."

We dashed through an early afternoon sun and rain to the riverfront to join a throng of damp tourists boarding the *Mississippi Queen*. Daughter's face, while gazing at the giant riverboat, beamed an excitement reminiscent of her fifth birthday at Disney World when I bought her satin Princess Jasmine shoes. Or like the time when she was seven and we visited Chef John Giurini in Hollywood, Florida, and he lovingly made her an Italian ham sandwich while she beamed with awe and apprehension. (She didn't like ham, but she ate the sandwich lustily.)

The riverboat tour would give us an overview, a gradual penetration of the city. Then we'd narrow our focus to the nitty-gritty. It was important that Daughter love it here, because New Orleans is a place easy to hate for some (like the obnoxious guy on the bus from the airport on my trip in '87). Daughter had apparently had a good start liking the city on her trip here alone to tour Loyola the previous month. I'd picked her up at the airport the next day and a few spacey words escaped her obviously hungover lips: *Smoothie Shop, Grayson Capps, Southern Blues Rock, Chickie Wah Wah, Taco Truck, Night, Magical, This Guy*. It wasn't unlike her toddler-speak of years long past: *Maw, Hamaburger*. I got that the city had won her over, and that—cringe—she had gotten laid.

The rain stayed onshore as the paddlewheel began its trek upriver. I bought us two beers in the boat's bar and joined her on the bench along the starboard deck, the onshore rain slight through sun-rimmed clouds. We sat silent, staring at the misted shore before us.

Cruising the Mississippi, the first view of major importance was looking over the levee and down upon New Orleans from the boat's deck. Most people, informed now by Hurricane Katrina, understand that New Orleans is below sea level. But to look over the levee down into the city from a riverboat is actual, visual proof of this fact, like viewing Earth from space is actual, visual proof of its roundness.

We remained silent, like two lovers sharing a moment, holding our plastic cups of beer in our laps, gazing at the French Quarter, my mind going miles faster than the boat. The young, insecure chef and excitement junkie was buried beneath a veneer of success and motherhood. For twenty years I tried to set a good example, but she was practically an adult now, so surely I could let her know I'm human, right?

I began the tour. *See, that's the rest of the Quarter, look up there—that's Jax Brewery, used to be a derelict building when I lived here, now a fancy shopping place. Oh! And there's downtown; there's the Top of the Mart, a rotating restaurant, quaint, I know, but a great view. Oh, there! That's where Expo was; before Expo, it was just run-down warehouses and now it's more shopping . . . there used to be a place over there with a bar from Al Capone's restaurant in Chicago.* And on went the tour, a film rolling my past before us, Daughter nodding, her face beaming with the excitement of it all while looking at the broken-up sky, the broken-up city, drinking her beer, listening to her mom babble nostalgically.

Then the stories began. Moving to New Orleans at twenty-one in search of something. My line-cooking debut at Arnaud's, more cooking, always frustrated, never getting what I felt I deserved, then Armand, the fights, the drugs, the drinking, the escape. Being back here with her dad, post-Expo, how she could've been born here if a chef's job had been available for me here and not in Destin.

"Can you believe I actually turned out okay? Finally?" We were on our third beer now, feeling buzzy, the river whizzing by us, the air moist on our skin.

She put her hand on my knee, as if she were the mother and me, the child. "You are who you are, Mom. This has all made you that special person."

Her validation relaxed me a bit.

Once Uptown at the Audubon Zoo, the paddlewheel turned and headed back in the other direction—downriver, past the French Quarter again toward Chalmette—low green countryside, much of it under bayous of swamp water, interrupted by massive rusty oil refineries coughing up plumes of gray smoke. It was a bewildering scene, this man-made devastation marring the riverbanks like a disease.

"A land of extremes," I said by way of an excuse, as we cruised on toward the Chalmette Battlefield.

Back in the French Quarter, legs vibrating from the ship's engine, we went to Acme Oyster House for an early dinner. Daughter was a puddle of putty, her excitement so huge, and she was game to try oysters. My picky eater? Oysters? Well, she'd be twenty-one in two days; maybe her taste buds were finally changing. The supposed taste-bud-changing event had apparently been skipped when she had turned fourteen, when I'd thought she'd eat tomatoes again.

In the din of the old oyster house, we took seats at the bar, ordered beers, and gazed at the mounds of oysters piled up on crushed ice under the length of bar top. For a time we watched the bartender/shucker expertly pry open the mollusks, flick the knife to separate meat from shell, and arrange the shiny beauties symmetrically on plates. I thought of Seattle briefly, my first oyster at nineteen, Daughter's first oyster now at twenty-one, if she didn't chicken out; her aversion to textures was still quite strong. But there was a look of awe on her face, dumbstruck by such food ceremony. Yep, she was ready.

There was no way *not* to like the salty, juicy, cold, sweet oysters, and Daughter appreciated the sensation and drama of this partaking. She took pictures of the tray of oysters and of me, no doubt sending them to her friends in Sarasota with a proud text: *Look what I'm doing with my mom.* We both slurped and smacked and I felt so proud, like a veteran mountain climber or brain surgeon passing along expertise to the next generation.

The dark-skinned oyster shucker/bartender was named Hollywood. He had a bright smile and wore an enviable look of calm as he emoted, "I love my job." We began to chat, me about the old days of course, my sentences starting with "Thirty years ago" and Hollywood telling us about his way up through the ranks of professional shuckers in the Quarter and how he was in a movie—hence his name—and that he was "one bad motha shucka." He handed us each a card: "Michael Hollywood Broadway."

A memory crawled into my beer-slogged mind and I had to validate it. "Hey, Hollywood, thirty years ago, in a bar on lower Bourbon—I forget the name—there was a shucker called Airborne because he flipped the oysters in the air from their shells and yelled, 'Airborne!' The tourists loved it."

Hollywood's face got serious. "Yeah," he said. "Wuz my mentor. Taught me everything I know. Died a few years ago, a big funeral for him." Daughter at this point was still gripping his business card and grinning like a loon. Where else in the world is oyster shucking such a revered, historic, and passionate profession?

Our bellies full, we were ready for the nitty-gritty city tour. We had already walked by my old apartments—the slave quarters where I lived with Dona on Dumaine and the haunted apartment on St. Peter. We'd gotten the city's overview from the boat and had eaten the best meal in the French Quarter. We had a communal beer buzz. It was time to go barhopping—and tell more stories from the past.

The old Chartroom bar on the corner of Charters and Bienville is always a time warp. The venerable place had doorways open to both streets and we wandered in, passing the small bar along one wall. A thirty-something guy wearing checked chef's pants and a T-shirt, half his butt on a barstool and his other leg grounded into the age-stained floor, smoked a cigarette and stared at his half-empty rocks glass, the unmistakable, post-kitchen-stress-disorder plastered on his face.

"Ohhh," I moaned in recognition, thinking of that Sunday afternoon after my first line shift at Arnaud's. *A guy will always be a better line cook than a girl,* Grant had said.

"What, Mom?"

"Look," I said, jerking my head toward the guy. "That used to be me."

"Not anymore, Mom," Daughter said proudly.

I breathed a silent sigh of relief.

She sat at the wood banquette across from the bar and I got us drinks from the bartender. Still cheap, still poured strong. Then, as if a master puppeteer from the past was pulling my strings, I set the drinks on the table in front of her and went over to the jukebox alcove and began to peruse the CDs, the modernized version of the old 45s from years ago. The music was the same in a way, New Orleans classic artists like Professor Longhair, Louis Armstrong, Marsha Ball, Lil' Queenie, and the Neville Brothers along with newer tunes, all the way up to the eighties: Blondie, Elvis Costello, Pretenders. Oddly, these albums had been in my collection when I lived here, but eighties music had been uncool back then and the jukebox had only gone up to the sixties.

"I guess eighties music is cool now," I said, sitting next to Daughter and taking my drink, "or the Chartroom wouldn't have it on the box. I wonder what happened to shoulder pads anyway."

I believe I detected a shudder at this mention, as Daughter looked around the tiny dive bar.

Lil' Queenie's "My Darlin' New Orleans" cranked up. "You know, this is your second time here," I said to Daughter.

"What?"

"Yeah, when you were an infant, Dona came from California with Kristina to check out cute infant you and we drove here from Destin. We cruised up and down Bourbon, you in your stroller, little Kristina holding Dona's hand. We were both thinking, 'Look at us now, barflies of yesterday are now mothers.' Anyway, we wound up here for old times' sake, and the bartender was very accommodating—no kids inside of course—but he let us take chairs outside. You slept in your stroller, Kristina slept along two chairs put together, and us bad mothers drank on the sidewalk 'til, I don't know, 2 a.m. or something. Only in New Orleans, you know?" I raised my glass and she raised hers.

We went to more bars that night, played more jukeboxes, and I talked about the city's collective soul. How in '81 Professor Longhair had been dead for a year, but you could still feel the sadness everywhere. It all had felt so poignant back then. How five years after Hurricane Katrina, you could still feel that angst and sadness and defiant sense of pride. The city wears its vibe on its sleeve. The city has guts. The city is not fake.

New Orleans, unlike any person or any kitchen job, had made me feel alive back when I was so dead inside. At the Abbey on Dumaine I told stories about the Abbey on Dumaine. At the Old Blacksmith's Shop I told stories about the Old Blacksmith's Shop. I told Daughter about Ruthie the Duck Lady, the crazy Bead Lady, the old sign at the now gentrified A&P: "No Drunks, Derelicts or Dirty People." Then midnight found us giggling and running, barefoot in the rain, back to our rented apartment on Royal Street.

The following night, after a quiet, happy, hungover day securing an apartment and Daughter's Starbucks job transfer for the beginning of August, we found ourselves on Frenchmen Street, a place from my eighties past that was known to me and my peers as "dark and creepy." Seldom had Dona and I ventured past the furthermost streets of the Quarter, where lighted bars dropped off into the darkness of derelict eighteenth-century Creole houses and unknown street creatures of the Marigny. When we did venture yonder, we were too drunk to know any better and didn't much remember the jazz band we saw in a club resembling someone's living room.

But a tattered *Gambit* magazine perused at an Uptown restaurant listed several bands on and around Frenchmen Street, so apparently things had changed. Sure enough, on our second night in town when we crossed Esplanade behind the Quarter, we saw action on the other side: a few blocks clotted with people, music, and lights spilling from several bars, an eight-piece jazz band—complete with tuba—playing in the street. We parallel-parked a few blocks away and hustled toward the epicenter of Frenchmen Street.

It was a feast of good music, the two of us *ooh*ing and *aah*ing at each jazz band, Cajun band, and rock band we saw in the tiny, no-cover-charge clubs. The musicians busking on the street were just as good as the ones inside; we watched for a long time a train-hopping-looking trio tucked into a few steps between buildings, jamming on washboard, fiddle, Jew's harp, and guitar, playing old-style street blues. Daughter bought a CD of a band called Stalebread Scottie. We walked the three musical blocks and back, seeing homeless-looking guys selling art on street corners, and three geekily dressed poets-for-hire posted at old-fashioned typewriters perched upon fold-up TV trays. We went into one club long enough to watch a set of Lynn Drury's band, where I bought her CD. We drank beer and we were silent mostly, just taking in the whole Darwinian experiment of humanity, this complete community that embraced everyone: homeless weirdos, tattooed and pierced youngsters, talented musicians, and even the suited-up Uptown men and their aging debutante wives, stepping out for the evening, getting gritty in the Marigny.

When we thought there was no way to love Frenchmen Street even more, and that we had melted into its tapestry of craziness, an epic event occurred. Walking the three-block strip again, we saw people clustered around the spot where Scottie and his ragtag band played. Someone danced on the sidewalk in front of Scottie, a dancer playing a tambourine.

But what exactly was she doing with that tambourine? You couldn't actually see the tambourine because it was a blur, the old Black lady's moves so fast and furious, each percussive *hit-pop-whack* of the tambourine to hip, palm, shoulder, butt, the scene a personified drum set. It sounded like a drum set had been added to Scottie's repertoire, and people clapped and stomped and howled on the sidewalk and street. An enigmatic force pulled us in. A guy sitting on a bucket in the gutter kept time with a butter knife and a tin can. It was an impromptu street party of epic proportions.

Then at midnight, Daughter's actual birthday, we were elbows-to-assholes in the Three Muses, watching Glen David Andrews's aerobic horn antics on the tiny stage, and I said, "Happy birthday, dear, your turn to go to the bar and buy your mother a beer."

The next day at her birthday dinner, at MiLa, the waiter said the sweet-bread appetizer was like the hot fudge sundae of appetizers and shockingly, even after I told Daughter that sweetbreads are a glandular meat, she agreed to share the dish with me. I'd seen sweetbreads on menus the whole trip and described to her how we cooked the dish back when I worked at Arnaud's, thirty years ago: We'd blanch the breads in court bouillon, lay them out on a sheet pan, and cover them with cheesecloth before stacking salad plates on top to flatten them as they cooled in the walk-in. Then we'd peel off the membranes, dust with flour, sauté with butter and morel mushrooms, deglaze with brandy, and finish with heavy cream. The few times I worked the sauté line at Arnaud's at night, I envied whomever the dish was for and nabbed an elegant morsel of it for myself. I've never had the opportunity to cook them again or order them in a restaurant.

Daughter smiled at me after the waiter left with our orders.

"What?"

"Everything is 'thirty years ago' . . ."

"Well, everything *is* 'thirty years ago,' I suppose. Different times, not always great times, really, but now I feel fondly for them."

"I can tell. You've come a long way, Mother," she said with a grin.

And she was correct on that. Revisiting New Orleans with my daughter the same age as when I moved here showcased all I had accomplished. That which I had had no inkling of as I fought for recognition in the kitchen and cruised the bars and streets looking for something elusive. The next drink, the next joint, the next black-beauty buzz, the next man to take me to his bed, the next something to relieve the frustration of my self-consciousness.

My daughter was here to pursue her dreams: honors classes, people, writing, working to support herself. I take credit for this, you see; I did this. Through my struggles and defiance and loyalty to motherhood, I created this well-adjusted being. Her flaws made her even more perfect: her sadness from the divorce, then Stephen's death when she was fourteen, her mother's single-minded single parenting skills (or lack of), her penchant for brooding. But she was well-adjusted nonetheless, and driven to excel in all things. And she cracked eggs one-handed like her mother. And thankfully, she now ate real food.

The appetizer arrived, the sweetbreads piled atop creamy grits dotted with specks of black truffle drizzled with an amber sherry glaze. We looked at this holy thing between us, our eyes silently saying *let's begin*, and we each took a bite.

The buttery smooth, truffle- and bacon-spiced, creamy sweetbreads and grits massaging our taste buds signified all that was right, that everything in the past was worth it. This thing between us, this beautifully executed culinary symphony of flavors—to enjoy this with my grown daughter was my prize for all things accomplished. My prize for my fight up the rope to the top, where I could travel, go out to dinner in a nice restaurant, pay for college—things that would have been nonexistent as a chef.

I'd scrimped on my chef salary to send Daughter to dance classes. And when I started out as a kitchen designer, my draw against future commissions was about what I'd earned per year in high school working at the Sea Scoop. But being poor was not an option for me or for my daughter, and I rallied against that lifestyle of bad spaghetti and Chicken Delight that had been my childhood, dreading each day at my new job and each mistake I made, each judging look I'd get from a potential client as I cold-called restaurants with my insecure stutter. That fear of being poor had driven each clenched fist further up the rope, one above the other, until I got to the top, blisters and all.

So there I was sitting across from Daughter on her twenty-first birthday, a big smile on my face. I was content in my knowledge of all things kitchen and bar, my achievements in the anti-stress department, with lots of loyal clients now, a passion for reading and writing, finally a great man who loved me, a colorful past to reminisce about, and a fucking awesome plate of sweetbreads to share with my fucking awesome daughter. Realizing that somehow, through therapy, maturity, or blind drive, I had gotten happy.

CHAPTER 35

GHOSTS OF KITCHENS PAST

WHEN GOOGLING MY OLD New Orleans restaurants for this book—the Columns and Gautreau's, both of which are still in operation, and Upperline, which was a victim of the pandemic and has recently closed—something surprising emerged. Apparently, I'd been cooking in the midst of a revolution during 1980s New Orleans. Young chefs in small Uptown restaurants were making their mark on the ultratraditional New Orleans cooking by blurring the boundaries of Creole and Cajun cuisines and infusing other ingredients and international elements into the food. It was called New Garde Cuisine, a small but significant event in New Orleans cooking whose outside-the-box way of approaching indigenous ingredients has, over the years, inspired many young creative entrepreneurs to open exciting restaurants. Some chefs in this movement were Susan Spicer (a rare woman in the kitchen in those days), Frank Brigsten, Emeril Lagasse, and Armand Jonte.

Two things came from my online discovery. One, that it wasn't my imagination that things were pretty damn stodgy in New Orleans during the time. The chick-in-the-kitchen thing had been a chip on my shoulder, but the food we were cooking, mixing Cajun and Creole techniques and tossing in some Asian or Italian flavor for good measure, was a big deal to the sacred cows of New Orleans cooking tradition. History now tells us so.

The second thing: Where the hell was Armand Jonte, anyway? Online, he popped up under New Garde Cuisine, especially during those years he

was at Gautreau's. I once heard from visiting Mississippians in a sushi bar on
Maui of all places (such a small world) that he had gotten married. I knew
from further rumor in the late nineties that he had moved to Waveland and
worked weekends still at the Bay-Waveland Yacht Club, then opened his own
restaurant in Waveland called Armand's. While I was married to Stephen, I
fantasized about driving up to Mississippi and showing up at his restaurant
for dinner. I even drunk-dialed Armand's mom once. (I obviously had some
unresolved relationship issues during those years.)

Having the internet at your fingertips can evict some mysteries right
from your life. I learned that Anne Russell of Gautreau's had died. I learned
that Steve Manning of Columns Hotel and Eggs Back-a-Town fame had
continued on for years at Clancy's Uptown before moving to Harlem to
open a Creole Restaurant. I learned that Jacques and Claire Creppel still
owned the Columns. Jo Ann Clevenger still owned the Upperline, which
I didn't even need the internet for because there she was on an episode of
Treme, seating people the same way she did back when I nearly burned
down her restaurant.

But even in terms of the internet, Armand remained a ghost. All I could
discover was that his street in Waveland had been annihilated by Hurricane Katrina, and possibly he was holed up somewhere, still working at the
Bay-Waveland Yacht Club. This wouldn't have mattered to me, for I had outgrown the smitten chick syndrome and was now happily married to a man
who showered me with the love and affection I so craved; I was no longer
that needy girl who would sell her soul for love and recognition, and I had no
desire to stir up past torments. But I was visiting Daughter in New Orleans
a lot while she attended Loyola and I was writing this book, and I just wondered what had become of the passionate and creative New Orleans chef of
the eighties who had made such a mark on my life.

So before a trip to visit Daughter in August of 2012, I renewed my Google searches. What I found was this: Steve Manning was back in New Orleans
and had just opened a restaurant in the Warehouse District (former World's
Fair territory) called Annunciation.

Cooking techniques and styles evolve with time, much like music. Like
music, some foods are classic and shouldn't be messed with. A good rock riff
stands the test of time, and so does a perfectly fresh, perfectly fried soft-shell

crab with a lemony meunière sauce. Which is what I ordered at Annunciation when I visited in the fall of 2012. A thing of beauty! You just knew the crab was happy to sacrifice its life to sit so prettily and tastily, its crispiness basking in a bound lemon-butter sauce on a warm white plate placed near a flickering white candle. Exquisite to look at, heavenly to eat. Way to go, Steve Manning!

Steve recognized me when he emerged from the kitchen, untying his apron. We both said it at the same time: "You look the same!" Conversation was short, semiformal. I introduced him to Daughter, who was smiling up from our white-linen table. He showed me his tiny kitchen, his small and elegant restaurant, the dream of all of us back then—Steve, me, Armand. He asked what I was doing now; I told him and gave him my card. I wasn't embarrassed that I wasn't cooking. No sir-ee. Then the inevitable arose in the conversation as if he knew why I was there in the first place.

"Armand's cooking right up Magazine Street at Johnny V's. Just helping out for a while. You should go see him."

My daughter, a willing accomplice, was ready to jump into the time machine with me.

By the time we got there, Johnny V's restaurant was closed for the evening, but the adjoining Monkey Hill Bar was open, so we settled in at the bar for two import beers. And I was relieved in a way, for I wasn't prepared to just walk into a restaurant and ask for Armand Jonte. Daughter assessed the joint: dark hipster bar, a tad douchey. What was that playing on the speakers anyway? Some music that had evolved past the point of being discernible. George Harrison played backward, maybe.

I wondered what kind of restaurant would be attached to such a place. Daughter went off to the restroom, and I gazed up at the small chalkboard above the bar. Suddenly, disappointment and then embarrassment washed over me. The first item of bar food scrawled on the chalkboard, eggplant Eloise.

Daughter returned, sporting a look of grave concern. "What is it, Mom?"

I motioned with my head to the chalkboard. "Thirty years later and he's making the same food?" It was a good dish, but . . . heavy Creole fare? Now? In a hipster bar? "That's so eighties!" (Where *are* the shoulder pads?)

She shrugged and smiled at me, taking her beer and squinching up her face. "What's that playing on the speakers anyway, funereal rap?"

Halfway through our beers, an apparition appeared in the curtained doorway behind the bar, which obviously led to the kitchen. Checked pants, Hawaiian shirt, a pack of Marlboro Golds peeking out from the front packet. His back was turned to us, checking the kitchen one last time, backing out through the flip-up-bar door to sit two stools down from Daughter. A glass quarter-filled with amber liquid was placed in front of him along with a Heineken. There were the narrow-set eyes behind rimless glasses, serious and tired; everything about him and his mannerisms looked the same as when I'd been so in love with this man, except for the graying of his loosely curled hair. He engaged instantly in conversation with a young jock-looking guy. All this occurred behind Daughter.

"Mom?" She leaned in and grabbed my wrist. "What? Is he there?"

"Behind you." I shifted a little on my stool so he wouldn't see me. My daughter, my shield.

"You going to say hi to him?"

And what would I say? *You were such an asshole to me? Sorry I broke your Civil War soldiers?* Or how about, *I'm successful, are you? I'm happy, are you? I get to be in kitchens, but I don't have to stay in kitchens? I get to travel some and come home every night to a sweet man and you're still stuck cooking eighties food at ten at night?* "No," I said. "If he sees me and wants to say hi, he can come over here."

I was lucky, I suppose, to get a glimpse of the two sides of what could have been, had I remained in the kitchen. The ghosts of kitchens future and past had visited me. Steve Manning's pride in his new place, although he was still working so hard after all these years. Armand's temporary gig at a dark and unknown restaurant attached to a hipster bar, his embattled look as if life had whizzed by him, and grabbed some of him along the way. What would it have been like for me if I had remained in the kitchen? I know the answer to that, for at my last chef's job at Tournament Players Club, I was becoming a person I did not like. That chip on my shoulder had become a permanent tattoo of cynicism.

For half an hour, part of me peered around Daughter at him, wondering about where we wind up, the other part of me nearly hypnotized by Daughter's animated conversation. Then Armand rose and faced the front door. With the slightest nod, I instructed Daughter to have a look as he walked past us.

She surreptitiously watched him saunter past us, out of the bar and onto the moonless sidewalk. Daughter said, "He's just standing out there, smoking a cigarette."

"Waiting for a cab maybe."

"Humph." She shook her head. "You win, Mom."

AFTERWORD

THROUGHOUT THE PANDEMIC, my husband and I have searched out the best takeout and delivery places here in Sarasota to satisfy our need for good food prepared for us by others—and of course also to patronize local spots that are limping along during these difficult economic times. One of our favorites is a small Asian takeout restaurant housed in an old motel half a mile from our house. The man who owns the place takes your order, cooks your food, takes your money, and pleasantly orchestrates all these tasks seven days a week. We call him "Theoneguy." Several times a month I'll say to my husband, "Let's get shrimp mai fun and egg rolls from Theoneguy tonight." I don't know the man's name, only that he's from China, has no employees, and does not have family here. When I'm in there waiting for my stir-fry, I feel this deep need to go back and help him, or to replace his residential freezer with a free scratch-and-dent commercial unit. At my Christmas Eve party, with guests from my daughter's circle of service industry workers, I half jokingly said we should go help Theoneguy clean up and bring him over for some wine. I respect this man so much. I want him to succeed. I want him to be happy. I don't want him to burn out.

The pandemic has capsized the food service industry. We are no longer in times of gradual changes we barely notice, like the Crepells aging out of running the Columns and selling it in 2019. More drastic occurrences, like the Upperline closing recently after forty years, are now the norm. The future of the pandemic is unknown, and staffing shortages are real. What has not changed is that people still want good food, and they want to go out to eat.

Restaurants are evolving to meet this demand. Ghost kitchens are emerging with multiple menu delivery options. Food truck courts are becoming even more popular. In my realm of design, country clubs are creating more outdoor dining with small display kitchens, and the competition for staff is so strong that larger and better employee breakrooms are part of these designs. In some areas, wages are going up! It is up to us, the dining public, to continue to patronize our local spots. Be patient. Tip big. Smile at these hard workers. As for Theoneguy, I would wield a wok or clean out his deep fryer for him, if he wanted me to.

ABOUT THE AUTHOR

MARISA MANGANI was born and raised in Hawaii. Finding her niche as a culinarian at a young age, she cooked her way to New Orleans and some of that city's finest restaurants. A pivot put Marisa in the kitchen at World Expo '84, and from there she went on to manage high-volume international food concessions and restaurants at Expo '86 in Vancouver and Expo '88 in Brisbane. She is one of the eight featured chefs in Thrillist's "Why 8 Top Chefs Quit the Kitchen." This is her first book.

Made in the USA
Las Vegas, NV
23 March 2024

87668627R00163